Physical Security Assessment Handbook

Physical Security Assessment Handbook: An Insider's Guide to Securing a Business, Second Edition has been fully updated to help you identify threats to your organization and be able to mitigate such threats. The techniques in this comprehensive book outline a step-by-step approach to:

- Identify threats to your assets
- Assess physical security vulnerabilities
- Design systems and processes that mitigate the threats
- Set a budget for your project and present it to company managers
- Acquire the products through competitive bidding
- Implement the recommended solutions

Each chapter walks you through a step in the assessment process, providing valuable insight and guidance. There are illustrations and checklists that help simplify the process and ensure that the right course is taken to secure your company. This book provides seasoned advice on the competitive bidding process as well as legal issues involved in facility security. After reading it, you will know how to assess your security needs, specify the right products, and oversee and manage the project and installation. It concludes with project implementation, and the necessary follow-up after installation, to verify the proper use of the new security solutions.

Physical Security Assessment Handbook, Second Edition provides a structure for best practices in both specifying system components as well as managing the acquisition and implementation process. It represents the culmination of the author's 44 years of experience in the design, installation, and project management of security system solutions. This is a valuable resource for security managers, security consultants, and even experienced industry professionals to best approach and organize security assessment projects.

Physical Security Assessment Handbook

An Insider's Guide to Securing a Business

Second Edition

Michael Khairallah

CRC Press
Taylor & Francis Group
Boca Raton London New York

CRC Press is an imprint of the
Taylor & Francis Group, an **informa** business

Designed cover image: Shutterstock

Second edition published 2024
by CRC Press
2385 NW Executive Center Drive, Suite 320, Boca Raton FL 33431

and by CRC Press
4 Park Square, Milton Park, Abingdon, Oxon, OX14 4RN

CRC Press is an imprint of Taylor & Francis Group, LLC

First edition published by Butterworth-Heinemann 2005

Library of Congress Cataloging-in-Publication Data
Names: Khairallah, Michael, author.
Title: Physical security assessment handbook: an insider's guide to securing a business / Michael Khairallah.
Description: Second edition. | Boca Raton, FL : CRC Press, 2024. |
First edition published by Butterworth-Heinemann 2005. |
Includes bibliographical references and index.
Identifiers: LCCN 2024002690 (print) | LCCN 2024002691 (ebook) |
ISBN 9781032790770 (hardback) | ISBN 9781032790800 (paperback) |
ISBN 9781003490432 (ebook)
Subjects: LCSH: Business enterprises–Security measures. | Security systems. | Crime prevention.
Classification: LCC HD61.5 .K435 2024 (print) | LCC HD61.5 (ebook) |
DDC 658.4/73–dc23/eng/20240415
LC record available at https://lccn.loc.gov/2024002690
LC ebook record available at https://lccn.loc.gov/2024002691

ISBN: 9781032790770 (hbk)
ISBN: 9781032790800 (pbk)
ISBN: 9781003490432 (ebk)

DOI: 10.4324/9781003490432

Typeset in Times New Roman
by Newgen Publishing UK

Contents

About the Author

Michael Khairallah is a native of New Orleans and has served in the United States Navy as an Electronic Countermeasures Specialist. He was educated at the Louisiana State University at New Orleans where he earned a bachelor's degree in business. He entered the security industry in 1980 as a Manufacturer's Sales Representative and then founded Card Access Systems in 1981 where he served as the president and CEO for 17 years.

In 1998 he sold the company and became an Independent Physical Security Systems Consultant, forming a firm called Security Design Solutions LLC which manages all the elements of risk assessment and mitigation for clients.

Michael has been a member of ASIS International since 1980 and helped write the Professional Service Exam, Physical Security Professional (PSP). He is now a qualified "Lifetime" member of ASIS International based on his service to the security community. He is also a member of the International Association of Professional Security Consultants since September 2003 and a member of the National InfraGard Program since July 2004.

In his security career Khairallah has sat in every chair at the table. He has been the seller, the buyer and the consultant at different times in his work. He is a Board-Certified PSP and the author of the original work, *Physical Security Systems Handbook*. He is also a court-approved expert witness.

Introduction

WHAT IS THIS BOOK ABOUT?

This book is the second edition of a comprehensive guide to identifying the man-made threats to an organization, determining the vulnerabilities of the organization to those threats, specifying security upgrades to mitigate those threats and acquiring and implementing the recommended solutions. It represents the culmination of the author's 44 years of experience in the design, installation and project management of security system solutions.

The techniques presented in this book will help you conduct a physical security assessment and identify ways to mitigate identified threats and then specify a new security system or system addition to improve security conditions. The book also describes methods used in evaluating the survey data, proposing the recommended systems to company management, preparing a system bid and managing the bid process. The book concludes with a description of project implementation on how to follow up the implementation to verify proper use.

The depth of detail in the book assumes the reader is a security professional and has some experience and the technical skill necessary to create a basic security system design. The book organizes the process and provides an overall structure for best practices in specifying system components and managing the acquisition and implementation process.

The main emphasis of this book is to provide you with a guide for doing the right things at the right time throughout all phases of a physical security assessment. It is an aid to planning and documenting the studies necessary to establish needs and outlines the tasks for acquisitions and implementation of systems to deal with threats. Even the experienced professional will find this book helpful in organizing the approaches to security assessment projects.

HOW IS THIS EDITION DIFFERENT?

The original text was prepared and published in 2005 and focused primarily on electronic security systems; a lot has changed since then. Additionally it became obvious that more attention was needed in areas other than the security systems themselves. In fact, a broader view of "systems" was needed. A system is not

DOI: 10.4324/9781003490432-1

just the electronic or mechanical devices that are included in a physical security system, it is also the people, procedures and other tools that make up the complete picture.

All of the sections are updated to meet the industry conditions of 2023 and certain sections have been enhanced further. For example, the threat assessment section now contains a list of examples that can be used to identify potential sources of threats and analysis tools to help prioritize security threats.

There are new checklists throughout the book to improve data gathering in the field and make the job easier. Every effort has been made to ensure the reader has the most current tools and most useful approach.

There is a section on how to write a security policy providing a step-by-step guide to developing the policy and documenting your decisions. There is also a section on how to set up a response team; although this is not a book on security force management, it provides guidance on deciding how many security officers are needed, how to post them and some tips on scheduling.

What you will probably find most illuminating are suggestions on how to avoid lawsuits involving "reasonable care". The author has been approved by the courts as an expert witness and explains how your security preparation is viewed from the perspective of a litigant.

WHEN IS THIS BOOK MOST USEFUL?

This book is most useful when company management recognizes the need for an improved security system and requires a physical security assessment to identify and mitigate threats.

The most important milestone in beginning the physical security assessment process is company management's recognition that the company needs security improvements. You must help build "institutional will" to proceed with system design and evaluation. Throughout the process, management agreement must be part of implementing the new security system to provide funding and foster acceptance of procedural changes.

This book will provide clear and meaningful guidelines to determining threats, assessing vulnerabilities, selecting system components to accomplish security goals, choosing the appropriate vendor to supply components and implementing those components into a cohesive effective security system.

WHY IS THIS BOOK IMPORTANT TO YOU?

This book is a guide to planning a security system assessment to help avoid making expensive mistakes. Security system acquisition requires considerable planning of system details, coordinating vendor activity and comprehensive and adequate documentation. You must clearly communicate system objectives for the implementation to be a success. In most security systems, especially in access controls systems, an incorrect diagnosis of a problem or the failure to document those findings properly can result in costly errors. By using the techniques presented in this book, you will avoid many of the common mistakes experienced in security system implementations.

A friend of mine in the industry used to say, "Every time I make a mistake I get a little smarter … right now I am as smart as I ever want to be!".

This book will also help establish acceptance standards for getting the job done. These standards will be useful for the company and the vendors hired to perform the work. By providing standards in all security system projects, the company will save money and the project team will save time. Standards are essential for measuring vendor performance. Without appropriate standards, performance quality is just guesswork.

WHO SHOULD USE THIS BOOK?

Security system project managers will find this book most useful when confronted by a major project for the first time. This book will be an excellent guide to developing the security assessment plan and strategy, performing the assessment and conducting all the steps necessary to implement the recommendations of the assessment. Even if the security system project manager has years of experience, this book will be useful in organizing the steps necessary from need identification to implementation.

Security directors who are not project managers will find this book especially useful. It will provide a step-by-step process to identifying threats and vulnerabilities designing the right system to mitigate threats and implementing the solutions. Also, general managers who have taken on security as one of their responsibilities will find it useful in managing the work of the security personnel you assign to the job.

Using this book is not a substitute for the skills of a qualified security consultant. The reader may find that the level of expertise needed to conduct the required surveys may not be within their experience. In these cases, this book will serve as a guide to working with a professional security expert.

Chapter 1 presents the entire process overview and is an excellent place to start; even if you are an experienced security professional, it will give you insights into the rest of the book.

CHAPTER 1

The Process from 10,000 Feet

CONTENTS

1.1 INTRODUCTION: WHY DO YOU NEED A SECURITY ASSESSMENT?

Something has happened … there was an incident, you saw a news report about a company like yours where there was an incident, your boss asked you "are we prepared to handle a problem" or perhaps you are just conscientious and feel your company may not be prepared for an incident; whatever the case, you now feel you must test your company's ability to handle security problems. The key words in security preparedness are Deter, Detect, Delay and Respond to unwanted human activity. That is what this book is about.

You will note that "human" activity is added to the criteria; that is because there is more to protecting your business than just security. You must be prepared

 DOI: 10.4324/9781003490432-2

for catastrophic events such as weather, earthquakes, floods and other natural disasters; so there is more to being prepared than just security … but those issues should be addressed separately, here we will focus on human activity that may cause harm to your assets, both people and property.

Why not just double lock all the doors, hire a small army to guard every opening, seal everything up, then you will be secure! Forgive my sarcasm, of course you would not do that; in the first place it would be too expensive and in the second place it would be impractical. The most expensive element in any business is labor, personnel is an ongoing expense and the cost is high and getting higher. Would you spend a half million dollars a year to protect a million dollars of assets?, of course not, no business manager in a typical corporate or institutional environment would agree to budget that. To be sure, there are situations where unusually high security expense is justified but that is not the norm. So how should you budget for security, how much is "normal"? That is what a security assessment will tell you.

What about practicality … if your business is "sealed", how can the company personnel access the facility or use any of the company's assets? Of course you must allow access to selected personnel but at the same time monitor that access to confirm that only people allowed to reach an asset can do so. Therefore, you cannot be completely sealed and therein lies the challenge – deciding who, goes where and when they can go there. Again, that is the purpose of a security assessment.

Then there is the every present Sword of Damocles, the lawsuit. What if an employee or visitor is assaulted on your property because an unwanted intruder found them and caused harm or death? How much precaution should you have taken to prevent this? Then your security preparedness becomes a matter for the legal system, the courts will decide if you did enough. The matter is called Reasonable Care; it is adjudicated by a judge and jury based on evidence presented about your security efforts and how effective they were in preventing this crime. So, as you may now realize, there is more to your security measures than just the immediate protection of assets.

A Physical Threat Assessment examines and identifies the potential sources of man-made attacks. This examination includes a review of company records (usually in the security department) and extensive interviews with company personnel. The Physical Threat Assessment provides a careful assessment of the concerns of management and employees who work with the critical infrastructure of the business with the goal of identifying those company assets that are most critical to ongoing operations.

1.2 WHY THE "OLD WAY" DOESN'T WORK

We do it this way because we have always done it this way! There are lots of stories I am fond of telling my clients about how old ways of doing business has led to disaster. You must constantly be improving your approach because your advisories, the bad guys, are always learning. You should be too.

One story is the tale of Kodak cameras. Kodak was for many years the leader in consumer cameras. More to the point, they made their greatest profits from the sale of film and film developing equipment.

So in December 1975, when an employee named Steven Sasson approached his bosses with a discovery called the "digital camera", they flatly rejected his suggestion. After all, their biggest profit was from film and developing equipment and the digital camera would end that. So instead of moving ahead with the latest technology and getting in on the ground floor they doggedly stuck to the old way of doing business.

Sasson left Kodak and approached Sony with the idea. They embraced the idea and launched the digital camera age and flooded the market with the new product. Other electronic manufacturers soon followed suit. As a consequence, in January 2012, Kodak filed for bankruptcy. So Kodak went from the leading provider of consumer camera equipment to bankruptcy because they failed to keep up with the changing market.

In security there is always risks, so your approach to security must keep pace with the times. Doing something the same way in the face of changing conditions will only lead to a bad outcome. You must adapt your security measure to meet changes in the environment.

1.3 REASONABLE CARE

So what is the standard for budgeting and for openness in a facility: Reasonable Care. But what is Reasonable Care? The term is usually defined as follows: "Reasonable care is the degree of caution and concern an ordinarily prudent and rational person would use in similar circumstances". It is a standard used to determine a legal duty and whether such a duty was fulfilled. The criteria for making that determination are to compare the security measures required in a situation against those that are in place. Within reason, differences in needs and performance define achieving "Reasonable Care".

Along with Reasonable Care is Reasonable Anticipation, which is defined as follows:

> A concept used in security to anticipate unwanted acts; it assumes that a reasonable person would be able to predict or anticipate the ultimately harmful result of actions or lack of actions given a particular set of circumstances. It further assumes that this average person would have no special knowledge other than what is commonly known by the population of that area.

So the conclusion is if you took prudent steps to learn what may threaten your business, developed plans to defend against those threats and then implemented those plans effectively, then you have taken Reasonable Care. However, if you have failed in any of those steps, that is, not looking for threats, not planning to deal with them, or not effectively implementing those plans, then there is a good chance that an injured party will be able to collect damages from your company.

1.4 LET'S GET STARTED

That may sound like a logical approach and simple to implement, but the road ahead is filled with potholes and the purpose of this book is to help you navigate around those potholes. So where do we begin? Your first step is to identify your assets.

Assets are people and property … notice that "people" come first; they are not only the most expensive element of a business, they are also the hardest to replace. Begin by identifying who you are protecting and where they work; Chapter 2 will help you with that. Also in Chapter 2 you will find guidelines on conducting a "Goal Setting Meeting", that is, a policy setting exercise where you establish the boundaries of your protection. Security is not limited to just the security department, it touches every part of the entire company and so deciding on how best to secure the facility is a job for every leader of the company. In the case of employees, where does your duty to protect begin and where does it end? In most cases the demark is the company property line, when they are on company property they fall under the protection of the company, and when they are outside the company they have the right to choose their own level of protection.

The exception to this rule of thumb is Executive Protection. Some individuals are so valuable to a company that the loss of their personal expertise would result in a catastrophic failure of some portion of the company. This is usually the executives of the company (hence the name) but can also extend to other employees with special skills or knowledge. That is what the Goal Setting Meeting will determine.

Next you should identify the physical assets of the company, where they are located, how they are arrayed and how they are currently protected – these are some of the elements considered in Chapter 2. Next establish a value for these physical assets; the cost and trouble of replacement will help you decide how much to spend protecting them. For example, if you have a pump located outside the main structures, it is important but not vital, it is a small unit with a specialized purpose and cost $10,000 to replace (including labor). If your security measures cost more than the replacement cost, it would be better to use minimum security investments and simply have a spare pump on hand ready to be installed. On the contrary, if it is a vital component to the operation, cost becomes less important; or if it requires substantial effort to replace and the loss of this item results in a major disruption to the operation, then higher security costs can be easily justified.

As a security specialist, your opinion alone is not grounds for such justification; thus, you need to have members of the Goal Setting Meeting to help you determine the importance of this item to your overall security assessment.

Now you know what assets you have to protect, the value the company places on these assets and the impact losing any of these assets will have on the company's operation. So you are ready to begin your assessment.

1.5 WHAT THREATENS YOUR COMPANY?

That is not as easy as it may sound … sure, we can all name off a few of the obvious threats but what about the ones you didn't think of, what happens if you are surprised by something? The analysis tools at the end of Chapter 2 will help you identify those unlikely concerns.

"Unlikely", what is unlikely? The best example I can offer is a bank. Assume that you are a bank manager, your bank has never been robbed and no one has ever threatened to rob you, does that make robbery unlikely? Ask any banker and he will say "of course not". Because other banks have been robbed in the past, that puts his bank in the cross hairs of thieves; remember the old Bonnie and Clyde movie, "We rob banks because that is where the money is!". Well, you may have something somebody wants or something somebody takes issue with, in today's society it is not uncommon for people to act out against an organization because they do not like what the organization represents. It may not be justified, maybe they just believe something about your company that is not true but that does not make their acts any less harmful.

Additionally, some crimes are ones of passion and are directed against an employee. The most obvious is a disgruntled ex-employee seeking revenge for losing their job, or it may not be related to the company at all; it may be a spouse who has been hurt by an employee and wants to express their displeasure forcefully. It could even be something as simple as race or religious hatred and they want to make a public point by killing people. These are all threats that might not always come to mind. Chapter 2 will give you some examples to consider.

Of course there are the traditional sources of information such as internal incident reports and law enforcement crime reports; a brief examination of Internet sources may also provide food for thought, all of which is provided in Chapter 2.

1.6 THE GOAL SETTING MEETING

The process begins with a goal setting meeting. In this meeting the security professional helps company management review and establish firm policies for acceptable levels of risk to the company's operation. Defining the security policy with the management team ensures that the boundaries set for securing the facility represent the corporate or institutional goals. In the goal setting meeting, the security professional prepares for the Physical Threat Assessment by determining the following:

- Which employees are most susceptible to attack?
- What equipment is most critical to the operation?
- When are these assets most vulnerable?
- Are there off premise assets that also require attention?
- Are there are other vulnerable assets?
- Are there threats of damage to the assets of others?

The process culminates in a report to company management that describes:

- What threats concerns the company the most
- What threats "should" concern the company the most
- Which human assets are most threatened
- Which physical assets are most critical to continued business operations

1.7 HOW VULNERABLE IS THE COMPANY TO THOSE THREATS?

So here is where it gets interesting. Try to imagine you are the person acting out these threats and examine the company's protective measures AND procedures that bar your way. Are there unlocked doors or open windows, are the walls, doors and other barriers substantial enough to withstand an attack, how likely are you to get caught if you commit these acts? How about procedures, what do employees know about recognizing and reporting strangers on company property? How does the security force respond to potential threats? The methods used to examine these and other vulnerabilities are discussed in Chapter 3.

A vulnerability assessment is a comprehensive assessment of all current physical security measures and operational characteristics that affect the facility's ability to detect, deter, delay and respond to threats. It defines a protected perimeter and the nature of the perimeter barriers then identifies all openings in the protected perimeter and establishes the optimum means to control and monitor those openings. This book instructs the reader on the methods used in conducting a vulnerability assessment and the techniques for recording the information learned.

The vulnerability assessment begins with identifying critical assets of the operation and then establishing a protected perimeter around those assets. Chapter 3 discusses how to evaluate the material used to establish the perimeter and determine how well it can withstand attack from the perceived threats.

The vulnerability assessment identifies all openings in the perimeter and then suggests monitoring and control measures for each opening. In some cases, access to or egress from the opening is denied, while in other cases, electronic devices are suggested that grant access or egress based on user identification. The means for identification vary with each opening. A discussion of these variations is included in Chapter 3. The vulnerability assessment reviews the current physical condition of the facility. It may suggest enhancements in existing lighting and improvements in the structural elements of the building or perimeter fencing.

After developing a plan for protecting the company's assets, the vulnerability assessment describes how to identify threats to infrastructure resources. These are services that are critical to ongoing operations and include electrical service, communications, water, sewerage and other vital utilities. The company sometimes has a means to restore or supplement these resources if successfully attacked. The vulnerability assessment verifies these backup measures to confirm effectiveness. An example is emergency generators to supply power if the commercial power feed is lost.

The vulnerability assessment also examines the company's ability to respond to these threats. Chapter 3 shows how to examine where security personnel duty posts are and the ways and means to communicate the presence of a threat to the response team. It also addresses procedures currently used to instruct the force on how to respond to detected threats and the manpower skill level and availability for threat response. The goal is to determine the skill level needed for response and the training requirements for the existing force.

The vulnerability assessment examines security force surveillance needs and capabilities and provides ways to observe the force's ability to view events in all areas of the facility and properly classify the event (threat or no threat). You will learn how to use closed-circuit television equipment to expand the force's ability to quickly evaluate an event and provide a measured response.

Doors and windows are a given because we use them all the time and easily recognize their value in providing access but look closely. Examine the hinges and door latches, how are the doors locked, is it a dead bolt or a simple handle lock? The walls … there are security incidents where chain saws were used to cut a hole in a wall to gain access, in certain circumstances where the asset behind the wall is valuable enough to warrant that level of intrusion extra care must be taken to detect intrusion. Again, Chapter 3 will provide guidance on these issues.

So, we begin by establishing a secure perimeter. A secure perimeter is an unbroken line of walls, doors and other barricades that surround our assets. There is usually more than one perimeter; these are arrayed in concentric circles of protection, with each successive layer being more difficult to penetrate than the one that preceded it (Figure 1.1).

It is important to note when testing the perimeter that it is evaluated in "degrees" that is, how long and how much effort would it take to penetrate the doors, walls and other barricades such as fencing. The question that follows is: how long is long enough? Well, remember the key words in physical security: Deter, Delay, Detect and Respond. The perimeters should be able to withstand a deliberate attack by ordinary means for the time it takes the security staff to detect the attempt and respond appropriately.

Generally, the first perimeter is a fence line at the property line; these often have sensors to detect tampering or intrusion attempts and are sometimes made

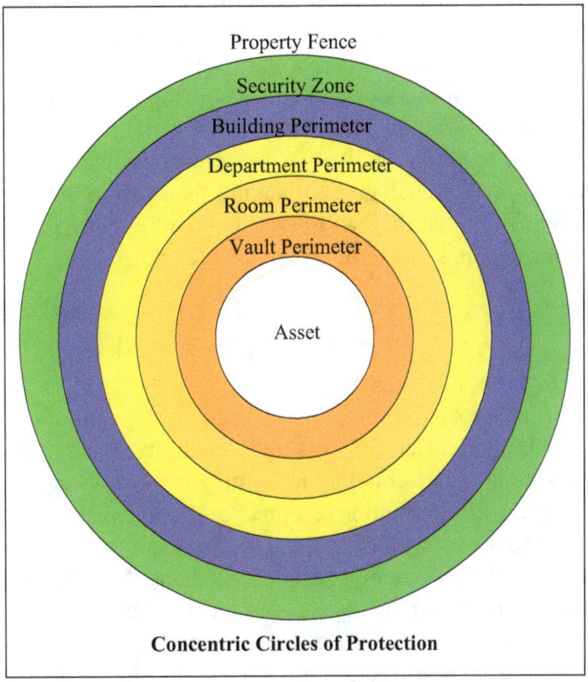

FIGURE 1.1 Concentric Circles of Protection.

of "climb-resistant" material (fence grids with holes that are too small to grip or high vertical sides that cannot easily be gripped). This can be a useful deterrent to intrusion attempts but no barrier is impenetrable, and you must assume that the fence line will be breached. Next focus on the detection of such a breach; if the asset value and the threat warrant it, a detection grid as the second perimeter may be needed. These are sensors that are above ground and some that are buried in the ground or provide a sensor net around the property, a kind of "no man's land" where activity can be easily detected.

Then examine the buildings which house the asset and look for ways to penetrate it; consider the delay factor closely in this part of the examination. For example, if you have a door with a 2-minute delay factor (it can withstand a 2-minute assault with bare hands or hand tools) and the alarm sensors can detect that attempt as soon as it starts AND it takes the security staff only one minute to reach that door, it is secure. However, if that door is located at a remote point and there are no security stations nearby, it may take 4 or 6 minutes to reach and the door is vulnerable. The point is that the delay factor should be great enough to delay successful penetration until a proper response can be made. Clearly, there are multiple variables; you can strengthen the door, station security personnel closer or increase the level of sensitivity of your sensors to detect the threat earlier.

Obviously, the use of the words "by ordinary means" is also important. Mentioned earlier was a case where chain saws were used to cut through a dry wall, there has even been a case where a forklift parked in the rear of a building was used to breach a roll up door and remove a safe located inside. These are unusual conditions and should only be considered if the asset is of particularly high value and the threat is likely. Also, the use of explosives is always a possibility but intruders are adverse to making their efforts obvious because it increases the likelihood that they will be caught. But explosives can be used to simply cause destruction, so it is not off the table completely.

1.8 THE COMMAND CENTER

After establishing the protective measures in the field, the vulnerability assessment determines if a Command Center exists and the ability of that center to gather, evaluate and disseminate information in a timely manner. There is a discussion of how to identify threat information resources and evaluate the protocols used to classify threats. The reader will understand how to determine the center's ability to communicate threat information to the force. Chapter 3 also provides a guideline to establishing and/or evaluating a Command Center.

At the Command Center all alarm information is presented and all control devices are managed, such as access control, elevator control, fire alarm detection and other basic building systems. This is also the primary observation point for video and audio surveillance and the radio control point for all security officers patrolling the facility. The Command Center's job is to know what is going on in the facility and direct resources and equipment to enforce company policy regarding the safety and security of the company.

1.9 CREATING THE DESIGN

At this point you now know which assets you must protect, the threats to those assets and the company's vulnerability to those threats; now it is time you create your initial security plan. Chapter 4 will help you analyze your findings, to reveal which areas need attention and the extent of that attention.

The information from the vulnerability assessment forms the basis of system design. Chapter 4 describes how to evaluate and document the data gathered during the vulnerability assessment in order to choose the right equipment to mitigate the threats uncovered. The chapter examines the best methods for recording a preliminary design and explains how these methods help to establish a well-defined bid. Good bid definition is essential in finding the right product at competitive prices.

The design establishes protected perimeters around critical assets using current floor plans and plot plans. Chapter 4 describes how to mark asset locations on the plans and then how to establish protected perimeters. It shows how to form protected perimeters in concentric circles around the assets using existing or planned structures as perimeter boundaries. A discussion follows on how to identify openings in the perimeters and the best way to secure them.

Chapter 4 also addresses selecting the proper type of alarm detection device for each opening and choosing the correct area sensor to use around protected assets to detect the presence of intruders.

Next mitigating steps will be selected to reduce or eliminate successful attacks for the anticipated threats. This assessment is more than just adding sophisticated electronics, and the recommendation may include altering the building configuration, sealing off doors or moving them, adding walls or changing procedures for the security staff or other employees. Standard company operations may need modification to make the company more secure and before announcing your plan, check with the managers of the affected departments to learn how your recommendations may adversely affect their ability to do their job.

Of course, you will probably be adding lots of technological devices because they reduce the labor needed to secure the facility and make the people you have now more effective at their job.

1.10 THE REST OF THE STORY

While all these steps are important, they are not the whole story. Chapter 5 will provide you with ideas on establishing the Command Center, organizing the response team and incident reporting. We will also cover employee identification, visitor controls and protocols with regulatory compliance. A guide is provided to help you set a security policy. Then there are brief discussions on communications, cybersecurity and, of course, litigation defense.

1.11 DOCUMENTING YOUR FINDINGS

You can do a first rate job at identifying the threats to your assets and having precise calculations on the vulnerabilities uncovered, but all of that will be for naught if no one understands your conclusions. Chapter 6 will help you with your documentation. You must convey not only your findings but also what it means to the company if they act or fail to act.

Your findings should include the immediate cost to the company if an attack is successful and suggest what the long-term ramifications might be. If you want this project to be funded, then everyone must have a clear understanding of the threats, how real they are and how likely they will occur.

Chapter 6 will also show you how to lay out your recommendation "graphically" so that the entire Goal Setting group will understand what areas of the company are affected by your proposals remembering that they will decide on funding your proposal. If there are serious legal consequences to a successful penetration by an attacker, that too should be included in your documentation. When all the analysis documentation is done, you are ready to present your security plan.

1.12 PRESENTING THE RECOMMENDATION

Your audience for this presentation is the management team you assembled for your Goal Setting Meeting. Here is where you tell them what you found in relation to the security goals they helped establish for the company. They will be interested in what you have to say but remember that security is not always at the top of their list; so job #1 is to get them interested!

Begin with the threats you identified … what are they, how likely are they to happen and what is the down side of those threats if they are successful? Statistics are helpful but relating the numbers and potential actions to company operations is the key to getting their attention; Chapter 7 can help you with that. If you are not used to making presentations to groups, you will find tips in Chapter 7 for assembling your visual presentation and your written "leave behind". Present your case and then provide a written package to all attendees to take with them. Take a phased approach because whatever your recommendation turns out to be, the price tag will usually give your audience sticker shock. By breaking up the implementation in distinct stages, putting the most important items first, you will demonstrate your awareness of budget limitations and increase your chances of acceptance.

1.13 TIME TO BUY

You did a great job, the team decided to accept the initial stages of your proposal; now it's time to make the vision a reality. This is a whole new challenge, there are over 400 substantial manufacturers of physical security products on the market today, and that is just the big guys, there are many more smaller but still viable manufacturers out there that will want your business. And to compound matters, there are multiple dealers that carry one or more of each of these product lines … how do you choose? More importantly, what are the ramifications of each choice?

The best place to start is with your purchasing department or purchasing agent; they know the company process and can guide your efforts. Unfortunately, you can't just hand him/her your recommendation and say "go buy it (!)"; there are still other steps that will require your efforts. Chapters 8, 9 and 10 can help you with that. But get your purchasing person on board early, they can save you some effort by telling you what they need to make this happen.

In Chapter 8 you will learn about the terms and conditions of Request For Proposal (RFP), Request For Quotations (RFQ), Request For Information (RFI) and other purchasing methods. Your purchasing department will help you determine company policy regarding the type of bid to use. The starting place for you with all of these approaches is the "Performance Specification". You will find suggestions in Chapter 9 on how to prepare these specifications.

Purchases of this size are often governed by internal rules that mandate certain actions; and if you are a government entity, those mandates are a matter of law, you must follow those guidelines. For example, the term above, "Performance Specification", is an important distinction. Chapter 9 addresses that and provides a comparison between Performance Specifications and Equipment Specifications. With a performance spec with you, do not say what equipment you want to buy; you say what you want the equipment to do. These types of specifications are usually released for bid using and RFP.

However, if you have an existing system and the new equipment must be compatible with the existing equipment, you can use an equipment spec. The equipment spec is easier to write, easier to evaluate and the bid documents are much easier to prepare; typically you would us the RFQ format. That approach assumes there are few variables, everyone is bidding on the same thing and you just want the best price.

Typically you are going to write the specification, not purchasing. Purchasing is good at following the rules for buying soliciting offers and can even be helpful in evaluating the bids, but they are not technology folks and the specifications describe the technology you need to do the job. You are the company expert on the job requirements so that task falls to you.

1.14 THE SYSTEM SPECIFICATION

So now you and the purchasing department have determined that you need to use an RFP because your organization's purchasing rules prohibit preselecting a product by brand and model. Consequently, you must describe the entire system with as much detail as possible because anything you don't describe will not be required. The description forms the basis of the contract with the vendor.

Chapter 9 will illustrate detail documents like the Door Detail Schedule and Camera Detail Schedule and will suggest ways of illustrating your requirements on floor plans and plot plans. Where necessary you can even use brand and model for some components to use "as examples only" to avoid having to list all of the characteristics of these devices.

Depending on the dialog you established in the Goal Setting Meeting you may want to package your completed plan and share it with the management team for final approval, but usually they will expect you to manage the entire process without further approval. When you think you are ready, you can then pass your specification package to purchasing for bid.

1.15 THE BID PROCESS

The purchasing department may need your help in identifying potential bidders if your company has not been previously active in the security market; Chapter 10 will provide some tips on finding and soliciting bids. One of the key elements of a successful bid is to have a long list of bidders.

Your specifications and the purchasing department's contract requirements will be released to the market to solicit offers; evaluating those offers can be a real challenge. Proper bid specification and "response requirements" described in Chapter 8 will help you in that evaluation process. Because you must use an RFP that also implies that your evaluation must be fair and even handed, you must be able to demonstrate that every bidder was given an equal opportunity to win your order. Of course, that makes the bid package that is much more important since your evaluation will depend on the information submitted. Chapter 10 will help you in your evaluation process.

1.16 THE AWARD OF CONTRACT

You've done it, the system was well defined and well documented, you received multiple bids and you were able to identify the best offer from among the bidders, now it is time to launch the project.

The purchasing department will have certain requirements for contract award but there is some preparation work for you too. When the legal and procedural matters are settled, call for a coordination meeting with the awardees; Chapter 11 will provide some tips on the process such as deciding on equipment storage, working hours and facility access. The vendor will want to deliver all the equipment as soon as possible and it may sit at your site for months waiting for installation. Ask how that will affect your warranty (it usually begins at delivery, not when it is put in service) and who will be responsible for the care of the equipment during that period? If the equipment is on your site, you are responsible and should something happen like a broken water pipe or a storm and the equipment is damaged, you may wind up buying the same equipment twice. Also consider billing (again look at Chapter 11); do you pay for equipment when delivered or when it is installed? The guiding principle is "caveat emptor", let the buyer beware.

After settling all the legal and logistical issues schedule an initial walkdown with the vendor and your maintenance staff. Visit every location for each piece of equipment, including the rooms where common equipment will be installed (control panels, wiring blocks, power supply locations, etc.) and discuss what is expected and solicit questions from the vendor. Involve the maintenance representative in the discussion especially for cable paths. Conclude the meeting with a request for a completion schedule and the requirements described in Chapter 11, such as as-built drawings and installation documentation and training.

1.17 FOLLOW UP

Inspect the job progress regularly to confirm that plans are moving forward as expected. If an issue arises, discuss it with the vendor's project manager, not the technicians on site. Monitor the schedule through to completion.

When the vendor declares the job "finished", it is time for commissioning. The formal definition of commissioning is as follows: "Project commissioning is the process of assuring that all systems and components of a building or industrial plant are designed, installed, tested, operated and maintained according to the operational requirements of the owner or final client". Observe and test all devices to ensure that they work as expected and the cosmetics of the installation is satisfactory; develop a punch list for all unsatisfactory items and present it to the vendor (see Chapter 11, System Acceptance for guidance).

After the system is accepted, schedule the training session for all users and plan for the users programming the system with the help of the vendor's technicians. When all are confident that the systems and the users are ready, notify the management team and then provide notice to the company about the start date of the new security program. On the start date apply power to all locks and other control devices.

During the next few weeks, periodically randomly check components, especially in sensitive areas, observe the use of controlled doors and how the system is responding, confirm the security personnel fully understand their jobs by observation and occasionally testing their knowledge. When you are satisfied that the implementation is complete, provide the management team with your final report.

So now let's begin the process!

CHAPTER 2

The Physical Threat Assessment

CONTENTS

2.1 SQUARE ONE

Usually some event raises company awareness toward the need for improved physical security in a facility or perhaps the general climate has become more threatening to company personnel or property. In any case, the company or their in-house security professional has determined that the physical security preparedness needs modification to deal with the current level of potential risk.

The first step in a security assessment is acceptance by the management team. You need to identify all the stakeholders in the process and bring them together for a discussion of the goals and limitations of the assessment. The best way to introduce the project to your team is through a "Scope of Work" (SOW), which is a proposed set of objectives; so everyone understands where this is going and what to expect as an end result. In the SOW you will define the ways in which improved physical security will protect the business operation, the security goals needed to achieve that protection and the means and methods to achieve those goals. The SOW is the introduction to the "Goal Setting Meeting"; that includes all the stakeholders in this project. Below is a sample index for your SOW (see Figure 2.1)

DOI: 10.4324/9781003490432-3

- Mission Objectives – the overall purpose of the assessment
- Study Approach – your basis for the assessment technique, this book, ASIS Guidelines, etc.
- Study Process – how you plan to carry out the assessment, the steps you will take
- Estimate of Probable Cost – how you plan to evaluate the cost of the recommendation
- Report Format – how you plan to structure the report that explains your findings
- Implementing the Study – what it will take to get started and initial costs you anticipate
- Follow Up – what will happen after the assessment is finished

The SOW will introduce your Goal Setting Meeting and begin to prepare the management team for your discussion. Goal setting is a management team review of the organization's security policy to identify or establish those policies for the assessment. Management employees in the policy-making capacity should attend along with interested parties from departments and outside agencies that have a vested interest in the development of the security policy. This forms the basis for the security assessment. Sample security policies are provided for each area of consideration. Figure 2.1 provides a sample agenda for the Goal Setting Meeting agenda.

The agenda provided a list of topics to discuss; not all may be required for your meeting, so review and carefully eliminate those areas that are of limited concern to your company, you don't want to bore your audience! You will note that policy-related topics have a proposed policy statement at the top of the topic list, this is not set in stone, it is merely a sample to suggest wording of your policy statements.

But you have some homework to do before requesting the meeting. Gather the information listed below:

- Contact information for all current security vendors but especially the companies that provide and service the existing security systems. Additionally, any guard or security monitoring companies that is currently being used.
- A copy of the following drawings for the existing buildings:
  - Plot plan for the entire property
  - Floor plan for each floor in each building in the study
  - Plans and specifications for any current changes planned for the facility that will materially affect walls, doors and windows

Usually, the physical plant or facilities department maintains these documents. If the company is located in a very old building and there are no plans readily available, the first step is to sketch the physical layout of

Security Goal Setting Meeting Agenda

Meeting Objective:

Goal setting is a management team review of the organization's security policy to identify or establish those policies for the consultant. Management employees in the policy making capacity should attend along with interested parties from departments and outside agencies that have a vested interest in the development of the security policy. This forms the basis for the security assessment. Sample security policies are provided for each area of consideration below.

Meeting Agenda

Assets

- Items of value or security concerns that will halt operations - show location on drawings

	○	Vulnerable executives
	○	Do you have "critical skills" employees at your facility? Where?
	○	mission critical assets (the loss will shut down the operation)
	○	High values items, what is the estimated total cost to replace
	○	Any hard assets to protect, i.e. server farm, main frame & data storage etc.
	○	explosive, corrosive or high flammable material
	○	controlled substances (drugs and other legally controlled items)
	○	Select Agents (biological hazards)

- Personnel:

	○	How many employees and staff will work in this facility?
	○	How many NON-employees work in this building, contract workers, contract service personnel etc?

- Facility Characteristics:

	○	What are the hours of operation, (days of the week, times of the day)?
	○	Any group of employee critical (would shut down operations in near terms)
	○	If the operation is not a standard business day, are there "shifts" and what are the periods of each shift?
	○	Are there "tenants" in this building, defined herein as independent entities who pay money to use the facility but are not connected to the prime occupant either financially or administratively?
	○	If there are tenants, who are they and how many people from their companies are expected to work in this building and where will they work?
	○	Are there considerations for neighboring properties with regard to light pollution on the exterior perimeter of the building?
	○	Given that a determined thief intends access to the building, what is the delay factor to allow proper response (typical is 2 minutes)? The question is intended to identify how substantial the doors must be and if door status monitoring is required for the security staff.
	○	In addition to breeching the security perimeter via a doorway, is there a concern that elements of threat will also attempt to gain entry by breaking into windows or glass walls surrounding the building?
	○	Do you have a receiving dock at this facility that periodically receives merchandise?
	○	Has there been shrinkage in material or equipment from your facility?
	○	On average, what is the police response time?

FIGURE 2.1 Sample Agenda for the Goal Setting Meeting.

the grounds and buildings. The best way to do this is to view the facility using Google Earth, capture the image of the campus (be careful with the scale, if the campus is large you may want to break it up into sections). Impose the captured image on a drawing program and trace the outer perimeter and each building perimeter, then add other immovable features on the site that may affect your security design decisions. Whether readymade drawings are used or sketches are developed for the facility, the same document types are needed. These documents are:

- Plot Plan – The plot plan is an illustration of the property boundaries of the company and, usually, fencing or other perimeter barricades used to restrict access to company grounds. The plot plan will generally contain an outline of all buildings on the property although without any detail regarding the specific characteristics of the building. In many cases, plot plans have been used as a “base document” to establish a description of facility-wide services. Such services would include telecommunications, data communications and existing security measures. See Figure 2.2 for an example of a plot plan.

- Floor Plan – A floor plan is an illustration of the walls and door locations of a building. It is essential to have a copy of the first floor of each building’s floor plan, but it may not be necessary to obtain copies of the upper floors if security measures will not be needed on those floors (Figure 2.3).

Building plans are generally arranged in “sets”. As a result, plan holders may ask you which “set” is needed. Request “floor plan only”, this is the most informative for vulnerability assessments.

- Copies of, or access to, the protocols currently used by the response team (if any).
- Copies of, or access to, any current written policies on security.
- Copies of, or access to, any incident reports over the past 3 years concerning security incidents.
- Prepare a sample letter of introduction to employees for top management.

Review these documents so that you are familiar with the physical layout of the company and a general idea of the previous security incidents. You may even want to begin marking your plans. I prefer to do this in a computer-assisted drawing (CAD) program, but if you are not CAD savvy, you can use paper with a red pencil.

Using the drawings described above, define each security perimeter. The security perimeter is always relevant to the protected assets. The physical threat assessment will identify those areas that are of most concern to the company. Establish the security perimeter based on the location of those assets. Obviously that has not yet been done, so you will not finish this step now but it will help you in the goal setting meeting if you start here (Figure 2.4). There is much more on this in the next chapter.

There may be several perimeters within a facility. The perimeters are loosely defined as concentric circles around protected assets. During the vulnerability assessment, it may be determined that there are insufficient barricades or too

Threat Assessment Defined by Management

Policy:	The Company shall identify all threats to its assets, both internal and external, and make preparations to mitigate those threats.
•	Internal
○	disgruntled employees
○	Industrial espionage
○	other internal threats?
•	External
○	Indigents
○	Crimes of opportunity
○	Professional thief
○	Terrorists (and related behaviors)
•	Should we perform an external threat assessment (adds at least $5,000 to cost)

Vulnerability Assessment

- **Exterior Perimeter**

Policy:	The exterior perimeter of the company property shall be protected by barriers to resist entry providing a resistance value of at least 4 minutes and by monitoring devices to register an alarm should the barrier be breached.
○	Do we control property boundaries
○	Parking security for passengers and the security of vehicles

- **Building Perimeter**

Policy:	All building openings will be locked and monitored except for the main entry which will be monitored by on-site personnel throughout the business day. The main entry door will be locked and monitored with all other openings after working hours. All openings will be barricaded by doors with a resistance value of at least 2 minutes.
○	Are all areas open to the public? Identify
○	Are offices locked down during an incident? How implemented? How notified?
○	Are we concerned with after hours intrusions?
○	Are we concerned about ramming threats?

- **Access Control**

Policy:	Only Authorized individuals will be permitted to enter company buildings and only a select set of individuals will be permitted to enter certain restricted areas that contain our most valuable assets. Regardless of the access permissions at an opening, any individual may exit that opening at any time. Access will be granted only during business hours and entry locations and times will be assigned individually.
○	How many employees do you have who require access to this facility?
○	Does everyone access all areas or do we limit by area / room? If not where are the restrictions?
○	Assumes controlled access and UNRESTRICTED egress or monitor egress?
○	What are the access hours for each group of occupants 24 / 7 business hours other?
○	Is there a concern that employees may intentionally or unintentionally permit others to use their access privilege?
○	Is there a concern that an employee may be held under duress and forced to permit an unauthorized person to gain access to a controlled area?
○	Method of ID: Keypad: dumb or programmable Credential reader: mag stripe, prox, fob, combined with keypad Biometric: print, hand, eye, voice

FIGURE 2.1 (Continued)

- **Remote Investigations CCTV and Audio**

Policy:	Monitoring will take place on company property 24 hours a day, 7 days a week. All openings to the company's buildings will be monitored as will all corridors and stairwells. Certain other areas containing critical assets will also be monitored from multiple angles.
•	Are we concerned about the area outside the outer perimeter security of the building? That is, do we wish to observe the sidewalks surrounding the building as well as the building perimeter for unwanted activity? How determined should that investigation be, do we want a patrol officer to examine situations in detail or will a view remotely be sufficient?

- Existing CCTV system

o	Locate cameras and views, FIXED / PTZ (requires Response Team)
o	All cameras IP
o	Common power camera service or POE
o	Where are the monitors

- New or Expanded CCTV system

o	Covert or overt cameras?
o	Monitor every access control point, which areas deserve special attention (spaces)
o	Who will do the monitoring? (required throughout the business day)
o	Where will the monitoring room be located?
o	Should we allow the monitor to have a dialog with a suspect?

- Recording Images for evidentiary data

o	All cameras connected to recorders, location
o	Recording retention time 30 days
o	Will archive recordings be required

- Existing Audio Surveillance system

o	Locate microphones and audio ranges (requires Response Team)
o	Where are the monitors

- **Alarm Monitoring and Response**

Policy:	The response team will monitor the status of all exterior and building perimeter openings and investigate any opening that appears to be unauthorized within 2 minutes of receiving an alarm. Additionally, the team will monitor enunciators for indications of employees in distress and respond as quickly as possible.
o	Exterior property perimeter (if required) locate the boundaries
o	Building perimeters
o	Asset perimeter interior areas (space sensors), if required
o	PANIC buttons
o	After hours intrusion detection required? Where is panel?
o	Lockdown Are there any "safe rooms" in the facility? Discuss Pod Controls.

FIGURE 2.1 (Continued)

- **Response Team and Incident Reporting**

Policy:	The company will have an in-house security presence who will monitor all areas around the exterior perimeter and building perimeter plus provide close attention to areas containing our most critical assets. This security team will classify all unusual activity as a "threat / no threat" and respond to all threats within 2 minutes of discovering an incident. The security team will be trained on apprehension and investigation and have a means to hold a suspect until public law enforcement arrives.
●	Will there be an employee position in the company that serves as a Director of Security? Has that person been named or hired yet, if not, when?
●	Is there a police presence on-site?
●	Is a response team planned for this facility (private security force, contract guards, paid details from the police department)? If yes, what is the extent of that service, how many guards, where are the stations, will there be roving patrols, how will they communicate etc.
●	If there is no response team, what type of response for a detected incident is required?
●	If no response team is provided, does the security policy of the company require video surveillance for evidentiary data (used for police investigations)?
○	Do you have a security station … location
●	Are their roving patrols, in what areas are they concentrated?

●	Incident Reporting Policy: Every incident that results in injury (employee or visitor) or loss of any company asset will be investigated and reported on the appropriate company form. All reports, photographs, recordings or other material pertinent to the incident will be stored in a controlled location and preserved for not less than 10 years.
○	Who investigates incident
○	Central reporting

- **Employee Identification**

Policy:	Every employee will be issued an identification badge that must be displayed at all times while on company premises.
○	Will it be necessary to identify employees with identity badges? Biometrics?
○	Will it be necessary to identify contract workers with identity badges?
○	What is the current process?
○	Are you satisfied with current process?
○	Do all occupants wear ID badges?
○	Are badges currently used for access control anywhere in the company?
○	Who issues ID badges, where?
○	See sample ID, can this be changed?
○	Other uses for credentials, copy machines, terminals etc.

- **Visitor Control**

Policy:	All visitors must obtain permission from the Main Entry Desk and be confirmed by the employee they are visiting before allowed on premises.
○	Visitors entry point and general destination
○	How many visitors are expected in this facility on a daily basis?
○	How do you distinguish authorized visitors from the general public?
○	Will visitor escorts be necessary, from what point (main lobby, department entrance etc.)?
○	Is permission from the staff required for a visitor to obtain access?
○	Can any employee authorize a visitor to enter the facility? If not, which groups can provide that authorization?
○	What items may a visitor NOT bring into the facility? How do you prevent this?
○	Will the visitor be permitted to drive a vehicle on company property
○	Will the Response Team be required to search visitor vehicles

FIGURE 2.1 (Continued)

•	Visitor Identification Policy: Information will be collected from all visitors before entering company property (define the elements of information required.
o	Will it be necessary to verify the identity of the visitors?
o	Do you want to control where visitors go
o	Would a time limit for visitors that automatically expires be useful?
o	Do you require the visitor to be escorted?
o	Have your employees found non-employees in sensitive areas?
o	What do employees do when unauthorized personnel are observed?
o	Identification credential verification, (such as a driver's license)
o	Should visitor credentials be held until departure?
o	Should visitors be photographed?

•	Visitor Badging Policy: all visitors must wear verified access badges while on company grounds.
o	Are visitors curently controlled at entrances, what is that control?
o	How many visitors do you see per day?
o	Will visitors be required to wear badges?
o	What information is currently captured from a visitor?
o	Do you now store invoration on visitors in the past, for how long?
o	Do badges expire

- **Protocols and Regulatory Compliance**

Policy:	The management staff will provide detailed instructions to all employees on how to respond to all recognized security threats and to identify and comply with all legal and corporate security requirements.
o	Do you have a written security PROCEDURE for alarm response and other incidents?
o	Are employees trained on security procedures, how? Are the procedures written?
o	Is the security training repeated at intervals?
o	Do you have mandates for security from external sources (regulations) or internal sources (upper management)?

Related Security Areas

- **Communications**

o	Is there communications between offices and the guards, what?
o	Do you have paging capabilities, automated announcements?
o	What is the protocol for an employee observing an incident?
o	How does security summon the police?
o	How does an occupant signal distress to security?

•	Lighting -Is there adequate lighting in all areas, including Parking?
•	Signage - Can a police officer who has never been here before know where to go when an incident is reported?
•	Blast Proximity - Are we concerned about proximity explosives?
•	Utilities and Emergency Power ENTRANCES- Any critical utilities to protect?

FIGURE 2.1 (Continued)

many openings in the protected perimeter to adequately secure the facility. The system design recommendations may include additional walls, doors or fence lines to create new perimeters later (Figure 2.5).

Start with the exterior perimeter – usually the outer boundaries of the company's property line – and then establish the protected perimeters for each of the internal areas based on the location of the assets protected. For instance, if there are four buildings in the facility, each building will have a potentially protected perimeter. Each inner layer will receive progressively higher grades of protection.

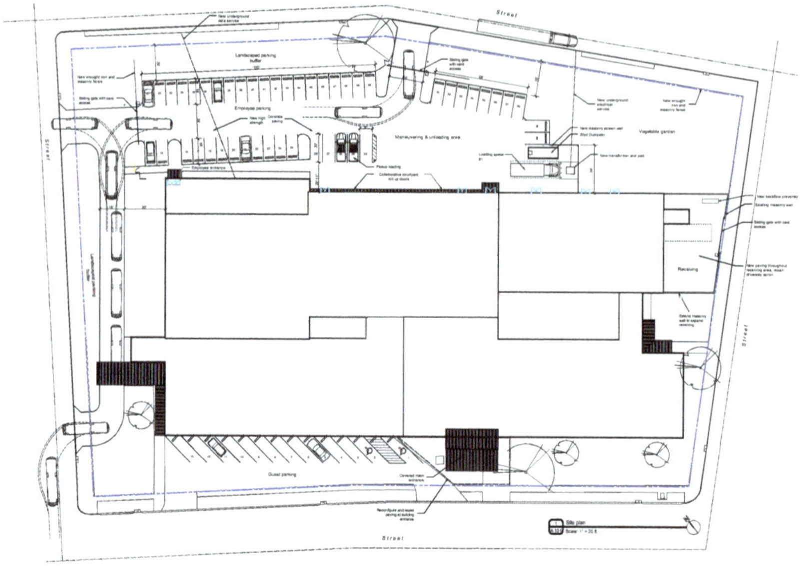

FIGURE 2.2 Example of Plot Plan.

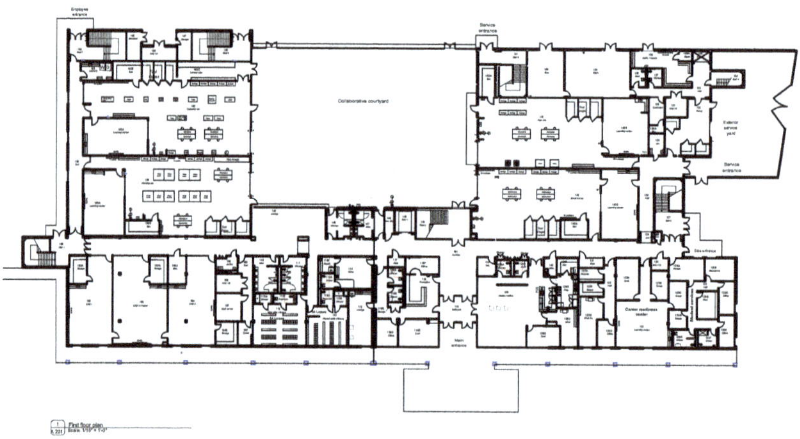

FIGURE 2.3 Example of a Floor Plan.

There are also circumstances, such as single facility office buildings where the outer perimeter is the building's outer walls and the internal perimeters are asset areas within the building. Each inner layer may have higher levels of security to protect highly sensitive assets. An example of such an arrangement would be to provide "building level" access control at the exterior perimeter and more restrictive access for a data processing center within the building. In the

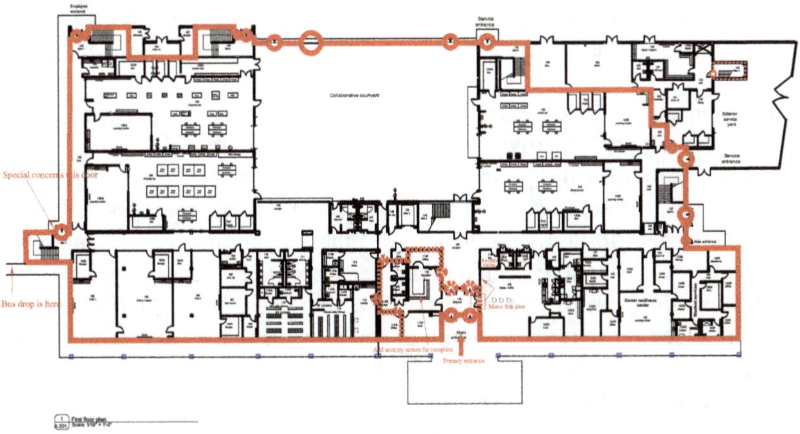

FIGURE 2.4 Sample Floor Plan with Perimeter Markings.

FIGURE 2.5 Concentric Circles of Protection as a Floor Plan.

data center, there may be highly sensitive information. Access control to these areas will require greater protective measures such as biometric identification devices.

Each progressively smaller circle should provide higher levels of security to protect the more sensitive assets. When creating this design, it is only important to establish the perimeters and the level of security needed within each area. It is not necessary to establish controls for these openings at this time but it is important to know the location of these openings. For example, in a fence line surrounding a protected perimeter, know where every opening exists in that fence line, even if the opening is seldom used. If the facility does not have a protected fence line, start with the outer walls that encompass the assets requiring protection. Be sure to include windows and other openings that may provide access to the facility. Do not assume that because an opening is rarely used, such as a "fire exit", it does not need protection. Consider any break in the perimeter as an opening.

2.2 THE GOAL SETTING MEETING

At this point you have already prepared your SOW, provided it to the management team along with an invitation to the Goal Setting Meeting and the agenda you prepared. Also, you are familiar with the company campus, building layouts and prior incidents; now it is time to set the security policy. During this process remember that the management team sets the goals and you guide them through the process. This is not something they think about all day nor should you expect them to have particular policy ideas in mind, although they sometimes do. Your agenda will navigate this decision process.

In many companies the security goals are not well established and only reflect reactions to past incidents, they do not often step back and consider the whole picture as you are making them do now. If the process becomes too laborious, suggest deferring details to a "committee" named by the management team and concentrate on the big picture in your meeting.

Also, setting policy required that you word those policies to limit the scope of what will be done. The simplest example is protecting personnel, you should restrict those protection efforts to company grounds and not extend beyond that point except where certain individuals fall under an Executive Protection requirement (more on that later). Part of this meeting is to identify the level of acceptable risk the company will assume; policy statements determine this risk level.

If the company has a current policy for security or acceptance risk, that would be an excellent place to start. Review each section of those statements to determine the level of risk associated with security concerns and, in the absence of an existing formal policy, the agenda guideline referred to earlier will provide examples.

In the meeting write statements that describe your understanding of the management team's assigned risk levels. An example might be as follows: "All employees are required to obtain and wear employee identification at all times while on company property" and another may be:

> The identity of all visitors on company property must be verified by company security before a visitor is permitted to enter company facilities. Visitors must present a valid picture ID to the receptionist and the information on that credential must be recorded along with the time, date and purpose of the visit.

These policy statements will set the stage for the threat assessment and vulnerability study. More on policy setting is presented in Chapter 5.

A policy mandates standards for acceptable conduct. Policies generally contain the following elements:

- Statement of need or rationale
- Statement of purpose
- General principles
- Definitions
- Procedure
- Statement of relationship to existing policies

Policies translate the abstract business values of the operation's mission statement into practical terms to shape the behavior of personnel. The goal is for personnel performance to be consistent with the company's mission statement and values.

The management team or policy development committee need to understand that a policy is never finished. Even though management approves the policy, it can be improved over time. New situations, new threats and methods of mitigation will necessitate policy revisions.

This meeting determines what the company is most concerned about with regard to threats to the operation. The second step in the process is to determine what threats the company "should be" concerned about regarding ongoing operations. This is usually determined by researching the crime statistics of the area, the steps taken by similar organizations to counter the threats that cause them concern and other factors as discussed later.

A note on litigation … threats from litigants will be covered in more detail later in Chapter 5, Litigation Defense, but for now remember that the company is exposed to civil action if you are not aware of the criminal environment that surrounds your location. By that I mean that if a person is injured or is killed by an assailant on your property, even if that person is a visitor not an employee, one of the first steps of a plaintiff is to examine “reasonable anticipation” and “reasonable care”. These are further defined in Chapter 5. The argument is simple, even if you did not know of a threat but “should have known” that such a threat might be possible, your company can be found guilty of failure to have reasonable anticipation and provide reasonable care against criminal acts. Thus, as part of your threat assessment, you should request a police report of the crimes in your area or at least engage a professional security consultant to make such a determination. While this may, or may not, influence your decision to act depending on the findings, it will serve you well by demonstrating that you sought information to develop reasonable anticipation of criminal activity and made plans to take reasonable care. It is a solid defense against litigation.

Management approval early in the process is essential to the success of the survey and any resulting recommendations. Obtaining management approval is not always easy; the historical view of security was that it is a “cost” to the operation. It will come as no surprise to security professionals with experience in the industry that security is usually under-funded and undermanned. Company resources tend to flow toward elements of the business that created profit. One of your role is to help the company see that profits and the long-term viability of the operation may be in jeopardy if the company does not take adequate security measures.

Moreover, employees and visitors must feel that the company has provided a safe and threat-free environment in which to conduct business. The presence of adequate security measures in today’s threat-filled environment can become a true asset in attracting and retaining top-quality employees.

It would also be helpful to start a second list of “security solutions” identified by the committee. In today’s “movie magic” security world, company employees that work with the security problems on a daily basis often learn about ideas or products that they feel would be ideal in their circumstance. Although some of these suggestions may be inappropriate, the “wish list” will help to surface more information about the company’s security problems. Remember that you are there to guide, advise and recommend. Investigate all ideas for reasonable application and budget constraints. The company managers will make the final decision as to which of these options most closely meet their objectives based, in part, on your recommendations.

When beginning a security improvement project, companies will frequently call for a security vendor to perform their security assessment. There are pitfalls in this process that are usually not obvious to the company’s management team. Security vendors are there to sell products, not perform an independent assessment. Product vendors will usually limit their recommendations to the products they sell and not provide an overall comprehensive assessment of security needs.

Security system sales personnel will often portray themselves as "consultants" but their primary mission is to sell equipment or services. Many are quick to recommend expensive equipment solutions when threats or vulnerabilities are identified, but they fail to examine the consequences of inaction. For example, if doors to a particular area are unmonitored, an equipment salesperson may recommend the use of card readers and electric locks to secure the door. They may not consider the assets behind the door nor the frequency with which the door is used.

One of the key questions to answer when deciding to apply a card reader to a door is if there is something of value behind the door (people or property) and if the door is high traffic. If the door restricts access to a storage area that contains inexpensive cleaning supplies, then a simple door status switch may be a better solution. If the door were opened only once a week during business hours, a standard lock with a metal key would be a more cost-effective protection method.

"Consequences of loss" is an another important element of physical threat assessment. It is helpful to orient the management team members attending the meeting to view the process as a mission of discovery for all possible threats and not just ones that can be solved using particular pieces of equipment.

To conclude the initial goal setting meeting, you should reiterate the problem areas identified, and help the committee establish a priority or level of importance for each item listed. This list becomes the goals of the security improvement project. Some examples of identified goals with respect to the problems identified earlier are as follows:

- Control access to sensitive areas and require proper authorization for entry.
- Establish corridors for visitor access and prevent unauthorized entry.
- Prevent unauthorized personnel from entering specific employee areas.
- Provide a means to expand and extend security officers' presence to all areas of the facility.
- Control the use of emergency exit doors and limit access and egress to "emergency only".
- Protect valuable company assets from unauthorized use and observation.

End the discussion with what information you will provide the committee for their decisions. Document the results of the initial meeting to firmly establish what was discussed and what were the resulting decisions of the management team. A complete record of company decisions will help in defining why you took the steps that followed the meeting. Here is an example of meeting minutes (Figure 2.6).

In addition to the minutes of the meeting, prepare and request approval of a letter of introduction to other company employees not included in the goal setting meeting. Transmit a copy of that letter to all interviewees before the scheduled interviews. Here is a sample letter of introduction (Figure 2.7).

Minutes of Initial Meeting (Date)
Physical Security System Improvement Project

Date
Consultant Name and Title
Consulting Firm Name

The Physical Security Improvement Committee met for the first time on (date). The agenda for the meeting accompanies this report.

Those attending the meeting were:

Name	Dept / Company	Phone
(List each member)		

The committee convened and reviewed the process to be used in executing the physical security improvement project. The role of the consultant and the committee was discussed and the purpose of this project was described as follows:

Develop specifications for a new physical security system to meet the following goals and then implement the most effective system found within budget to achieve these goals:

- Control access to sensitive areas and require proper authorization for entry
- Establish corridors for visitor access and prevent unauthorized entry
- Prevent unauthorized personnel from entering specific employee areas
- Provide a means to expand and extend security officer presence to all areas of the facility
- Control the use of emergency exit doors and limit access and egress to "emergency only"
- Protect valuable company assets from unauthorized use and observation

The project time line was discussed. It was noted that if all matters proceed as planned, the project will take approximately (number) months to complete, with completion being defined as an installed, working system.

The process for equipment specification and evaluation was then reviewed. That process included a two-phase approach, covering system features, the business plan offered by the vendors and the service capability of the vendors. The Committee was in agreement with the methodology presented by the consultant.

A Threat Analysis was discussed and it was decided by the committee that company managers were keenly aware of the threats to the organization and external research was not required in the threat analysis. An interview list of company personnel was established for the consultant to identify the personnel and hard assets to be protected.

Goals were set for the next committee meeting and included:

- Results of the management-defined Threat Analysis
- An overview of the company's vulnerabilities as these relate to identified threats
- A budget for addressing these vulnerabilities
- A decision to proceed with system acquisition and implementation

END OF REPORT

FIGURE 2.6 Initial Meeting Minutes.

Date

LETTER OF INTRODUCTION

This is to introduce (Consultant) and members of the consulting firm of (Company Name). (Company Name) has been engaged to study the security systems and protocols used in our facility and report those findings to security management.

Please extend every courtesy to (Consultant) and his staff. They are authorized to review and copy incident reports, security logs, post orders, videotapes and other similar records maintained by our security staff during the course of their work for our company. The staff of (Company Name) may enter secure areas of the facility in the same manner as any of the company's employees. In areas where sensitive information is kept or critical systems are in use, (Company Name) has been informed that a company escort may be required.

The purpose of (Company Name) review is to help us better define our security needs and formulate a recommendation to improve our security systems, policies and procedures. Your full cooperation will be appreciated. Please advise my office of any concerns you have regarding this access to our facility and records.

Sincerely

Security Manager

FIGURE 2.7 Sample Introduction Letter.

2.3 THE SELECTION COMMITTEE

While you have the management team assembled, you will want to begin to develop "buy-in" for the conclusions you reach and the actions you plan to take. The best way to garner that support from the management team is to ask for volunteers for a selection committee. Before the meeting consider the most appropriate personnel for that role … they would be the managers with the greatest stake in the outcome of the upgraded security systems. Suggest these few management team members (at least two) become your co-designers. You will provide the technical and security expertise and they will view your decisions from the management perspective.

2.4 IDENTIFYING ASSETS

The company's assets must be clearly defined so that the security assessment will protect the important elements of the company and the threats to those assets can be clearly identified. Threat identification leads to a recognition of vulnerability and an estimate potential loss comes from knowing the consequences of failing to mitigate those threats. This will establish the value of the solutions. Without this regimented approach, system component selection will be uncertain.

In the goal setting meeting, the assets that concerned the company the most were defined in "broad stokes". Before beginning interviews, make a detailed

Threat Analysis Department Questionnaire

Company Name:	Project:	Date of Survey:

Contact:

Department Name:	
Manager's Name:	
Manager's Title:	
Phone Number:	
E-Mail:	

Department Area	
Building	Floor

Department Data:

Number of employees in this department:		
Approximate area of department:		Sq Feet
Are visitors permitted in this area (yes / no):		
Are deliveries received in this area (yes / no):		

What critical operational personnel and assets are in this department:

Primary Security Concerns: Vulnerable times, off-premise assets, threats from adjacent facilities

1	
2	
3	
4	
5	

FIGURE 2.8 Department Questionnaire.

list of these assets (including personnel) and prepare to expand on this list as the interview process unfolds.

Prepare an outline for interviews with company personnel. Here is a sample data gathering form (Figure 2.8).

2.4.1 Which Employees Are Most Susceptible to Attack?

All employees are valuable to a company but in most cases perpetrators are interested in those employees that represent high hostage value or are mission-critical personnel. Department management can best direct attention to those employees that are the most obvious targets for hostile action. Additional consideration should be given to the protection of employees who are most threatened and are candidates for "Executive Protection". While the name implies a management role, these individuals may also be engineers, product developers and other essential personnel whose absence would have a substantial effect on company operations. An example of this kind of employee is a key mid-level manager who is responsible for product development decisions.

In these cases, protection may extend off company premises and in a few of these cases that protection may result in a personal protector who is always nearby to protect the most valuable employee. The level and type of protection will be discussed later, but for now, identifying these individuals is the goal.

2.4.2 What Equipment Is Most Critical to the Operation?

To determine what equipment is most critical to the operation, it is best to discuss the operational process with production or operations managers. Ask them what a perpetrator could do to effectively disable the operation. In most instances, you need to have a "criminal mentality" and try to imagine what the criminal would do, having insider knowledge, to disrupt the flow of business. You can help the operations managers establish an order of priority for those assets that are most critical to the business. This will help focus attention on those assets when designing the security system.

An example of such a situation would be an oil refinery with a production critical processor. The failure of this device will cause the entire plant to shut down even though other facilities on the plant are operational. This would be a top priority and deserve the most attention.

Given that same example the loss of an engineering office or quality testing office in the plant might pose a disruption in the production process but would not instantly shut down the entire plant. This would be a less important priority and may deserve less attention. A third example would be an administrative office. Damage or disruption to this part of the facility may prove a serious inconvenience to the operation but may not stop production. In all cases, however, we assume that there is damage to the physical asset and not to personnel. Protection of personnel is always a top priority.

2.4.3 When Are These Assets Most Vulnerable?

Most businesses operate on cycles with critical timing elements. An example of this is a retail operation just before or during the Christmas shopping period. While business disruptions during any time of the year can create serious hardship for a business, retail operations make the majority of their earned revenues during the Christmas season.

Disruption to most retail operations is more severe during the Christmas shopping cycle. Additionally, certain times of the day render businesses more susceptible to crime. An example of this would be a law office with sensitive case files. While this office is vulnerable to attack 24 hours a day, surreptitious entry and the seizure of vital information would, in most cases, seem to be prevalent after normal working hours.

Most managers will consider the 24-hour day cycle but give little thought to the annual changes in business activity. It would be most helpful to remind facility managers when conducting these discussions to also think on this broader scale.

2.4.4 Are There Off-Premise Assets That Also Require Attention?

In addition to discussions with operations managers, some accounting personnel can provide information about off-premise assets. A comprehensive physical security plan must also consider these assets.

The Physical Threat Assessment will establish a list of all of assets that can be destroyed or damaged, resulting in significant business interruption. However, a comprehensive security plan will include provisions for damage due to natural threats such as hurricanes, floods, earthquakes and similar catastrophes. We will not address other natural threats; the focus of this work is to assess "man-made" threats.

Begin with the assumption that there are perpetrators with deliberation and intent who seek to cause harm to the facility or to the individuals that work or visit the company. The objective of the physical security assessment is to establish the means for detection, deterrence, delay and response to man-made threats.

2.4.5 Other Vulnerable Assets

Determine what other assets or services are imperative to company operation. An example is public utilities such as communications, gas, water and power. These are non-owned facilities but are essential to continued operation. What disruption can occur in the operations if these assets were successfully attacked?

2.4.6 Threats from Damage to the Assets of Others

Take the same approach with examining external threat data. Some information like generalized local crime statistics can be obtained with relative ease from public records. However, industry-specific data may require a special report from a qualified firm and some of these reports can be costly. In addition, collecting industry information from comparable business operations can be labor intensive and expensive. Before committing to the collection and analysis of industry threat data or acquiring reports of industry-specific crime statistics, discuss the cost–benefit relationship with the company management. Determine the value of the additional information and allow company management to decide if these additional investments are worth the additional confidence they will add to conclusions about potential threats.

In addition to harm that would result from direct attacks on company assets, also consider consequential damage of attacks to the assets of others in the surrounding area. For example, if a chemical plant was located next to company property and a perpetrator successfully attacked the plant, assess the harm that could result to company assets from the damage or destruction of the neighboring facility. Toxic chemical spills and harmful vapors can be as deadly a threat as a direct attack on the company.

Here are some other threats to consider:

- Domestic Activist – Picket
- Domestic Activist – Vandalism
- Domestic Partner Assault
- Domestic Violent Extremist Active Shooter
- Domestic Violent Extremist Arson
- Domestic Violent Extremist Assault
- Domestic Violent Extremist Explosive Attack
- Employee Assault on Employee
- Employee Assault on Visitor
- Gang Member Assault
- Gang Member Vandalism
- Larceny/Theft – canteen, cafeteria or loading dock items
- Outsider Surveillance
- Outsider Assault on Employee
- Outsider Assault on Visitor
- Robbery of Employee
- Terrorism/Violent Extremists Disrupt Operations
- Terrorism/Violent Extremists Mass Casualty
- Theft – Drugs
- Theft of Money/Bursar/Canteen
- Theft of HVAC/Electrical Utility for Scrap Value
- Theft/Larceny – Maintenance/Contractor Tools and Materials
- Theft/Larceny – Office Equipment
- Utility Shutdown – Disrupt Operations
- Vehicle Break-in/Theft
- Violent Extremists Hostage Takeover

2.5 CYBER THREATS

This book is not intended to address cyber threats; we are only concerned here with physical threats but threats from cyberattack can be just as damaging. Cyber threats can shut down operations, rob funds and destroy customer good will. While it is not a subject for discussion here, this does not mean that it is not important.

Please add a cyber defense to your security plan and seek the guidance of a cyber expert on how best to approach the subject.

2.6 THE THREAT ASSESSMENT INTERVIEWS

Now you understand what assets the management team views as critical to the company's operation, it is time to review these assets with those who use them, specifically department heads and group managers. You have already prepared your interview guide and you have a letter of introduction; send that letter along with your meeting invitation to the appropriate personnel and begin your reviews. Depending on your corporate culture, you may also want to send a copy of the interview guide so that the person you are meeting will be better prepared to answer your questions. Conduct the interviews, gather your data and catalog it for further review.

Interviews with the company's front-line employees may not be necessary but be prepared to discuss security with anyone who expresses concerns. Each level of employee may have a different perspective on the possible threats to their portion of operational responsibilities. Each successive level of interviews provides greater comprehension in the overall assessment.

Interviews at lower administrative levels will not always reveal a substantially greater degree of information. There is a concept used by accountants and economists that describe this relationship, called "the point of diminishing returns". It is an economic law, also called the law of diminishing marginal returns, which expresses a relationship between input and output. It states that adding units of any one input (labor, capital, etc.) to fixed amounts of the others will yield successively smaller increments of output. In common usage, the "point of diminishing returns" is a supposed point at which additional effort or investment in a given endeavor will not yield correspondingly increased results.

The objectives in this interview process are to determine the primary security concerns of the interviewee. Ask if there are specific ideas or suggestions that the interviewee has for employing security devices in his or her area. Security has become a hot topic in the news and in fictional productions today. People see a variety of exotic devices and think that that would be an ideal solution for a problem they have. While you must examine any recommendation shared by company employees, you are not there to ask, "What do you want to have"? Rather, their answer to the questions will reveal concerns they have about the security of the company assets and their charge. You can then use those statements as a springboard to other lines of inquiry.

2.7 INSIDER THREATS

Establishing an insider threat program begins with agreeing to a definition within your organization. However, to be effective, an insider threat program must consider the expansive universe of actors that can make up the set of insiders. It must include contractors and vendors that are provided access to your facilities or systems. The three pillars of any action are:

1. The motivation or reason driving the action
2. The mechanism or method used to carry out the action
3. The result or consequences of taking that action.

Your goal setting meeting should have revealed the concerns of management on insider threats but such insights can also come from department heads. Insider threats are the hardest to deal with because the "insider" knows the system and can exploit weaknesses.

2.8 INTERNAL INCIDENT ASSESSMENTS

If the company has an existing security force, it is likely that the security force has a record of incidents in the form of reports on file. Even if there is no on-site security force, it is likely that there are incident reports to provide the history of unwanted activity on-site. The threat assessment should include a review of these reports dating back at least 3 years (Figure 2.9).

Begin your incident report assessment by listing all reports (an Excel worksheet is very helpful for this) and then assign, if it has not already been done, a category of each type of incident and the time and location where the incident occurred. Look for patterns in the data, are there trouble spots, do most incidents happen at a certain time of day, certain days of the week, consider the number of each type of incident; all these characteristics will help focus your attention on the vulnerabilities covered in the next chapter.

2.9 EXTERNAL INCIDENT DATA

Police reports are a good source of information, especially if internal records are not available. The local police department can furnish a list of these incidents (there is a cost) and if internal incident recordkeeping is weak or insufficient, it may be worth the investment. If you request police reports, don't limit your search to just the company's address, you want to be aware of the surroundings too. There are no hard and fast rules for deciding on the breadth of your search but consider the situation. If the company is the only facility on a lonely road, miles from the nearest population center, using just the company address may be sufficient. Conversely, there are cases where the company is located in the middle of a heavily populated and dense commercial area such as the French Quarter in New Orleans; that case may only require a one-block radius for reliable information. Each case is different, so expand your search to get a good feel for the area, not just the company's location.

Additionally, there are services that monitor and record national crime data and make those reports available for a fee. Depending on the level of exposure

Incident Report Analysis 5 years

Incident Data

Location	Item	Month	Day	Year	Incident Type	Disposition
Fire Exit E	C06178-02	03	04	2019	Suspicious Person	4
Lobby	C20491-02	03	13	2019	Injury Accident	3
Lobby	G05918-·02	07	04	2019	Purse Snatching	4
Lab	G39724-02	07	22	2019	Injury Accident	2
Customer Svc	I01989-02	09	02	2019	F Fight	4
Lab	K28212-02	11	17	2019	Medical Emergency	4
Lab	L22232-02	12	13	2019	Medical Emergency	3
Maintenance	C13281-02	03	08	2020	Illegal Use of Weapons	4
Lobby	G13846-02	07	08	2020	Suspicious Person	4
Maintenance	G39724-02	07	22	2020	Drug Law Violation	2
Parking Lot	J13700-02	10	08	2020	F Fight	4
Containment	K39823-02	11	24	2020	Suspicious Person	4
Lobby	L39099-02	12	23	2020	Injury Accident	4
Fire Exit W	C38891-02	03	23	2021	Suspicious Person	4
Lobby	G13851-02	07	08	2021	Suspicious Person	3
Containment	H19979-02	08	12	2021	Aggravated Burglary	4
Parking Lot	J41645 ··02	10	25	2021	Purse Snatching	5
Lobby	K50908-02	11	30	2021	Simple Battery	4
Loading Dock	L29074-02	12	18	2021	Suspicious Person	3
Office Jones	C40550-02	03	24	2022	Purse Snatching	4
Customer Svc	G15623 -02	07	08	2022	F Fight	4
Rear Stair	H48529-02	08	28	2022	Suspicious Person	3
Parking Lot	I00052-02	09	01	2022	Theft From Interior of Auto	4
Lab	J46366 02	10	28	2022	Injury Accident	4
Lobby	L06952-02	12	05	2022	Injury Accident	4
Lobby	B38109-02	02	21	2023	Aggravated Burglary	4
Office Smith	F11237-02	06	07	2023	Purse Snatching	4
Loading Dock	G23737 ·- 02	07	13	2023	Auto Accident	4
Containment	I01963-02	09	02	2023	Aggravated Burglary	4
Lobby	K12395-02	11	08	2023	Simple Battery	4
Parking Lot	L20085-02	12	12	2023	Suspicious Person	4

Analysis

Location	Count
Fire Exit E	1
Containment	3
Customer Svc	2
Fire Exit W	1
Lab	4
Loading Dock	2
Lobby	9
Maintenance	2
Office Jones	1
Office Smith	1
Parking Lot	4
Rear Stair	1

Year	Count
2019	7
2020	6
2021	6
2022	6
2023	6

Incident Type	Count
Aggravated Burglary	3
Auto Accident	1
Drug Law Violation	1
F Fight	3
Illegal Use of Weapons	1
Injury Accident	5
Medical Emergency	2
Purse Snatching	4
Simple Battery	2
Suspicious Person	8
Suspicious Person	8
Theft from Interior of Auto	1

FIGURE 2.9 Incident Report Assessment.

(see Tools to Analyze Threats in Section 2.11) you may want to consider how crime is trending in a city, state or the entire country to anticipate potential threats to the company. Figure 2.10 presents an example of a report from the CAP Index (https://capindex.com/).

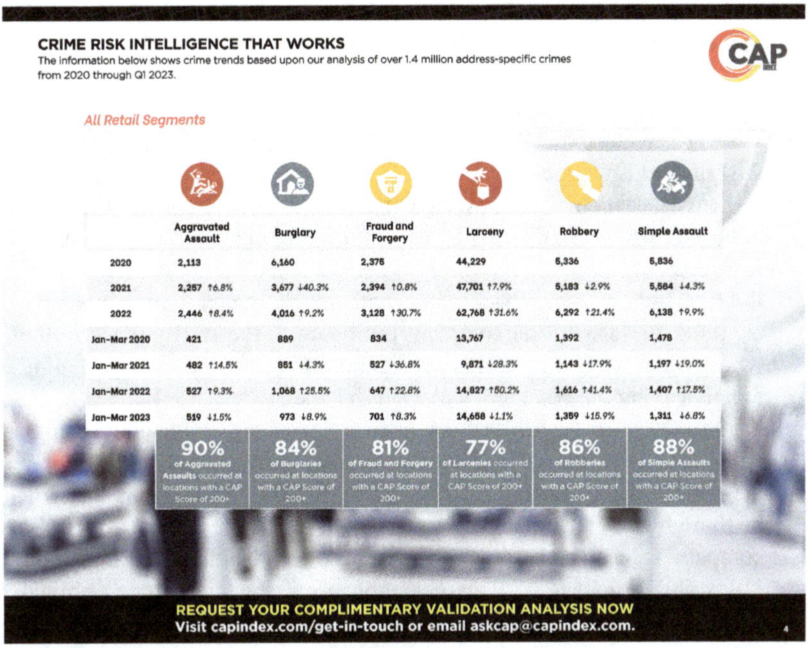

CRIME RISK INTELLIGENCE THAT WORKS

The information below shows crime trends based upon our analysis of over 1.4 million address-specific crimes from 2020 through Q1 2023.

All Retail Segments

	Aggravated Assault	Burglary	Fraud and Forgery	Larceny	Robbery	Simple Assault
2020	2,113	6,160	2,375	44,229	5,336	5,836
2021	2,257 ↑6.8%	3,677 ↓40.3%	2,394 ↑0.8%	47,701 ↑7.9%	5,183 ↓2.9%	5,584 ↓4.3%
2022	2,446 ↑8.4%	4,016 ↑9.2%	3,128 ↑30.7%	62,768 ↑31.6%	6,292 ↑21.4%	6,138 ↑9.9%
Jan-Mar 2020	421	889	834	13,767	1,392	1,478
Jan-Mar 2021	482 ↑14.5%	851 ↓4.3%	527 ↓36.8%	9,871 ↓28.3%	1,143 ↓17.9%	1,197 ↓19.0%
Jan-Mar 2022	527 ↑9.3%	1,068 ↑25.5%	647 ↑22.8%	14,827 ↑50.2%	1,616 ↑41.4%	1,407 ↑17.5%
Jan-Mar 2023	519 ↓1.5%	973 ↓8.9%	701 ↑8.3%	14,658 ↓1.1%	1,359 ↓15.9%	1,311 ↓6.8%
	90% of Aggravated Assaults occurred at locations with a CAP Score of 200+	84% of Burglaries occurred at locations with a CAP Score of 200+	81% of Fraud and Forgery occurred at locations with a CAP Score of 200+	77% of Larcenies occurred at locations with a CAP Score of 200+	86% of Robberies occurred at locations with a CAP Score of 200+	88% of Simple Assaults occurred at locations with a CAP Score of 200+

FIGURE 2.10 Sample CAP Crime Report.

2.10 OTHER POTENTIAL THREATS AND SOURCES

A truly comprehensive examination of threats also considers elements where crimes have not necessarily been recorded but are nonetheless present. Here are some examples:

- Terrorism – your company may be in the crosshairs of a terrorist group because of what the company represents and has nothing to do with the operation
- Domestic Violent Extremist (DVE) Groups
- Racially or Ethnically Motivated Violent Extremism (RMVE)
- Anti-Government/Anti-Authority Violent Extremism
    - The Sovereign Citizen Movement:
    - Militia Extremists
    - Antifa (Anti-Fascist)
    - Boogaloo Concept
    - Animal Rights/Environmental Violent Extremism
- Crime – The company may be targets of simple criminal activity, again having nothing to do with the operation, they just happen to be at the

wrong location at the wrong time. This is why your police report search looked outside the company boundaries for criminal activity.

- Drugs
- Gangs
- Disgruntled Customers
- Disgruntled Employees
- Cyber Crime – This is a growing concern and must be considered but is outside the scope of this work. We are limiting our assessment to physical security.
- Public Safety – This considers riots and protests, again it might not have anything to do with the company but being in the wrong place at the wrong time. A big part of this consideration is employee safety coming to and leaving the company's place of business.
- Natural Disasters — While this work does not focus on the direct causes and remedies of natural disasters, your assessment should consider how the public will act during a disaster. Are there company assets that will be in high demand should a disaster befall the community in which the company is located? How will people behave when they are desperate?
- Industrial Espionage — This goes above and beyond simple criminal conduct, this is a direct assault on company assets for the purpose of aiding competing firms. It is not limited to taking information but also includes destroying valuable material or data to prevent the company from using it.

2.11 TOOLS TO ANALYZE THREATS AND THEIR ADVANTAGES

In the goal setting meeting the management team described what security threats they ARE concerned about; your research has defined what security threats they SHOULD BE concerned about; now let's see how those threats can impact the company's assets.

Collecting threat data can sometimes result in a wide assortment of disjointed and unrelated information that is difficult to decipher when trying to form a comprehensive picture of what you must give priority to and the level of importance of each threat discovered. Some tools exist to help sort out this information. They are not always needed but if the task becomes voluminous, these tools can be most helpful.

When security is an issue, does money ever stand in the way? While we'd like to think money is not a problem when there is a security need, in reality, money is always an issue. How do we choose where to spend limited funds? Chief security officers and security managers don't only have to justify why they've spent funds, but, in the event of an incident, they may need to explain why funds were not spent, or why funds were spent at one location and not another.

CARVER Matrix

TARGET	CRITICALITY	ACCESSIBILITY	RECUPERABILITY	VULNERABILITY	EFFECT ON POPULATION	RECOGNIZABILITY	TOTAL
Water intake	1	1	3	4	2	1	12
Sanitation processors	3	2	1	5	5	2	18
Power center	2	3	1	2	2	1	11

FIGURE 2.11 CARVER Matrix Example.

2.11.1 CARVER Matrix

The CARVER matrix was developed by the United States Army Special Forces during the Vietnam War. CARVER is an acronym that stands for Criticality, Accessibility, Recuperability, Vulnerability, Effect and Recognizability and is a system to identify and rank specific targets so that attack resources can be efficiently used. CARVER was originally developed in World War II by the Office of Strategic Services (OSS) for the French field agents as a simple, uniform and somewhat quantifiable means of selecting targets for possible interdiction. CARVER can be used from an offensive (what to attack) or defensive (what to protect) perspective.

Use CARVER to establish the importance of each target or vulnerable point. This will help set the priorities for the level of efforts needed at each of the various areas of concern.

In target selection and Risk/Vulnerability assessments you calculate the value of a given potential target and the ease with which such a target could be neutralized. Or in other words, it's a logical way of looking at what one might want to do and whether or not it is possible, based on the resources one has to work with. These factors are also the acronym of the system name CARVER: Criticality, Accessibility, Recuperability, Vulnerability, Effect and Recognizability. In the offensive, employing the CARVER matrix can help identify targets that are vulnerable to attack and for defensive purposes the Carver matrix can indicate "High Risk" targets that require additional security assets allotted to them to prevent the degradation of said assets via enemy assault or terrorist action. Figure 2.11 presents an example of such a matrix that uses the CARVER system for striking a water sanitation center.

2.11.2 MEVA

The Modular Effectiveness Vulnerability Assessment (MEVA) is an engineering tool for assessing the vulnerability of ground targets to conventional weapon attack. MEVA may be used to configure a model for more detailed type studies where more precision is desired. Critical components within targets may be modeled and assigned to fault trees providing a means for assessing functional damage to a target.

MISSION ESSENTIAL VULNERABILITY ASSESSMENT (MEVA) Threat Index

THREAT CAPABILITY	WEAPON	LOCATION	THREAT PROBABILITY (Highest # is most probable)	THREAT SEVERITY (Highest # is most severe)	THREAT PRIORITY (Prob x Severity)	THREAT PRIORITY INSIDE PERIMETER (lowest number is highest priority)	THREAT PRIORITY OUTSIDE PERIMETER (lowest number is highest priority)
Domestic Violent Extremist (DVE) - Active Shooter	Handgun/assault weapon	In parking lot	2	8	16		3
Domestic Violent Extremist (DVE) -	Knife/club	In parking lot	3	7	21		2
Assault - Patient on employee	Physical Altercation	In parking lot	5	6	30		1
Assault - Patient on employee	Club/Knife	In parking lot	2	6	12		4
Domestic Activist - Picket	Physical blockade	In parking lot	2	4	8		5
Assault - on employee	Club/Knife	Inside building	2	7	14	3	
Assault - visitor	Club/Knife	Inside building	1	7	7	4	
Domestic Violent Extremist (DVE) - Active Shooter	Handgun/assault weapon	Inside building	4	8	32	1	
Assault - Patient on employee	Physical Altercation	Inside building	3	6	18	2	

FIGURE 2.12 MEVA Example.

The purpose of a MEVA assessment is to provide justification for protecting one vulnerability over another. MEVA assigns relative values to threats based on their probibility. The scale for MEVA assignements is as follows:

- 10 (Very High) – Exceptionally grave consequences (e.g. extensive loss of life, widespread severe injuries, or total loss of primary services, core processes, and functions)
- 8–9 (High) – Grave consequences (loss of file, severe injuries, loss of primary services)
- 7 (Medium High) – Serious consequences (serious injuries, or impairment of core processes and functions for an extended period of time)
- 5–6 (Medium) – Moderate to serious consequences.
- 4 (Medium Low) – Moderate consequences (minor injuries or minor impairment of core functions and processes)
- 2–3 (Low) – Minor consequences or impact
- 1 (Very Low) – Negligible consequences or impact.

Threats are listed relative to the vulnerabilities defined and each is examined for the impact of the threat on the target (Figure 2.12).

2.11.3 MSHARPP

Mission, Symbolism, History, Accessibility, Recognizability, Population, and Proximity (MSHARPP) is a test for perceived vulnerabilities and can be used to predict attacks based on the perceived value of a target. In this context, we must underline the specific difference between risk and vulnerability which arises from threats (origins/causes) and characterize the consequences of their results (loss, damage and suffering). The perception of the consequences and the likelihood of threats is the focus. Vulnerability relates to the subject of the exposure to threats

Mission, Symbolism, History, Accessibility, Recognizability, Population, and Proximity

TARGET	MISSION	SYMBOLISM	HISTORY OF THEFT/TERRORISM	ACCESSIBILITY	RECOGNIZABILITY	POPULATION	PROXIMITY	TOTAL
Security Office	1	10	1	10	10	8	10	50
Admin Building	1	2	1	8	10	10	8	40
Research Lab	3	6	2	5	5	7	6	34
Testing Facility	3	6	2	5	5	7	6	34
Primate Containment	2	7	4	4	7	1	4	29
Controlled Substance Lab	7	4	3	1	2	2	3	22
Controlled Substance Storage	10	4	3	1	2	2	3	25
Drug Dispensary	4	2	7	1	2	2	2	20
Isolation	10	2	1	2	1	1	1	18

FIGURE 2.13 MSHARPP.

as characterized by the type and level of susceptibility, the reaction to the loss from those threats.

Analysis of the risks pertaining to critical infrastructure is therefore connected with the general problem of decision-making under conditions of uncertainty. The risks do not exist on an objective manner, but are "built" by the decision-makers, while the parties involved in the decision-making process, possibly nonparticipants in the process but targets of the effects thereof, could perceive this phenomenon as a threat. All of the methodologies and techniques of risk assessment rely on probability of outcome while MSHARPP is based on perception. This type of approach is a subjective one, but enables a higher degree of generalization and is less restrictive (Figure 2.13).

These tools are most useful when assessing threats and vulnerabilities in environments where the security designer's judgment is subject to close review. In other words, when you not only need to say what must be done but justify your decision to an uninformed audience.

2.12 THE NEXT STEP

Now we know the assets to protect and the threats to those assets; the next step is to determine the vulnerability of the assets to the threats. We will cover that in Chapter 3.

CHAPTER 3

The Vulnerability Assessment

CONTENTS

3.1 VULNERABILITIES – INTRODUCTION

You now know what the security goals are for the company and the potential threats to its assets, so now it's time to assess how vulnerable the company is to those threats. You will perform a thorough review of the company's facility to determine the likelihood that any one of these threats can be successfully carried out.

This assessment is also a comprehensive review of all current physical security measures and operational characteristics that affect the facility's ability to detect, deter, delay and respond to the threats. This includes an examination of the physical security systems such as access control, alarm monitoring and closed-circuit television (CCTV) plus the procedures used to manage the systems and respond to identified threats. A part of this examination is to verify the life safety features of the systems, such as unrestricted egress on controlled doors. For example, a company may have an existing access control system and, in some high-security situations, egress is also controlled. If so, such egress controls may be a violation of life safety protocols. There is usually an interface between the electric locking systems and the building's fire alarm to offset the egress control such that in the case of a fire detection the egress control will be overridden. This is done so that exits where egress is controlled meet fire code requirements. You should test this interface during the vulnerability assessment to ensure proper operation.

 DOI: 10.4324/9781003490432-4

More on this process can be found in Chapter 11, Section 11.5, of this book for a new system.

3.2 THE VULNERABILITY ASSESSMENT PLAN

Begin with a review of the assets and threats you uncovered in the previous steps. Develop a written plan to help keep the assessment on track; decide where to go and what to look for; you will find many distractions while conducting the assessment, a written plan helps to carry out the proper steps in sequence to completion.

When doing your inspection the goal is to take an adversarial perspective and ask, "What can you do to disable or destroy the asset under consideration?" Can you use tools or explosives to cause enough damage? Once you've considered the potential damage, then ask, "Who needs to use this asset and how are they vetted?". This will help you get a handle on access control design which we will cover in the next chapter.

If tools are required to do damage, then ask yourself, "What tools would you need to do damage?" How would you get those tools to the asset? Now you are beginning to focus on the nature of the perpetrator.

Perimeter protection is the first line in the defense to detect an intruder. The most common points you should equip with sensing devices for perimeter protection are doors, windows, vents, skylights, or any opening to the facility. More than 80% of all break-ins occur through these openings and so deserve the most attention. Most alarm systems can be used to provide this type of protection. The major advantage of perimeter protection is its simple design. The major disadvantage is that it protects only the openings. If the intruder bursts through a wall, comes through the ventilation system or stays behind after closing, perimeter protection is useless. But we will begin with outsider threats, so let's look at establishing our perimeters and then we can consider ways in which it can be defeated.

3.2.1 The Plot Plan

Take out your plot plan (from your preparation for the goal setting meeting), this will identify the property boundaries for you and establish your first perimeter. Begin by locating the protected assets on the drawing and marking those locations. In many cases, the assets are simply the areas where work is taking place and the assets are "people". Now look at the plot plan and find the farthest edge that surrounds those assets on company grounds, that will be the property line and this will be your outside perimeter.

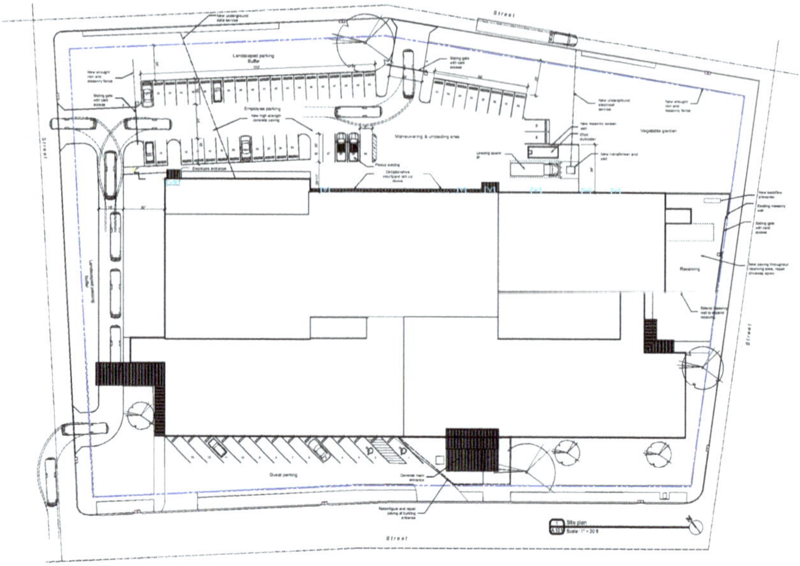

FIGURE 3.1 Example of Unmarked Plot Plan.

For this example, we will use a complex environment with a campus containing multiple buildings and multiple asset locations. Your environment may be simpler such as a commercial building in a population area; in that case your outer perimeter may just be the company's building (Figure 3.1). Please adjust your planning as needed to disregard unnecessary steps.

We are starting to establish physical security perimeters. These are placed in concentric circles beginning at the outer perimeter that encircles all assets with each succeeding circle narrowing and having progressively higher levels of security up to the individual assets (Figure 3.2). In that way, the most valuable resources received the greatest focus of security system measures.

What is a perimeter … it is a contiguous line of barricades and controlled openings that resists intrusion to a protected area. The "types" of barricades and methods to control openings will be discussed later. Not all perimeters are "controlled" or complete; for example, the company may be a bank, you would want people who are not part of the company to enter the premises during the day but be restricted from some areas of the bank. At night, that outer perimeter may be closed. Conversely, the company may be a manufacturing or research facility where strangers would not be welcomed on company grounds without vetting and may even need an escort. So the outer perimeter is a consideration only in certain circumstances.

One of the more unique perimeter configurations is in a K-12 school. The exterior security perimeter is usually twofold, there is an outer perimeter that is generally defined by the property line and a "student" perimeter defined as the area where students are permitted but un-vetted visitors are not permitted.

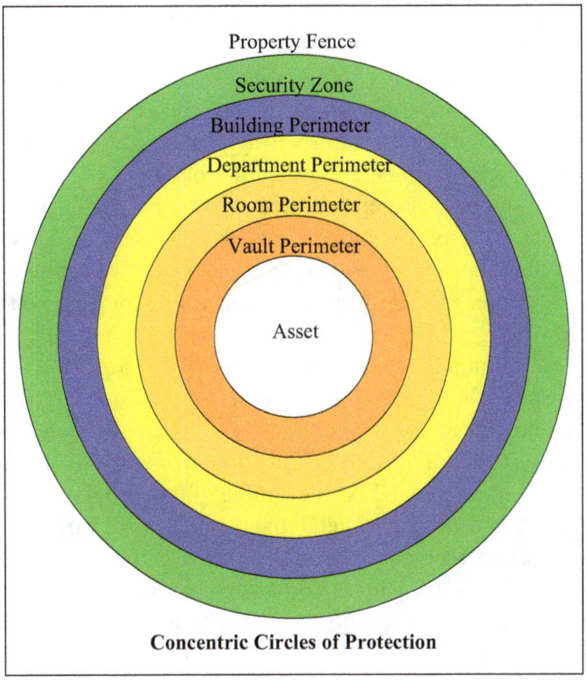

FIGURE 3.2 Concentric Circles.

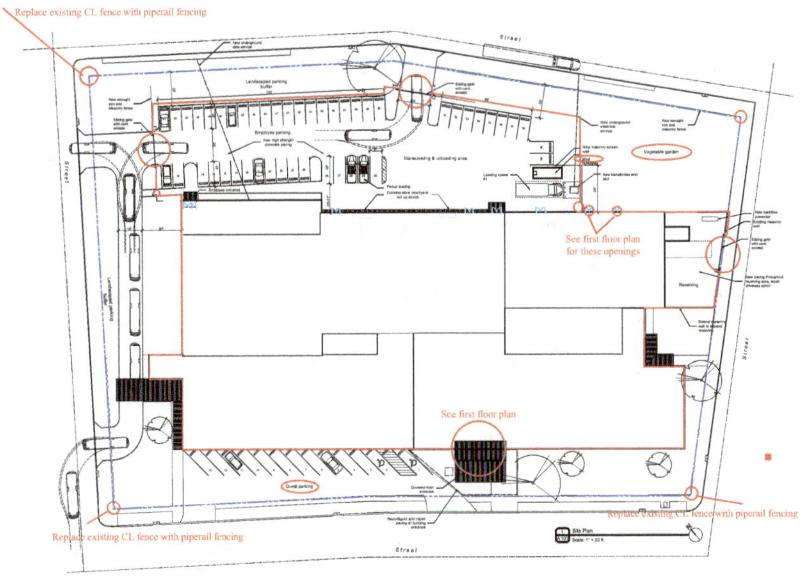

FIGURE 3.3 Plot Plan with Perimeter Markings.

The outer perimeter is to restrict vehicles from driving on school grounds but is usually open to pedestrians. Additionally, those restrictions are lifted during school hours and driveway gates are left open for access by visitors and service personnel such as trash collectors and food suppliers. This means that anyone can drive on campus during the day but driveway gates are closed outside of school hours to restrict vehicles from entering school grounds.

However, the student perimeter restricts everyone from entering areas where there are students. This is usually accomplished by fencing or using existing barriers such as buildings. The goal in school security is to require everyone who is not a student to enter through a control point where they are vetted by school administration.

The simplest technique is to mark your "controlled" perimeter on the drawing with a solid line and where there is an opening in the perimeter, place a circle to which the perimeter line attaches on either side. Again, some outer perimeters are never controlled and do not need to be marked but if they are closed during any condition, mark them. Figure 3.3 is an example of the technique.

Now move to the next perimeter using concentric circles as discussed earlier. In some cases that may be an open area between the first perimeter and the nearest building. Consider making that a detection zone, a kind of No Man's Land where anyone crossing this area will be detected; more on this will be discussed later. Such protection zones are themselves considered a perimeter. To goal is to detect the presence of an individual before they actually become a threat.

The next perimeter is a usually a building wall for one or more of the buildings on campus. You may have one large perimeter with several smaller independent perimeters inside. Once all the exterior perimeters are established, you now must look at "smaller circles" inside buildings.

3.2.2 Building Floor Plans

Now using the floor plans you obtained for each building on campus, again identify the assets on each drawing. Then identify the perimeters from outside the building leading up to the assets using the existing walls as your perimeter boundaries. Use the same marking techniques on the floor plans that were used for the plot plan (Figure 3.4). In the analysis step we will discuss recommending changes in the walls to better facilitate controls. For now, use what is in place.

When deciding on controls for these perimeters, a natural inclination is to rigorously provide insurmountable obstacles to threats at all possible levels. However, the practical application of this approach is expensive and can adversely affect the operation of the facility. It is more likely that a tailored approach would win greater acceptance from management. Some typical elements of perimeter development include:

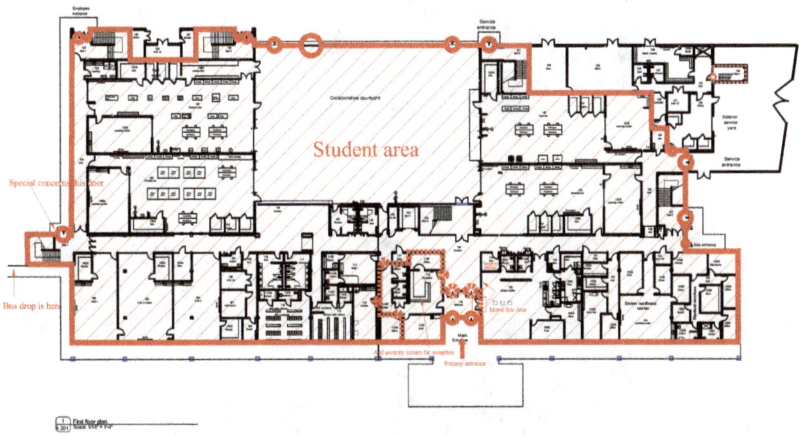

FIGURE 3.4 Marked Building Floor Plans.

- The facility's mission and objectives
- An assessment of the likelihood of intrusion by unauthorized personnel to areas of critical assets (people or property)
- A determination of consequences of loss from perpetrators with deliberation and intent
- A review of existing countermeasures to threats, including emergency procedures and insurance reimbursement as a result of anticipated losses

3.2.3 Threat by Proximity (Explosives)

Establishing a perimeter generally implies that the threats are stopped at the perimeter but that is not the case with explosives. A perpetrator can park a "loaded" vehicle next to perimeter, detonate it and cause nearly as much damage as if the explosive was inside the perimeter (Figure 3.5).

So, as you are evaluating your perimeter, consider parking and vehicle access along your perimeter. You may find that moving the "personnel perimeter fencing" further in on company grounds, then restricting vehicle access to the areas around and outside of the personnel perimeter is a good solution. Of course, this implies that the buildings are not already sent up next to the property line, in that case there is little you can do other than consider expensive reinforcement of building walls. The best protection against explosives is distance.

3.3 PERIMETER INTEGRITY

It is not enough to simply have a barrier between the good guys and the bad guys to create a secure environment, the "resistance value" of that barrier must also

The bombing of the Alfred P. Murrah Federal Building in Oklahoma City on April 19, 1995 was the deadliest act of homegrown terrorism in U.S. history, resulting in the deaths of 168 people.

FIGURE 3.5 Oklahoma City Bombing.

be evaluated. Resistance value is the time needed for an individual with nothing more than hand tools to breach a perimeter. Each perimeter type has a resistance value and, within those types, each material selection has a value. The objective of your assessment is to look for ways to defeat the perimeters. Let's examine the most popular types and see if we can find weaknesses in the perimeter or the controlled openings.

3.3.1 Fencing

Fencing is usually used on outer perimeters as the first line of defense against intrusion. It is usually the company property line but doesn't have to be. The fence line can be set back to make control easier or more certain but generally it is the outer boundary. If you were the bad guy, how would you defeat a fence? You'd go over it, under it or simply cut through it.

3.3.1.1 Going over It

Evaluation of penetration times of chain-link fencing have been conducted by the U.S. Army Mobility Equipment Research and Development Command. Chain-link fences with extension poles installed have been subjected to climbing attacks by fit young men to estimate the effectiveness of fences as barriers against penetration. The 8ft fence mounted on poles has been penetrated by a man with another man assisting without the use of aids in 4 seconds and was climbed by a man with three men assisting in 2.5 seconds. A 6ft fence was climbed unassisted and without the use of aids in 3 seconds, and with one man assisting without the use of other aids was 1.5 seconds.

Chain-link fences with barbed wire top were penetrated with one man assisting without the use of aids in 4 seconds for a 7.5ft fence and 5 seconds with one assistant.

3.3.1.2 Going through it

A chain-link fence is neither crash rated nor intended to stop forcible entry. In most cases, a chain-link fence can be easily penetrated by a normal passenger vehicle. As a consequence, target hardening must be installed for facilities where forcible vehicular entry is an issue. A chain-link fence may be enhanced with the aid of crash-rated tension wires threaded through the fence, or with concrete crash structures, or simply by digging a trench around the perimeter of the fence to stop vehicles from reaching the fence. There are crash-rated fences from manufacturers like:

- Ameristar / Assa Abloy
- AMICO
- Barrier 1
- Cochrane High Security Perimeter Barriers
- ELGO
- Perimeter Security Solutions
- Ross Technology Corporation

If your first perimeter is a property boundary, evaluate that perimeter, and if there is fencing consider using a product more substantial than simple chain link from one of these manufacturers.

3.3.1.3 Going under It

Obviously, if the foregoing means are not practical the tunneling is the next best option. It takes longer, it is more involved and requires tools. The usual remedy for tunneling is a fence foundation (sometimes referred to as a chain wall). The preparation of the ground for a fence is important in making the final product effective. Fence installations can provide dig resistance by either using a continuous foundation going several feet below ground level or adding a concrete or asphalt sidewalk adjacent of the base of the fence so that digging requires a long tunnel. Either of these methods requires construction that is resistant to movement from frost heaving.

The ground along the fence line should drain well by ensuring the ground slopes away from the bottom of the fence. This area should be properly maintained as vegetation such as plants and shrubs can hide attackers. A surface that resists plants establishing themselves is ideal. The ground on either side of a fence without an anti-tunneling barrier should have compacted gravel to a depth of at least 1 foot and extending at least 3 feet on either side. This should eliminate the possibility of erosion or heaving of the fence and posts and prevent gaps from developing under the fencing. This is especially important where the fence fabric cannot be buried due to environmental conditions.

Pay close attention to the existing terrain. I had a client where I was assessing his fence line. The contractor did not install a foundation and used standard chain-link fencing. There were natural swales that ran perpendicular to the fence line in several locations and were constantly refreshed by rain runoff. This provided "ready-made" tunnels under the fence line with no effort. The ground under the fence line should be flat and even.

3.3.1.4 Gates

If you have a fence line you will always have an opening. The level of resistance of the opening should equal the same level as the fence and one might say it should be greater, since that is the most likely point of attack. The first consideration is material … it follows that if a certain level of fencing is sufficient for the perimeter, that same level should be sufficient for the gate. The next significant question is the type of gate to use. But now we are getting into design and that will be covered in the next chapter. For now, look at the fence line right up to the opening and remember that you need to continue that level of protection across this opening.

3.3.2 Wall Construction

That same approach can be used for wall perimeters (buildings). You usually can't go over or under exterior walls but you can go through them. The penetration point is generally an existing opening but I have had cases where the bad guy went "through" the wall. They made their own opening. So we must look at penetration resistance for building walls too. However, this problem becomes far more pronounced for interior walls. In most commercial buildings the walls do not go up to the floor above but instead stop at a suspended ceiling. The have the appearance of being full height but one can simply remove a ceiling tile and go over a wall. So let's look at interior walls.

Ideally, walls defining perimeters should be designed as full partitions extending floor-to-floor above to minimize opportunity for easy access through drop ceilings. In low-risk applications and situations where the primary design objective is to simply delay the perpetrator's access, drop ceilings may be sufficient. Attackers most often use visually obvious portals (e.g., doors and windows) as their main pathways for movement but drop ceilings are certainly possible for a determined adversary.

Walls should ideally resist forced intrusion with similar delay times as doors, locks and windows. In many commercial and academic facilities, walls protecting rooms commonly designated for use as safe rooms (e.g., offices, conference rooms, and classrooms) are often secured by little more than two layers of gypsum board on wooden studs. Two-layered drywall partitions can be penetrated in 60 seconds by an adversary without using any equipment and in 30 seconds with the assistance of hand tools. Despite the poor performance of gypsum board walls (also known as sheet rock), they may be used in some situations, considering the rare frequency of active shooter attacks where walls have been used as a point of entry into locked rooms. In low-risk applications or situations where budget limits retrofit options, replacement or upgrade of existing drywall should not be required.

In medium- to high-risk applications and safe room designs with delay time objectives over 45 seconds, walls should be constructed using intrusion-resistant materials. Some options for protective wall construction include reinforced concrete, filled masonry block, expanded metal mesh, and polycarbonate-composite wall panels.

Reinforced concrete walls provide the best delay time performance against adversaries using limited toolsets. According to tests documented by Sandia Laboratories, 4-inches of reinforced concrete with No. 5 rebar on 6-inch centers will provide approximately 4.7 minutes of delay against penetration with hand tools (including saw). If the threat definition is an adversary relying solely on firearm penetration and blunt object impact, reinforced concrete of any dimensions will provide almost indefinite delay.

Unfilled concrete masonry unit (CMU) block walls provide minimal delay against forced entry and only slightly better performance than drywall against some methods of penetration. According to data published in the *Barrier Technology Handbook*, the mean delay time for penetrating an unfilled CMU block wall is only 36 seconds by the use of a sledgehammer. Unfilled CMU block walls are also susceptible to damage by rifle projectiles and may crumble when struck repeatedly by gunfire. For better performance in delaying forced entry, CMU block walls should be fully grouted and reinforced with rebar.

Supplementing exterior drywall layers with a securely attached inner layer of expanded metal mesh is one of the most common methods of retrofitting existing walls for improved resistance against forced entry. Expanded steel constructed of 9-gauge 3/4-inch diamond mesh is a common material specification for this purpose. In this type of wall design, the expanded metal mesh is installed on the inside of the protected room and secured to wall studs by using deep screws and fasteners specially designed for this purpose. The expanded metal barrier layer is then overlaid with gypsum board or plywood. According to Sandia, a wall constructed of two layers of 3/4-inch plywood, two layers of gypsum board, and an expanded metal mesh interlayer can provide as much as 6.5 minutes of delay against penetration with hand tools.

Several manufacturers currently offer polycarbonate composite wall panel products marketed for security applications. Most products of this type are composed of a thin polycarbonate layer (0.08–0.125 inch) bonded to gypsum or cement board. Manufacturers of polycarbonate composite wall systems are generally cautious about describing the capabilities of these products. Although the concept of these products is very appealing, their use in performance-based protective design is discouraged.

3.3.2.1 Doors

Considering the cost of security doors and the number of rooms often desired for availability as safe rooms during armed attacks, many organizations do not have the budget or risk justification required for implementing security doors rated under forced entry standards. In this situation, you may choose commercial door hardware with security features adequate to accomplish the design objective or retrofitting existing doors with cost-consciously selected upgrades for maximum benefit.

As a general rule, outward-swinging doors provide the best protection against exterior ramming force due to resistance of the rebate within the frame. Additionally, adversaries attempting to pull open locked outward-swinging doors without the aid of tools are at a great mechanical disadvantage. If rooms earmarked as potential safe rooms feature existing inward-swinging doors, door hardware (e.g., locks, strikes, and frames) should be carefully specified to ensure adequate resistance against ramming force.

Most security doors certified under forced entry standards are constructed of steel. However, indoor rooms potentially earmarked for use as safe rooms in office and academic facilities are often equipped with solid core wood or solid wooden doors. Solid core doors are constructed with a composite wood core and overlaid with hardwood veneer for aesthetic appearance. Considering the materials involved, solid wooden doors are preferable to solid core doors. For application against a gunman employing impact force without additional tools, solid door leafs (regardless of construction) are unlikely to be the point of failure when compared to the potential vulnerability of locks, strikes, wooden frames and vision panels.

Doors featuring glass vision panels are often highly vulnerable to forced entry. Tempered safety glass panels only provide about 10 seconds of delay against a gunman. Once broken, the intruder can simply reach through the window and use the interior door handle or lock to gain entry. To limit this vulnerability, vision panels should be no wider than 1.5″ (3.8 cm) or constructed of intrusion-resistant glazing such as laminated glass, polycarbonate, or reinforced with anti-shatter film. If the delay time objective exceeds a few minutes, vision panels should be avoided completely.

3.3.2.2 Locks

As a prerequisite, all mechanical locks on safe room doors should feature thumbwheels for ease of locking under stress. In several previous active shooter attacks, critical doors on rooms where people were seeking refuge remained unlocked during the event because the lock required a key. Additionally, good preparation for active shooter events should anticipate the occupants will be under high stress impairing cognitive function and fine motor coordination. These negative effects can interfere with even simple tasks such as locating and manipulating keys.

Surface-mounted deadbolt locks are generally superior to mortise and bored locks in resisting forced entry, especially if the mounting screws penetrate all the way into the door frame and not just on the surface molding. Surface-mounted deadbolt locks can incorporate bolts unconstrained by the thickness of doors and require the adversary to entirely penetrate the door leaf to access the lock. Surface-mounted deadbolt systems are also less vulnerable to prying due to the increased force necessary to lever the entire door frame.

Many surface-mounted deadbolt systems designed for high-security applications feature auto-bolting locks. Auto-bolting systems lock automatically when the door is closed and often disengage automatically when the inside handle is operated for exit. Manually bolted surface-mounted deadbolts require a manual unlocking operation to permit exit. Building and life safety codes should be reviewed to ensure life safety code compliance before installing manually bolted surface-mounted locks.

For organizations without the budget and/or risk justification to equip safe rooms with door sets rated under ballistic resistance standards, the next best option is installing surface-mounted deadbolt locks on the inside of solid wooden or steel doors. Although most solid wooden and steel pedestrian doors are vulnerable to penetration by small arms, the door material will provide some reduction in bullet velocity and conceal location of the lock to reduce hit probability. Conventional steel wrap-around door knob plates are not bullet-resistant, but may offer a marginal benefit by reducing projectile velocity.

3.3.2.3 Electrified Locks and Access Control Design

If a facility is employing/or planning to use electrified locks on potential safe room doors, careful consideration should be used in configuration of the access control system and hardware specification. Although access control systems offer great versatility in security design, they often suffer from vulnerabilities in real-world application, which can be problematic during active shooter attacks.

Many buildings were designed as large workspaces with few offices, storage rooms or conference rooms suitable for use as safe rooms. In some of these facilities, permissions were broadly granted to employees through the facility's access control system to allow convenient access to conference rooms and shared offices. During an attack by an internal active shooter, doors with broadly applied access privileges will not provide useful protection. Likewise, if the access control system in the facility employs card readers and an outsider adversary recovers an access badge from a fallen employee, all doors with universal access will be compromised.

Another common problem relates to the fail-safe/secure configuration of electrified locking systems. Building and life safety codes require that egress doors equipped with electromagnetic locks be "fail safe" (unlocked) during power outages and controlled unlocking during fire alarms. Although safe room doors in most situations will not be classified as egress doors, other controlled doors in facilities where all access-controlled doors were universally configured to fail safe means that if any fire alarm pull station is used, all doors would be compromised. This is a very real concern. Further, in a real life exercise in a school shooting mock up, the individual playing the bad guy used a real gun and real ammunition (blanks) and the smoke from the gunfire triggered the fire alarm which then unlocked the controlled doors. Hence, as part of your design you should include disabling the fire alarm lock interface in any "lockdown" trigger design.

3.3.2.4 Windows

As a general rule, window and door glazing should be avoided in high-risk situations or applications where long delays are desired. Although there are glazing products capable of high delay times, such systems are quite expensive by comparison to the price of wall construction and doors. In low- to medium-risk applications and situations where glazing is an unavoidable element of architectural aesthetics, windows should be designed to adequately resist intrusion. Consequentially, the performance of glazing should be a top priority and may even exceed the importance of delay provided by barriers along less obvious intrusion paths such as walls, floors and ceilings.

Laminated glass is a composite material constructed of two or more layers of glass bonded to a poly vinyl butyral (PVB) or polycarbonate interlayer. Manufacturers of these products rate their resistance value and the product manufacturer and model selection should be based on the rating desired.

Polycarbonate is another option for intrusion-resistant windows. Polycarbonate is relatively inexpensive and can be purchased as sheets and cut to dimensions as needed. The main disadvantages of polycarbonate are its limited resistance to scratch damage and susceptibility to discoloration and degradation from UV exposure. Some tests also suggest polycarbonate may be vulnerable to fragmentation and shatter critically when penetrated by a 12-gauge shotgun.

In low-risk situations or circumstances where budget does not permit replacing existing glazing, anti-shatter film properly attached and anchored to tempered or annealed glass may be a cost-effective alternative. If anti-shatter film is chosen as an upgrade, specifications should require mechanical or cement bond frame attachment.

3.3.2.5 Ceilings and Floors

Although penetration through ceilings or floors is possible, such paths of entry are least likely considering typical construction characteristics. However, in high-risk design applications, floors and ceilings should provide balanced protection according to the safe room's specified delay time objectives. For this purpose, Sandia Lab's *Barrier Technology Handbook* provides a good survey of penetration times for a wide range of ceiling and floor construction variations. For instance, if the threat is intrusion by a perpetrator walking on company grounds, then sufficient distance is required to detect the intruder and, using video surveillance, classify the threat. If the threat is an explosive device, greater distances will be required.

3.4 WHAT YOU SHOULD LOOK FOR

Your plan should include at least the following:

- Review of written security response procedures
- An inspection of all identified assets as they relate to the threats identified
- Establishing protected perimeters starting with each asset out to the exterior perimeter
- An assessment of the physical barricades that comprise the protected perimeter
- An identification of each opening that provides human access (of any kind) to the asset and how that opening is used (ordinary access, emergency exit only, etc.)
- Means of control and monitoring for each opening in each protected perimeter
- Key management control
- Remote investigations
- Response team and incident reporting
- Lighting conditions around the protected perimeters
- Review of employee identification procedures

- Review of visitor controls
- An evaluation of the effectiveness of existing security systems and panic alarms
- Compliance with protocols and applicable regulation
- Communications methods for the staff with security
- Signage to direct first responders around the campus or building
- Blast proximity, especially regarding parking
- Utilities and emergency power

The threat assessment may have uncovered some additional concerns that do not fall into one of the above categories. Review your threat assessment notes to ensure that you have included all reasonably foreseeable threats.

3.4.1 Review Existing Systems

Of course, as you conduct your assessment, look for existing means of threat mitigation – door status switches on perimeter doors, access control, CCTV cameras, etc. Note the location of these on your floor plans and plot plans. In Chapter 6, Documenting the System the System Design We will discuss how to distinguish between existing and planned system features, but for now it is important that you note what is in place.

You will also want to "test" these systems as part of your assessment. Some suggestions on how to test existing systems can be found in Chapter 11 System Implementation, Testing New Systems.

Of course testing the systems in place is a given but you must go further in your assessment, you must test the effectiveness of the original design. For example, you can have a door with sophisticated access control and locking systems but that same door has exposed hinges and the pins are not permanently set in place. Why would a perpetrator waste time defeating locks and access devices when he can simply remove the hinge pins to gain access.

Further, you may even have a case as I did once where the design called for door status switches but the contractor exposed the wiring for the switch on the outside of the door. The contact was not supervised so it would have been an easy matter to cut the cable and cross-connect the wiring to then open the door without an alarm.

So testing the operational aspects of a system is not enough, you must also look for ways to defeat it.

3.4.2 Review Security Procedures

Security procedures are twofold first, what instructions do employees have on how to respond to a perceived threat? What do you do when you see a stranger? What are your responsibilities for keeping the business secure? These are matters determined in the goal setting meeting and this is the time for verification that the written procedures meet the management goals. however, it is likely that you will find there are none or they are so general and wide sweeping that an employee would find it difficult to implement. There are suggestions in the next chapter in assessing these procedures, but this is the information gathering step so for now just collect the data.

The second procedural element is for the security staff or response team. Do they have instructions on how to handle an intruder? Are most common situations covered? Is there a training and refresher program to keep them up to date on the latest developments and management perspective? Comparing a private security force to law enforcement is a good exercise for you when reviewing security staff procedures. Law enforcement has "laws" that govern their performance and their job is to enforce those laws. The security procedures for private security take the place of those laws. As the security expert you are to guide management down the path of keeping their business safe while not violating public law. It is a narrow road and the next chapter provides some guidance on how to do that.

3.4.3 Inspect the Assets

It is one thing to be told about an asset, it is something entirely different to see it for yourself. Part of your plan in the early steps of the assessment is to view the assets that most concern the company. Sometimes vulnerabilities become obvious by just being there. So as an early step, plan to look at each asset when it is in operation; if the asset is personnel, observe the work being done; it will help in assessing the need for access control and alarm monitoring. Also note any space sensors that may be there … ultrasonic, passive infrared, laser beam, etc. that provides an alert if someone approaches an asset who may not be authorized.

3.4.4 Establishing the Perimeter Controls

All protected perimeters will have openings to permit routine business activity. Some of these openings are frequently used but in many cases they are usually closed and locked throughout the business day. They are opened only in special circumstances. An example of this is emergency exit doors in an office building. These doors are usually secured with mechanical locks. The vulnerability assessment must include all openings and the identification of mechanical locks as well as electric locks used in access control system. Here are some things to include in your plan to look for at these openings:

Door Type, e.g.: A – single or pair, opaque or glass, frameless glass

- Hinge Type: 3 point, 2 point, continuous
- Access Method: handle, push, etc.

- Egress Method: door handle hardware, panic bar, automatic, etc.
- Lock Sets: mechanical, electromechanical, power magnet, etc.
- Door Features: Door status monitors, fire alarm interface, external exit buttons, etc.
- Security Surveillance: exiting camera view the door, audio surveillance
- Door Use: is it a control for a closed room or does it lead to other areas?

This would also be a good time to note the material from which the door is made and includes the surrounding structures too. The entire perimeter should likewise be examined because your perimeter is only as strong as your weakest point.

Include all openings, regardless of use in the assessment and in the design phase we will determine how best to secure these doors. As suggested earlier, document these openings on your drawings with a circle around the opening and connect the circle openings with lines that follow the contiguous barriers (walls or fencing) to the next opening. In the end, you should have a complete circle that defines each perimeter with smaller circles that define each opening in that perimeter. The earlier illustration is shown in Figure 3.6.

All doors on the protected perimeter should be controlled and monitored. Control is sometimes a simple mechanical lock and key while at others it is a more sophisticated access control device. Door status switches are usually used to monitor most doors, look for them in your assessment. In addition to door openings, there are also windows and freight openings in the protected perimeter

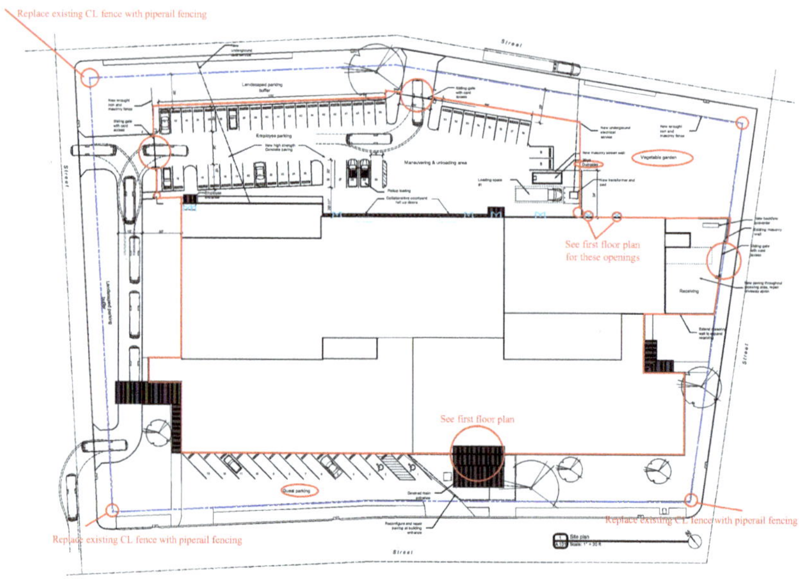

FIGURE 3.6 Plot Plan with Perimeter Markings.

that likewise require some form of detection monitoring to determine the status of the opening. Your job is to confirm that some form of monitoring exists.

3.4.5 Key Management Controls

Mechanical doors require keys to unlock. Interview the person who assigns those keys, what is the criteria for issuance … when (if ever) are the keys returned? How often are locks rekeyed and where are the spare keys kept? How do you stop an employee, who is assigned a key, from making multiple duplicates and sharing them with others? These are all part of the interview process. Your goal is to understand if good controls exist over the keys for mechanical locks.

3.4.6 Find Observation Points (Remote Investigations)

The function of remote investigations is to permit security forces to gather information about an incident without actually having to go to the incident location to classify it as a threat or non-threat. This is most often accomplished using CCTV cameras. The application of remote monitoring will be dependent on the goals established for the alarm response team.

Security personnel can't be everywhere, always … trying to do so would be cost prohibitive and wasteful. So instead of putting a guard at every vulnerable point your plan should include identifying vulnerable areas and finding ways to observe these areas remotely. Then use roving guards to respond to potential threats coordinated with the command center. More on the solutions will be presented later but for now your plan should include finding good points of observation for your video and audio monitors during your perimeter assessment.

In so doing, remember the sun! Avoid scenes where the camera is facing the direction of the sun as it move across the sky, direct sunlight on a camera can distort images and damage cameras. There is a clever cell phone app called "Sun Seeker" that allows you to see the arc of the sun anywhere on the planet so you can see if sunlight at a different time of day than your assessment trip will have an impact on your camera placement. At this step you will simply find locations for your cameras.

3.4.7 Response Team and Incident Reporting

The primary goal of private physical security is to detect, deter, delay and respond to breaches in security. The element of "response" is important in the assessment because without a means to respond the other goals have little value. A related objective in providing an enhanced physical security system is to provide the company's security force with information and control over the protected area.

Evaluating the Company's ability to respond includes interviews with security force management.

An effective physical security system will allow security force management to cover more area in less time and do a more comprehensive job of securing the facility without needing to increase the security staff. Further, an effectively designed physical security system will change the nature of the job done by the security force. Security officers will no longer stand in front of a door just to verify that authorized personnel enter. A security officer's work will focus more on response and less on deterrence, detection and delay.

To achieve improvements in the area of "response", review security procedures, watch post instructions, reporting methods and other security force protocols that enable the company's security force to respond to threats. Without adequate response and reporting, much of the company's investment in these new security tools will be lost. One of the easiest tools to use for this report is a "Guard Tour" device. More on this is given in the next chapter. Essentially it is a shorthand way for a guard to report an observed incident or situation and the action they took to mitigate it.

There is also software that mimics government crime reporting systems. While some companies find the government process tedious, it is a good place to start in identifying what data the security force should capture about an incident so that management can make informed decisions on how best to improve security in the facility. At the end of the assessment you should know what data is being captured and if it meets the management goals for evaluating security incidents.

3.4.8 Lighting

Document light levels around and on the protected perimeter. Ample lighting can be a significant deterrence to physical security threats and will be a consideration in selecting the type of CCTV equipment recommended. Review existing light levels around the protected asset and consider how it will deter the identified threat.

The most common measurement of light output (or luminous flux) is the lumen. A lumen is a unit of light flow or luminous flux. The lumen rating of a lamp is a measure of the total light output of the lamp. Light sources are labeled with an output rating in lumens. For example, a R30 65-Watt indoor flood lamp may have a rating of 750 lumens. Similarly, a light fixture's output can be expressed in lumens. As lamps and fixtures age and become dirty, their lumen output decreases and lumen depreciation occurs. In addition, the farther away the light source, the lower the light levels.

Sufficient light must be available for CCTV equipment so that an observer can perceive and classify an event. CCTV equipment cost is lower if ample light is available for standard grade cameras. Low light CCTV equipment can overcome low ambient light levels but it is more expensive. Manufacturers of CCTV equipment provide lumen requirements for their equipment.

Measure the available light using a light meter. Begin with your plot plan or floor plan (depending on the area you are examining). Layout a grid of approximately 20 feet by 20 feet covering all areas around the asset or perimeter opening. In the case of parking lots it is best to include the entire lot. During busy times an employee or visitor may have to park at the extreme edge of a parking area. Obviously you will make this assessment after sunset but that assumes the facility is open during hours of darkness. In the case of companies that are closed before dark, remember to consider employees who may work late and be mindful of their need to return to their parked vehicles in the dark (Figure 3.7).

In the case of companies that do not operate after dark and have no employees at risk after dark you still should identify lighting for all perimeter openings for after-hours intrusions. Adequate lighting will discourage perpetrators and provide illumination for camera observations and recordings.

When planning your reading date consider the weather and phases of the moon. Obviously you want the worst possible light conditions, so look for a dark night with limited atmospheric conditions … that is, clear skies. When it is

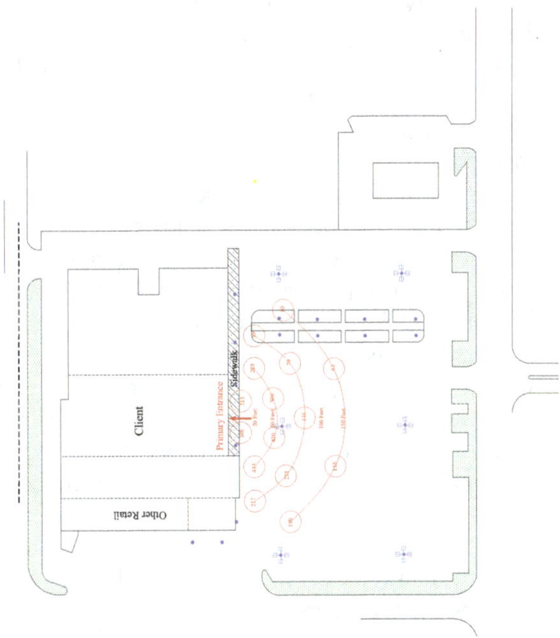

FIGURE 3.7 Light Reading Grid.

overcast, moisture droplets in the air can reflect ground lighting from other areas into your study area, giving you a higher than normal light reading.

To actually do the readings and superimpose your grid on the area in question, use a laser-based measuring device or some other device that is visually based. A very useful, inexpensive tool is a golf distance sighting tool. The accuracy has a wide variance (about a foot plus or minus) but it is easy to use and provides distance measurements that are within tolerances for this purpose. It is also useful to bring a tripod like the kind used in photography and mount a target on the top of the tripod, like a plastic or cardboard image you can use for sighting your measuring tool.

Start with a known point that matches your grid. Measure the light level at approximately 3 feet from the ground; plant your tripod at that point then move 20 feet to your next grid point, measure it, mark it then move your tripod to that point and start again with the next point on the grid.

Your recommendations for additional lighting will provide illumination for CCTV equipment and provide "deterrence" in secured areas.

3.4.9 Employee Identification

The primary purpose of employee identification is to distinguish between authorized and unauthorized individuals within the facility. Consider how the company identifies employees in the facility. Begin by reviewing the means used to recognize employees, the methods for issuing and controlling the identity credentials and the challenges used by all employees.

Most often, employees are identified by means of a pictured identity card and just as often, the company requires employees to wear these cards outside their clothing while on company premises. There are variations in this rule but it is the most secure approach.

The weakness in this method is that a skilled intruder with deliberation and intent can duplicate these identity badges and pass as an employee in large organizations. Examine the card format, it may require redesign to make it difficult to duplicate. You will not stop every effort at falsification but as in all areas of private security your goal is to construct impediments to the bad guys. For example, the more personal a badge design is, the less likely it is to be copied. A digital photo with at least 300 dpi resolution, fingerprint, or digital signature adds a more personal touch that is unique to each card holder. Other secure design elements to consider in your card design include watermarks, ghosted images, fine lines, and micro-text. A ghost image is a semi-transparent copy of the main digital photo on the ID badge that is hard to replicate. The image can be a slightly smaller or larger image embedded in the background with other design elements.

Highly secure credentials typically include design elements that are invisible to the naked eye. Micro-text is a feature that cannot be seen without a magnifying glass or with the card system. It is very difficult to replicate, so it is used as an added security feature in things like currencies and passports. At first, it looks like a thin line printed on the ID badge, but when examined through a magnifying glass the text presents a phrase or word in very fine print.

Next consider how these cards are produced. The most secure method is "in-house" and under tight controls. Often, this function is assigned to the Personnel Department or Security Department. Examine the protocols and observe the process to ensure tight controls of the card stock, imaging equipment and authorization to use the imaging equipment.

Finally, review the security protocols and enlist the help of a confederate who is not part of the organization or is visually known to the employees as part of your team. Determine if there is a company approved challenge to strangers and what action is to be taken if an unknown individual is seen on site. You will certainly want to inform the top manager in your chain of command of your test and the top security officer but you should not make this test well known. You want to see how employees will address an unknown individual and what steps they will take to deal with the situation. You must decide if the means of identifying non-employees are adequate.

3.4.10 Visitor Control

The primary purpose of Visitor Control is to permit authorized individuals to access specific areas on site for legitimate reasons but to restrict those same individuals from entering areas for which permission has not been granted. The security management goals for Visitor Control are to be able to:

- Distinguish authorized visitors from the general public
- Provide a time limit for visitor permission that automatically expires and notifies the staff that the visitor permission has ended
- Provide a means for an authorized visitor to access only the areas within which they have permission to enter

During the goal setting meeting you determine the criteria for admitting visitors to the facility. Most companies permit individuals who are not employees to conduct business on company grounds. Examples are sales representatives and customers. Establish where the visitors are permitted access and the verifications used to challenge the visitor to determine their intent on company grounds. Look for the records of visitor entry and note what information company personnel gather from the visitor before granting access.

You should have also determined how that access is granted. Examine the access procedures to determine if the company requires an escort for the visitor or are they simply permitted to walk onto company premises after passing the first challenge. In earlier visitor controls, a log was kept with manual entries indicating information about the visitor. Currently the most desired approach is to use a visitor management system (Figure 3.8).

Such systems allow you to capture data from identity cards (such as a driver's license) and photograph the visitor's face. Most of these systems also provide a way to print adhesive badges the visitor is then required to wear while on company premises. As an added safety measure, some systems can use a type of paper that is chemically treated so that when the backing is removed and the badge placed over clothing the badge begins to transform. In some cases the printed images dissolve over time, while in others the badge begins to turn to a solid color obliterating the printed data. The chemical process is set so that the badge can expire in a specified amount of time, most often it is 24 hours but some badges can expire sooner (Figure 3.9).

FIGURE 3.8 Visitor Management Systems.

FIGURE 3.9 Expiring Visitor Badges.

Once a visitor has been admitted to the facility the company policy toward visitors becomes much more important. If a visitor is permitted unescorted access to the facility, you now must consider threats from hostile actors posing as a legitimate visitor. It is not difficult if the "challenge" at the reception desk is modest.

For example, many companies do not require employees to notify reception of their expected visitors and equally likely that the receptionist will not call the employee if a visitor claims they need to see them. The burden of verification becomes troublesome and such controls are often overlooked or simply ignored. Sometimes a visitor comes so often that they are familiar to the staff and admitted without formal vetting. These are obvious mistakes but the consequence is the same, a non-employee wandering the halls who is technically uninvited.

Therefore, if your situation is "No Escort Required", then assume a perpetrator has penetrated the primary perimeter and look at the immediate access to the high-value assets in the company. A good example of this is a Data Center. Although all employees may have access to the company building, only a few have access to the Data Center. Likewise, of people permitted in the data center only a few have access to the primary server farm or record storage devices. This is a very good example of concentric circles of protection. In visitor controls you want to be certain that there are additional controls stopping an unescorted visitor from access to a high-value asset.

You should gather enough information to determine if the company's visitor controls are adequate.

3.4.11 Evaluate the Existing Security Systems

If the company has an existing physical security system, document where the components of those systems are located and the monitoring and display methods incorporated in the systems. This would include access control, alarm monitoring systems and CCTV. Of course, not any special conditions covered by unique applications. You will need to test these systems and should do so following the recommended test procedures for a new system (see Chapter 11). Determine if the existing system requires upgrades.

3.4.12 Protocols and Regulations

Most companies are governed internally but some have strict rules imposed on them by governments or their customers. So in addition to providing good internal security you must also consider what is required by others for the security of the operation or data. Obtain a copy of guidelines or protocols required by outside forces, review and confirm the requirements are met.

3.4.13 Communications

Although your job is not to evaluate the internal communications system it does include confirming that adequate communications methods exists for the staff and visitors to report security issues to the response team. Some of the most common items to look for are as follows:

- Is the phone number for security posted through the facility (for use with cell phones) for employees and visitors?
- Do employees have quick and easy references at their work station for reaching the response team?
- Does the response team have adequate facilities for receiving the anticipated volume of calls?
- Is there adequate staff to answer calls in a timely manner?
- Does the command center have an effective and efficient way to reach roving patrols?
- How does the command center know where each roving patrol is during the business day?

The goal is to provide as near "immediate" a response as possible to an incident unfolding.

3.4.14 Signage

Generally speaking, employees "know" where everything is in the company and they know the "code words" that represent various departments. But what about first responders? When you call for an ambulance or a policeman or a fireman, how do they know where things are? The answer is signage. The best example is an active shooter situation. Imagine someone calls the police (911) because they see an armed gunman walking through the building. They know he is in the Bio-Research Lab but that doesn't mean a thing to an arriving officer. Most people are too stressed to think clearly while a life-threatening incident is unfolding, so you must think for them. Assume they are cognizant enough to at least give the department name before they stop talking to hide from the shooter. You may expect the police to enter the front of the building, so plan your signage from that vantage point. Remember, the simpler the better. Your job at this point is to evaluate the signage for an un-oriented first responder.

3.4.15 Blast Proximity

As mentioned earlier someone does not have to enter the property to cause harm with explosives. Remember the bombing of the Alfred P. Murrah Federal

Building in Oklahoma City on April 19, 1995 by Timothy McVeigh. Timothy McVeigh parked a rented Ryder truck in front of the Alfred P. Murrah Federal Building in downtown Oklahoma City.

Inside the vehicle was a powerful bomb made out of a deadly cocktail of agricultural fertilizer, diesel fuel, and other chemicals. McVeigh got out, locked the door, and headed towards his getaway car. He ignited one timed fuse, then another. At precisely 9:02 a.m., the bomb exploded. Within moments, the surrounding area looked like a war zone. A third of the building had been reduced to rubble, with many floors flattened like pancakes. Dozens of cars were incinerated and more than 300 nearby buildings were damaged or destroyed. The human toll was still more devastating: 168 souls lost, including 19 children, with several hundred more injured. This is what you are trying to prevent with your assessment.

The best defense against blasts is distance. This means that you look for parking near the building and try to move that parking further away. More on this is presented in the next chapter but for now know that you should observe the building perimeters with blast in mind.

3.4.16 Company Utilities

All companies rely on electricity – it is an essential ingredient in running most business operations. Many companies also rely on communications and other public utilities. While it is useful at this step to confirm that power to your security tools is adequate and consistently available, you should also examine the power and communications entry points. In high-security applications a recommended approach is to feed from two separate locations that are not related in any way. Each entry point should be substantially protected and resistant to attack. More on protection methods is discussed in the next chapter but for now you should be looking for vulnerabilities in the source of these services.

3.5 GETTING IT DONE

Well, your plan is ready, you know what to look for, it's time to begin the assessment. There are two possible perspectives: the first is that you are an employee of the company. This means that you have an office on site and anything you need will be close by. There are some things you will want to carry with you (those are marked with a "C" on the list below). The others simply need to be near for easy reference. Second, you are assessing a client's site or a remote site for your company. The harder of the two is when your office is not close by, then you have to bring just about anything you might need with you. Gather your tools … here are a few suggestions:

- Your planning document
- C, Your checklist on what to look for and your path through the facility
- C, A small flashlight (the light on your cell phone works pretty well for this)
- C, A small digital camera (a 35-mm DSLR is an overkill, you just need to take some snaps)
- Spare batteries for the camera
- C, A writing pad, make sure it has lots of pages left
- C, A pencil (you can erase pencil marks and a spare pencil); I prefer 5-mm mechanical pencils
- Distance sighting tool and measuring devices
- C, Your introductory letter signed by company management
- C, ID badge (if you have one)
- C, Business cards (if you use them) just a few in case you are challenged
- C, Plot plans and floor plans (carry only what you need for the immediate trek that day)
- C, Interview outlines (if you are going to meet with employees for interviews that day)

Dress comfortably and wear good walking shoes, you will be on your feet all day!

Begin the physical survey by establishing a "walkthrough" schedule that includes a management representative of the operating department for that area and a representative of the physical plant or facilities department. If the security professional's role in the company is not in security management, a company security manager should accompany the security professional on this physical survey. When starting the survey, write the names and titles of the parties participating in the survey and the date the survey was done for later reference.

3.5.1 On Site

You are on site ... Begin with an examination of each asset and the area surrounding it. Then examine the perimeters. I like to start at the outer perimeter. Your first stop is the primary entrance. Inspect the opening, is it controlled, if so how. Photograph the opening and the areas on either side, pay special attention to support posts and other material that frame the opening, the pictures will help later when you will do the analysis of the data you gathered. Mark your copy of the plot plan or floor plan for the company's facility. A quick checklist is illustrated in Figure 3.10.

Begin walking the perimeter in a clockwise direction (counter-clockwise is OK too) and follow the entire path of the barricades around the facility. Stop at every opening in the perimeter, note it on the drawing (approximate location) and photograph it. If it is a valid opening, not simply a break in the perimeter,

Got	On-site Checklist
	Planning document
	Checklist on what to look for and your path through the facility
	Small flashlight
	Small digital camera
	Spare batteries for camera
	Writing pad
	Pencil
	* Distance sighting tool and measuring devices
	Introductory letter signed by company management
	ID badge
	Business cards
	Plot plans and floor plans
	Interview outlines

Note: You can subtitute a "tablet" with images of the drawings

* if you do not have scaled drawings

FIGURE 3.10 On-Site Checklist.

treat it as you did at the primary entrance with photographs and markings on the drawing. Remember that a window is an opening in the perimeter too. Depending on the threats you will need to consider if the widow is operable or just plate glass and if it is just glass consider if the threat will impact that window. Continue until you arrive back at your starting point. In some cases the campus is huge (I had one that was 6.2 miles). Often on such big campuses the security or maintenance force has small vehicles that they use to get around. When setting up your visit you may want to ask for the use of one such vehicle to save time.

After completing the outer perimeter, move to the next inner perimeter and do exactly the same thing. Continue inward, inspecting each perimeter in detail (that is why in your preparation for the goal setting meeting it was suggested that you mark the perimeters beforehand … it helps to find your way).

As you move further into the buildings you will encounter doors that were perhaps not on the floor plan (most likely added after the initial construction). You will need to enter those doors to confirm that the perimeter is contiguous.

When you are finally at the asset, consider camera views of and around the asset. This may not have response implications but will be most useful as evidentiary data should an incident occur.

Before leaving, review your notes and your plan markings, make sure you have complete circles around each asset. It is helpful to review your pictures too. The one mistake I always seem to make is not taking enough pictures or worse … during the analysis step there is something I want to know and I took a picture of everything around it but not of the item that is holding my interest. Digital pictures are "free", you can always "not take enough" but you can never take too many!

3.5.2 Examine Internal Security Conditions

Well, that wraps up the perimeters and now it is time to examine the internal security features. It is likely you will do this in a subsequent visit. Begin with Key Controls. As discussed earlier, determine who is in charge of key management (it may be no one or multiple people). Cover the aspects discussed earlier in Section 3.4.5. You can use this visit to also examine the blast proximity found and the utility entrances as previously discussed.

Next, conduct your interviews with security personnel. Follow that with a review of the Employee Identification protocols and methods discussed and visitor controls. This would also be a good time to examine the communications capabilities.

Then plan a night visit with your light meter (I use the Leaton model L830 Lux Meter), bring your grid as described earlier and take your after dark readings and note the atmospheric conditions as previously described.

On your next visit, evaluate the existing security systems and, of course, the protocols used.

Now that you have this mountain of data, it is time to assess what you have found.

CHAPTER 4

Analyzing the Data and System Design

CONTENTS

4.1 INTRODUCTION: ASSESSING AND MITIGATING THE VULNERABILITIES

Let's review at this point you have established your scope of work, met with the management team to set security goals and examined the threats to the company. You just completed gathering data on the company's vulnerabilities to those threats and now it is time to assess those vulnerabilities and decide how best to mitigate them. The simple reality is that not all threats can be stopped, your best effort is to anticipate the most likely attacks, and for highly sensitive areas, go beyond "likely" and consider all possible avenues that a determined perpetrator may take.

There is a dual purpose to your assessment and you must consider both perspectives simultaneously. The first is obvious, protect the company from harm, but the second is more subtle but just as consequential, protect the company from liabilities as a result of a successful attack. Lawsuits can cost the company millions in damages and it is much easier to loose in court with a sympathetic jury

DOI: 10.4324/9781003490432-5

than you might think. Litigation defense will be covered in the next chapter, but for now, remember that it must always be a consideration, so let's get into mitigating the vulnerabilities.

4.2 NEW CONSTRUCTION

We have thus far taken the perspective that the assessment is being done of an existing facility but what about new construction, is there a way to approach security in a new building design that will make subsequent mitigation efforts easier?

The best place to start is crime prevention through environmental design (CPTED). See the CPTED website: www.cpted.net/; it says,

> Crime Prevention Through Environmental Design (CPTED) is a multidisciplinary approach of crime prevention that uses urban and architectural design and the management of built and natural environments. CPTED strategies aim to reduce victimization, deter offender decisions that precede criminal acts, and build a sense of community among inhabitants so they can gain territorial control of areas, reduce crime, and minimize fear of crime. CPTED is pronounced 'sep-ted' and it is also known around the world as Designing Out Crime, defensible space, and other similar terms.

This association will introduce you to design principles for new construction and for building renovation. The topic is too extensive to list all the facets here and that is not the purpose of this book, but you should examine these principles and incorporate them in new building design criteria.

As a final note on this topic, building security into a new building is much easier than retrofitting it later. So always be aware of the company's plans for new construction and introduce your security mitigation effort early in the process.

4.3 PERIMETER CONSTRUCTION

As with the assessment survey, start with the perimeters. You inspected each perimeter in concentric circles that surround the assets and you discovered that there is not one perimeter but many (perimeters within perimeters). You also found that the assets were not conveniently grouped in a single area but were scattered around the facility; so while you may have one large outer perimeter, you found several smaller perimeters and still other smaller perimeters within those. Each of these were marked on your drawings of the plot plan and floor plan. You also have pictures of each perimeter to indicate the type of material used and the openings in those perimeters. At this step you are looking for the resistance vale of the material used in constructing these perimeters.

"Resistance Value" … what is that? Not all walls are created equally! For example, a simple drywall, like the petitions you find in most office buildings, are 2X4 studs (some are aluminum, not wood) with a sheet of gypsum board (or sheetrock) on both sides. They are good visual barriers and to some extent sound barriers, provide privacy and a measure of control for access, but a determined perpetrator would have little trouble with small tools penetrating that wall. So it would make little sense to have an armored door with herculean locks and door hardware mounted on a simple dry wall. The bad guy would just go through the wall.

Each type of wall material has a level of ability to stop or deter a deliberate attack. There are several variables in this equation that determine that material's ability to resist penetration by a variety of means. The more determined the perpetrator, the more a wall's ability to withstand an attack must be. Some references were provided in the last chapter, so review Chapter 3. There are detailed studies available that give seemingly precise measurements of the resistance value of each type of wall material when attacked in a variety of ways. If you are dealing with critical situations or very high value assets, you will need to be that exacting. But for most applications, a basic understanding of construction techniques and material properties should be sufficient.

A part of the system recommendation may include "hardening" the perimeter structures to prevent forced entry. An example of this may be to use wall mesh to reinforce drywall construction or improved perimeter fence lines. So at this step verify information about the protected perimeter's material, consider first the asset value and then the threat level and determine if a perimeter must be hardened based on the resistance value of the perimeter structure. Assess the degree of difficulty needed to breach the perimeter structure or defeat it in some meaningful way. For example, fence lines can be scaled or cut. If the perceived threat suggests that a perpetrator with deliberation and intent may attempt to climb this fence line and, after so doing, pose an immediate threat to a protected asset, additional security measures are required. More on this was also provided in Chapter 3.

Take an extreme view to defeat perceived threats when assets are highly vulnerable and located adjacent to perimeter fence lines. In those situations, a perpetrator with an explosive device may seek to damage the facility by placing that device near the protected asset, thereby causing the desired damage without actually having to defeat the perimeter line. In such cases, it will be necessary to harden that perimeter line with structural reinforcements to protect against those threats.

Consider the resistance value of the barricades used to control the openings. Sometimes it is impractical to reinforce an opening with sufficient resistance to prevent a deliberate attempt to access the perimeter. In addition to the physical security concerns, most businesses are also concerned about the cosmetic impact of security measures. An example of this would be the installation of "burglar bars" on windows. The company may consider this cosmetically unacceptable and, in some cases, it poses a violation to fire code egress rules.

Life safety issues are an important concern when securing a facility, pedestrians use openings to exit a facility as well as enter one. Hardened structures added to a security perimeter may prohibit egress from the facility in an emergency. Therefore, in lieu of hardening these access openings, it is often more acceptable to provide monitoring devices to detect and report specific threats when an unauthorized access to the facility is attempted.

When assessing the perimeters be sure to include interior perimeters such as telephone rooms, security common equipment and data communications and processing devices.

4.3.1 Perimeter Blast Proximity

When determining the resistance value of a perimeter the first consideration is saving lives. Protection of assets begins with protection of employees and then extends to the security of the physical assets of the facility. A threat most often overlooked is blast. The term referred to in most blast-resistant studies is the "elastic region". The elastic region is the range within which the walls or other perimeter structures will withstand a blast force and then return to the original shape. A wall with a higher elastic region value will not have permanent structural damage from a blast with a given force. However, a blast-resistant design must assume that the structure needs to exceed the elastic region limits.

Proximity of the blast is a factor in blast elasticity. Therefore, an effective resistance to blast is standoff distance. Standoff distance is that distance at which a structure can safely withstand a blast of a given magnitude. In establishing protected outer perimeters, the standoff distance is usually the first consideration in the placement of the perimeter line.

To determine the blast resistance of the structure, first determine the threat a particular facility faces and whether or not blast threats are an important part of their security profile. This information should have been uncovered in the physical threat assessment. Standoff distance is usually the best choice for resisting blast attacks. It is less expensive and easier to employ attempting to harden the physical perimeter of structures. When in doubt, employ structural engineers to evaluate the integrity of a structure and determine its blast resistance value.

4.3.2 The Outer Perimeter

Outer perimeters are usually secured by security fencing. Security fencing is one of the most important forms of property protection. It can be used in industrial or commercial environments to provide maximum security for assets, storage areas as well as open spaces on the property. A security fence is a barrier, railing or other upright structure made of any material enclosing an area of ground to control or prevent unauthorized access to the protected area. There are many types of fence materials and installation methods, but the most common security application is the "chain link" fence.

A chain link fence is a fence of heavy steel wire woven to form a diamond-shaped mesh. Chain-link fences require little maintenance, however, wire mesh fencing requires even less maintenance. It is made out of weather-resistant materials, which can last a lifetime, even in areas that often experience severe weather. The chain link is the most economical and is the most widely used. There are different types of chain-link fencing available on the market, each with its own unique benefits and drawbacks. The most common types are: Galvanized chain-link fencing and PVC coated chain-link fencing (Figure 4.1).

The Chain Link Fence Manufacturers Institute (CLFMI), https://chainlinkinfo.org/, produces standards for chain link fencing and provides test data on various materials that can be used for the fence line. For example, the use of ASTM F2781:

FIGURE 4.1 Image of Chain Link Fencing.

By using ASTM F2781 testing standards, which compared security grade chain link's performance against that of other products, the security and fence industries now have data to verify the effectiveness of security grade chain link fence products in deterring and delaying intruders in high security applications. The tests showed select security grades of chain link significantly outperformed other products in resisting low and medium force entry efforts, and one grade was comparable in High Aggressive Threat Levels involving powerful gasoline powered equipment. In addition, impact testing (a 4000 lb. vehicle traveling 20 mph) has shown security grade chain link to be effective in absorbing the impact of a vehicle, which establishes it as an effective safety barrier for parks, schools, and other public places. The testing was conducted by one of the nation's most respected independent testing organizations, the Southwest Research Institute in San Antonio, Texas, and the empirical test data and finding of the testing shows:

- Security grade chain link fence can be effective in deterring and delaying intruders and providing protection from vehicular impact in high security applications when properly specified and installed (design engineers should also adhere to ASTM guidelines for appropriate framework and fittings).
- Properly specified and installed security grade chain link fence provides superior resistance to both low and medium grade forced-entry threats and significantly outperformed a competing expanded metal [1/2"-13R (.188)] panel fence system in both categories
- Security grade chain link offers different products, fabrics, and gauges for different levels of threats when establishing perimeters and measuring performance in vehicular impact resistance
- Security grade, small mesh chain link fence is designed to preclude toeholds and finger penetration, serves as an effective barrier to the passage of weapons, and provides good visibility for the detection of breaching attempts
- Subjecting security grade chain link fence to ASTM testing standards through an independent testing organization provides the security and fence industries with data and test results needed for good, defensible decision-making.

Use security fencing on outer perimeters and around assets in the interior of the protected areas where additional security is needed.

4.3.3 Bollards

Once you have established the standoff distance you can use fencing or devices call "bollards" to keep vehicles at a safe distance from structures. Bollards with deeply embedded footings provide impact advantage. Their resistance is based on

FIGURE 4.2 Image of Bollards.

the physics of the portion of the bollard that lies beneath the ground. Crash-rated embedded bollards have specially engineered footings sunk into the substrate. A bollard barrier system is less intrusive than fence lines if it is short in length and thoughtfully integrated into the entire perimeter security system. The bollard materials should harmonize with the building architecture. Opportunities to add a palette of elements, such as varied bollard types, engineered sculptured forms, hardened street furniture, low walls, and judicious landscaping can all assist in creating a functional yet attractive barrier that will enhance the setting. Solutions that integrate a number of appropriate perimeter barriers into the overall site design will be more successful (Figure 4.2).

Use bollards as standoffs for blast protection and to prevent vehicles from ramming buildings and other structures that are adjacent to public areas and are vulnerable to attack.

4.3.4 Perimeter Alarms

Let's look again at the objectives of private security … DETECT, deter, delay and respond to unwanted human activity. While we are building this "fortress" we must remember that detection is our second line of defense. We discussed fence lines as the outer perimeter and you should expect that no matter how well you have done your job the bad guy will attempt to penetrate this perimeter. It may be surreptitious or they may simply enter an authorized opening disguised as a non-threatening entity but in any case you must assume that the first perimeter will be breached. Depending on the assets you are protecting and the threats you anticipate you may want to increase your ability to detect an intrusion.

Begin with detecting an attempt to attack your first perimeter (fence line). There are fence detection systems available that send vibrations in the fence line and generate an alarm for the security staff (Figure 4.3).

Senstar offers a range of fence sensors and other types of sensors

FIGURE 4.3 Fence Detection Device.

SOUTHWEST MICROWAVE, INC INTREPID Model 336-POE-S

FIGURE 4.4 Perimeter Microwave.

But again, the penetration of the first perimeter may be undetected because of the methods used by the attacker. So now we consider a second detection area, a kind of "no-man's land" between the fence line and the first building perimeter. There are several approaches you can use, each with their own cost–benefit ratio – for example, microwave (Figure 4.4).

These devices set up a detection zone and an object moving through the zone will set off the alarm. Another approach is e-field. E-Field is a proprietary terrain following perimeter sensor, not dependent on "line of site" operation. It is designed to be attached to existing chain link fences, walls, or installed as a free-standing sensor (usually positioned in a clear zone between two physical barriers). E-Field can also be attached to buildings, and go around or over roof tops. It can be configured to provide intruder detection in any irregular terrain-following situation. It is an active sensor system consisting of a field generator which excites one or more field wires. Parallel sense wires detect changes in the coupling from these field wires when an intruder enters the electrostatic field. If these changes have certain pre-determined characteristics, an alarm signal is generated. E-Field detects a compound signal consisting of:

- Amplitude Change = mass of the intruder
- Rate of Change = motion of the intruder
- Time of disturbance = time the intruder is in the electrostatic field.

Any E-Field system consists of three basic elements (Figure 4.5):

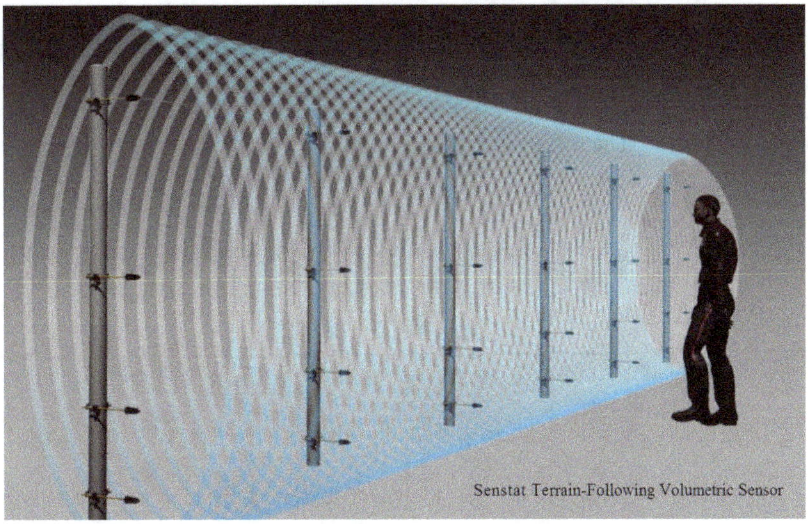

FIGURE 4.5 E-Field Perimeter Protection.

1. The field and sense wires, the hardware by which they are mounted to a fence, free-standing poles or a building, and the terminators which supervise the integrity of the wires
2. The sense filters which serve as both the mechanical and electrical interface between the wires and the signal processor
3. Processor which contains the field generator, signal processing circuitry, supervisor circuitry, alarm circuitry and power supplies.

4.3.5 Exterior Perimeter Openings

Since our exterior perimeter is usually a fence line we must also examine these perimeter openings. The most "positive" control for pedestrian passage is the full height turnstile (Figure 4.6).

A full height turnstile has the advantage of restricting "tailgating", that is, another person walking through a controlled opening with an authorized person. Consider turnstiles if you plan to use only access control at an opening and you want to ensure that only authorized personnel enter.

Of course, this approach can be defeated with a confederate who is an authorized person and they are using a physical credential. The credential can be passed back to the second person, thus defeating the turnstile's single entry feature. However, access control systems have control features that deter this by using a feature called anti-passback. It requires that a person badge out before they can badge in again and you can add a delay interval to the return so as to delay the conspiring pair while generating an anti-passback alarm for the security force. The attempted violation can be examined by security to evaluate it as a threat or no threat.

In addition to people, vehicles must sometimes be admitted to the facility through the exterior perimeter. These are usually controlled by gates. There are several types of gates and we discussed gate material earlier but now we must look at gate types. The most popular gates are:

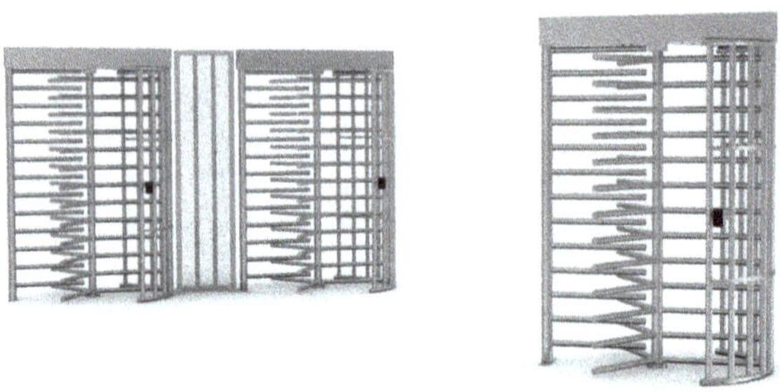

FIGURE 4.6 Full Height Turnstiles.

- Swing gates (Figure 4.7)
- Slide gates
- Suspended gates
- Lift gates

The swing gate is fairly common in non-security applications and is often manually operated but can be motorized and connected to an access control device. Swing gates can be opened either way, which allows easier access for pedestrians and vehicles approaching from either side. Swing gates are generally the more budget-friendly option. Fewer moving parts, less setup required at the side of the fence and no floor track make them cheaper to install. However, swing gates have a maximum opening of about 16 feet and tend to sag on their hinges and become misaligned over time. Often, there is no latching mechanism at the end of a mechanized swing gate and so can be defeated by a pedestrian fairly easily in some cases.

Slide gates usually do not have a fixed opening length because they are riding on a track (Figure 4.8). However, the practical limit is about 20 feet. These gates can be motorized but there is a problem. As the gate travels on its track, it sometimes jumps the track and will fail to open or close properly. Manual slide gates do not share this limitation since a person is operating it. But when motorized the gate must function properly without intervention. You will find that motorized slide gates can become problematic over time.

Suspended gates or cantilever gates are most often recommended for security applications that involve security fence openings. Instead of sliding along a track, a cantilever gate is supported by rollers that are tucked behind the fencing and remains suspended when opening and closing (Figure 4.9).

All three traditional swing, sliding and cantilever gates can be constructed using a variety of materials, including iron, steel, aluminum, wood and composite.

FIGURE 4.7 Swing Gate.

FIGURE 4.8 Slide Gate.

FIGURE 4.9 Cantilever Gate.

Suspended gates can easily be motorized and tend to perform well in most environments.

4.3.6 Interior Perimeter Openings

After identifying the protected perimeters, locate all of the openings on the perimeter line of each area. These are usually doors and windows. Some openings may not be frequently used (such as emergency exits) but are a part of the system. During the physical survey you evaluated the types of physical barricades used at these openings with special attention to the types of doors, locks and doorframes used to seal the openings.

But don't only take the wide view, also consider the smaller details. For example, there are telephone and network closets and rooms that house common equipment for security devices. Accessing these rooms by an unauthorized person can lead to disaster. So consider the security equipment, communications equipment and other vital services for the business as assets you must also protect.

Like perimeter walls, door construction can vary with each facility. The challenge is to understand how that barricade may be threatened and if the barricade is substantial enough to resist that threat. An example of such a comparison is a hollow metal door as compared to a hollow wood door. If the Physical Threat Assessment indicates that the highest concern for security at an opening is ordinary passage by a pedestrian without tools or high motivation, a hollow wood door may be sufficient to deter access. However, if perpetrators with deliberation and intent to gain access to the protected area threaten the facility and forced entry is expected, a hollow wood door would be of little deterrence. Metal doors with metal frames will provide greater deterrence and would delay the perpetrator longer allowing early detection and response. See Chapter 3 for additional information on this. In such cases, the system design recommendation will include replacement of doors to provide sufficient delay and deterrence to intruders.

When assessing perimeter controls and egress control is a consideration, remember fire/life safety. Refer to the National Fire Protection Association (NFPA), which is a US-based international nonprofit organization devoted to eliminating death, injury, property, and economic loss due to fire, electrical and related hazards. Their website, www.nfpa.org/About-NFPA, says,

> NFPA is widely known as a codes and standards organization — that's the backbone of what we do, and it always will be. Our mission is to provide you with the information and knowledge you need to do your job well in today's ever-changing environment. Our 300 codes and standards are designed to minimize the risk and effects of fire by establishing criteria for building, processing, design, service, and

> installation around the world. The more than 250 technical committees, comprised of approximately 9,000 volunteers, review public inputs and vote on the revisions in a process that is accredited by the American National Standards Institute. NFPA provides free online access to its codes and standards..

Security and life safety are frequently at odds when modifying a facility. Most state Fire Marshals (if not all) subscribe to the NFPA guidelines and instruct their inspectors to be mindful of NFPA guideline violations. Thus, if you design a system that has good and practical security reasons to prevent egress from a certain space and that egress is a fire exit, the Fire Marshal has the authority to "close" the building until the violations are corrected; in effect, shut down the business. While this rarely happens, it is a real possibility. There are some cases where egress control is permitted, such as penitentiaries and mental institutions, but those circumstances are pre-approved violations. If your requirement is essential, you may correspond (though the building owner or architect) with the Fire Marshal for exceptions.

Consider each opening in the protected perimeter and determine the following characteristics of the opening to decide if the opening requires an access control device:

1. Is there something behind the door of significant value to the company, either "people" or "property"?
2. Is there dangerous or hazardous material behind the opening that could be a liability to the company if accessed by unauthorized personnel?
3. Are there privacy issues regarding elements behind the opening?

If the opening requires an access control device, then consider the following questions to decide how to handle the opening:

1. When should this door be locked?
2. When this door is locked are there times when access should be permitted?
3. When this door is locked are there times when egress should be permitted?
4. Does management plan to monitor access or egress (or both) at this door by means of a security officer? If not, will the company need a record of entry or exit at this opening?
5. Is this a "primary exit door"? Note: in most buildings, an "Exit" sign above the door identifies a primary exit door. Fire code requirements in most states call for primary exit doors to be clearly marked and available for egress at all times.

6. Does this door lead to other doors that are considered primary exits and are there other avenues of escape to that exit without passing through the subject door?
7. Are there select individuals (as opposed to all company employees) that are permitted to use this door?

4.4 DOOR SECURITY

In Chapter 3 and again here we've discussed concerns about walls and doors but we know that a perimeter is no stronger than the weakest part and that is the openings. When a breach occurs it is usually at a door. And while sometimes the door itself is defeated, more often it is the means and methods to operate and control the door that is attacked and defeated. So now let's examine the devices used to operate and lock a door and see how we can mitigate threats to these openings.

4.4.1 Door Hinges

A typical door is hinged on one side permitting the occupants to open and close the door easily by swinging it on its hinges. But all hinges are not created equally. Some doors have two hinges, some have three or four depending on the height of the door. Also, the style of hinge will vary depending on the original designer's aesthetic and cost requirements. Fortunately, you do not normally have to specify hinges, only to understand their weaknesses when evaluating the vulnerability of an opening. There are occasions when it might be necessary to include a hinge recommendation for a high-security application.

The most common hinge is the butt hinge (Figure 4.10).

This type of door hardware can be defeated by attacking the hinge pin unless the specifier required a permanent hinge pin or the hinge is mortised into the door frame and completely concealed. To complicate matters, primary egress doors from commercial buildings are out swinging doors for fire egress purposes often times necessitating the hinge pin to be on the outside.

So in cases where your circumstance requires high security levels and ordinary hinges are used, it is sometimes best recommended changing the hinge to a continuous hinge. As shown in the illustration, a continuous hinge runs the entire length of the door, making it nearly impossible to successfully breach the door by attacking the hinge (Figure 4.11).

Additionally, how is the hinge mounted to the door opening? Do the screws that hold the hinge in place just penetrate the door frame or do they penetrate all the way into the door studs? The problem with "frame only" penetration is that door frames are not meant to withstand a great deal of force, they are mostly cosmetic. So for security applications, ensure that the screws which mount the

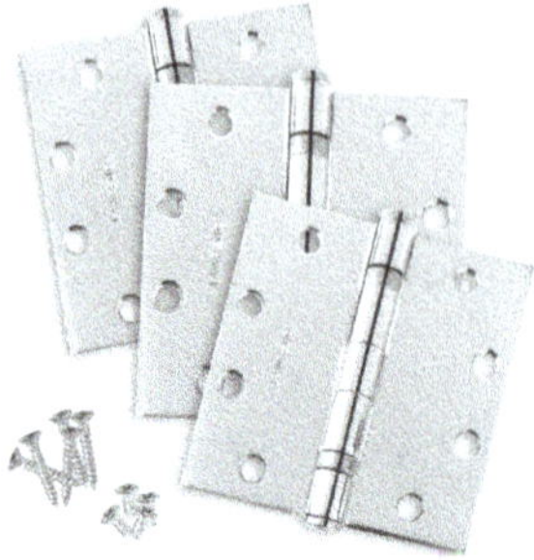

FIGURE 4.10 Butt Hinge.

FIGURE 4.11 Continuous Hinge.

hinges to the door penetrate all the way into the studs that form the opening for the door.

4.4.2 Door Latching Devices

So if your door and wall material are sufficient barriers and the door hinges are secure, what about the latch that keeps the door closed? Typically there is door handle hardware and sometimes some form of dead bolt, both of which are intended to prevent the door from swinging freely on the hinge. These latching devices and control knobs often have locking mechanisms to secure the door when not in use. Access in these cases is provided by means of a metal key that unlocks the door or electric lock control from an access control device.

The problem with this arrangement is the “key”. Keys can be duplicated by ordinary means and shared with others who may not have the access privilege granted to them by the company. Moreover, once a person has a key they may not return it even if asked, so anyone who ever had access will always have access until the lock is changed or rekeyed. But changing or rekeying locks is a time-consuming, costly proposition; and when you’re done you haven’t solved the problem, you just reset the starting point. It will happen again.

Some factors to consider when you review your choice for electric locks (and mechanical locks for that matter) are:

1. How is the lock mounted? Do the screws that hold the lock in place just penetrate the door frame or do they penetrate all the way into the door studs? The problem with “frame only” penetration is that door frames are not meant to withstand a great deal of force, they are mostly cosmetic. So for security applications, ensure that the screws which mount the strike plate to the door penetrate all the way into the studs that form the opening for the door.
2. Is there an anti-pick device built into the lock? These are features that prevent someone from using credit cards or similar objects to slide between the door keeper (the thing that holds the door closed) and the strike plate to force the keeper to retract. If one is not present, you can upgrade the lock or add and anti-pick cover to the door handle area to discourage defeating the lock.
3. Does the keeper move freely in and out of the door? Sometimes, due to wear or poor installation the keepers will stick in the open position. This defeats the lock and leaves the door unsecure.
4. Bolt throw … that is the term used for the length of the keeper. In most residential applications the bolt throw is only long enough to get the keeper just inside the strike plate. Ordinarily that is sufficient if all you want to do is keep a door closed. But in a commercial application with elevated security, that is simply not enough.

I had a case once where the client was a hotel and a guest was attacked in his room. It seems the door had cracked (it was an old, historic hotel with very old wooden doors) and had some deflection (you could bend it). The perpetrator applied pressure to the door, it flexed in the middle and the keeper was only ¼” in the strike plate. That was enough to defeat the lock and the door opened. Even with that old door, had the throw been at least a half inch, the intrusion would not have occurred.

So if simple locks are not enough now we must enter the world of access control.

4.4.3 Access and Egress Control Devices

An access/egress control device is a card reader; PIN pad, biometric measuring device or other identification devices that use a characteristic of an individual or the properties of a credential the individual possesses to identify the person requesting access or egress. The criteria for deciding that an access control device belongs on a door are simple but very important; a door must have two characteristics: something behind it is important (people or property) AND it must be high traffic. So you may have a door that controls access to the communications network of the entire business (certainly important) but a single technician goes in and out that door about once a month. Not high traffic so an access control device is usually not required.

But as in so many examples, there are exceptions. Perhaps access to this equipment (behind the door) is tightly controlled. Management wants to know who went in the door to access the equipment and when, even if that access is only once a year (!). Under these circumstances an access control device IS called for since it records who went in the door and when. Further, the access control system can restrict who has access better than controlling it with a metal key and when that person may enter.

4.4.4 Egress Control

Usually this is neither warranted nor desired. You will rarely want to restrict how a person exits a space because it is a safety concern (not to mention often a fire code violation) and largely unnecessary. But there are exceptions … again take our example above and assume that more than one technician enters the very high security space at the same time. Management may want to know how long a person was in the space, who was last to leave, etc., to do that you need egress control. A person must badge in and must badge out so that now we know what time each person entered and each person left.

Now you might say … Well they came in together and left together, what do I do then? If your application is so rigorous that the tracking and recording must be accurate, there are devices that can help. First, most access control systems have feature called "Anti-Passback" or a similar name. It is a software requirement that for certain readers (presumably the doors with access and egress readers) the doors are "paired" in the system and one must use the access reader to gain access but cannot access a second time until they have first used the egress reader to leave the controlled space.

But that still does not stop both going in together, for that you need an anti-tailgate sensor (Figure 4.12). These are devices that observe an opening,

FIGURE 4.12 Tailgate Sensors.

recognize that an individual has been granted access and permit a single passage. If another person tries to enter, the sensor triggers an alarm. Under very rigorous conditions this approach can be taken further to include man traps, revolving doors and other barriers that physically prevent tailgating. But this is taking the question to an extreme and is often very expensive and complex. You will not encounter these situations often.

4.4.5 Types of Access Control Devices

The lowest form of access control, the step just above a metal key is a mechanical keypad (Figure 4.13).

This device actually works much like a mechanical lock in that a certain combination of button presses aligns mechanisms that permit a thumbwheel or other device to turn and retract a keeper, thus granting access. The main strength of this device is that the code can be changed easily and users are to be told of the new code, so changing the keypad lock is simpler and less expensive than rekeying a mechanical lock with metal keys. Most models are all-in-one, so it is an access control device and a lock combined, plus it is the least cost option. The weakness of this device is that all users use the same code, so if one person must be removed from authorized access, every other user must have their code changed. Additionally, all users pressing the same buttons wears the buttons unevenly, so an astute observer can actually discern which numbers are included in the code and simply try all combinations of those numbers to gain unauthorized access.

The next step up is an electronic keypad (Figure 4.14).

FIGURE 4.13 Mechanical Pin Pad.

This device is similar to the mechanical keypad in that all that is required is pressing buttons in a certain order permits access. The strength of this device over mechanical keypads is that in most models there are unique codes for each user, a single user may be removed without affecting other users in the system. Additionally, most models have "scrambler" keys. This means that the button positions are not fixed, they are backlit buttons which display a numeral (one digit per button) so the position of each digit changes with each use, thereby making all buttons wear evenly and thwarting the observant criminal who either looks for button wear or watches a use key in their code. The main weaknesses of this device is that it requires wiring, electricity and usually a separate electrified lock to lock the door. Managing large populations with this device can be tedious and often each door is a separate system and must be programmed individually.

Integrated access control systems. These are computer-based devices with a wide range of options. In an access control system a computer program is used to

FIGURE 4.14 Electronic Keypad.

control electronic devices, which, in turn, receive input from readers and control locks (Figure 4.15).

Most access control systems today also serve as a multifunction command center tool. Their network devices have a variety of input monitors that can keep track of alarm points and signal the user when an alarm is triggered, such as a door status switch indicating a door was opened without authorization. They also have output relays that can be logically paired with alarms and other signals so that if an alarm is triggered a light can be turned on or some other device activated to automatically respond to unwanted human activity. In the more sophisticated systems alarms and door access can also be paired with closed-circuit television (CCTV) systems so that based on a specific criterion a camera image can be presented on the control screen next to an alarm signal or a door opening.

The identity criteria are broad with many options. We begin with the electronic keypad described above … you can have these keypads at many doors and control and program them all for a single computer station simultaneously. Most

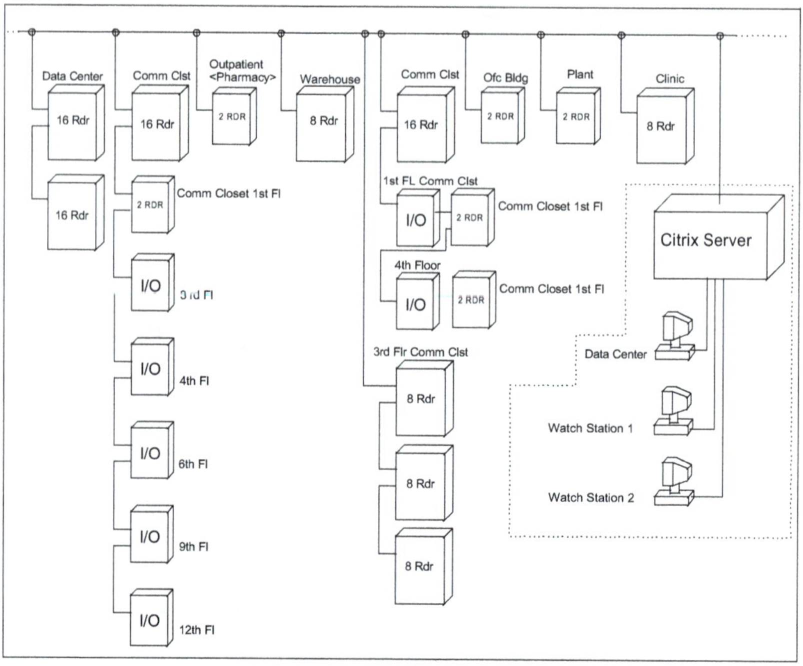

FIGURE 4.15 Access Control Network.

of this and the other devices discussed below are possible because of an industry "evolution" known as the wiegand effect reader.

(A Brief History Lesson)

John Richard Wiegand discovered the Wiegand effect, a physical phenomenon in which a special wire, called a "Wiegand wire", produces small magnetic fields. The accompanying Wiegand reader detects the magnetic pulses produced by the two-domain wire embedded within, typically, plastic cards. Wiegand discovered in the 1970s that wires made of a cobalt, iron and vanadium alloy will switch polarity when run through strong magnetic fields. Placing a sensor coil nearby will be capable of picking up the change in polarity as a high-voltage pulse, and then translate that pulse into data.

Well, so much for the science, the real story is that up until that time access control devices used magnetic stripe cards (which can easily be damaged and wear quickly) or barium ferrite insert cards (the readers of which had frequent mechanical problems) or proximity cards that required batteries and had a shelf life. The Wiegand reader changed all that. This reader was sealed, could not be affected by weather, dust or most other environmental factors that gave maintenance problems to competing technologies. In fact, when demonstrating the

Wiegand reader at trade shows, ambitious vendors would place the reader in a fish tank filled with water and reach in with a card to demonstrate how it reads!

Thus, Wiegand sold his technology to most of the access control manufacturers of the day and they adapted their systems to accommodate the Wiegand reader. The key point is that they all began using the Wiegand wiring scheme which was simple and easy to understand and so gained wide and immediate acceptance across industry boundaries. Now we had something we never had before, a de facto standard for credential readers. So every new technology that anyone invented only had to meet the Wiegand wiring standard which was not proprietary and commonly accepted and their device could be sold to the entire access control industry . That is why we have so many credential options in the market today.

Of course that change meant many companies offered Wiegand card readers which provided all the benefits described in the history lesson above but along came variations such as combined keypads and readers requiring the user to have the right credential plus know that access code associated with that credential. This thwarted perpetrators from stealing cards to gain access.

Of course, the mainstay of access control is the plastic credential. The Wiegand technology's dominance has given way to the passive proximity reader. The term "passive" is no longer used in the common lexicon of the industry and "passive proximity" was replaced with just "proximity". It was originally used to distinguish it from "active" proximity readers which were the first type to enter the market. Schlage created an active proximity cards, sometimes called vicinity cards, which were powered by an internal battery. They had a range, up to 2 meters (6 ft). However, the battery eventually ran down, and the range reduced to near contact and the card must then be replaced after 2 to 7 years. The passive card eliminated that and is now the dominant card type in the industry.

4.4.6 Biometrics

And then came biometrics. This is the science of reading the characteristic of an individual and, in some cases, can simply replace the card and keypad. It is probably the most secure form of credential currently available simply because it does not rely on something a person has (like a card) or knows (like a code) but who they are.

Biometric readers look for human characteristics that are unique for each individual. The industry now has fingerprint readers, hand readers, eye readers and (as of today) the hottest technology is facial recognition. Entire chapters can be devoted to each of these technologies but the purpose of this book is how to plan, execute and implement security improvements. You are urged to learn more about each of these technologies and the best place to start is with vendors of these products (Figure 4.16).

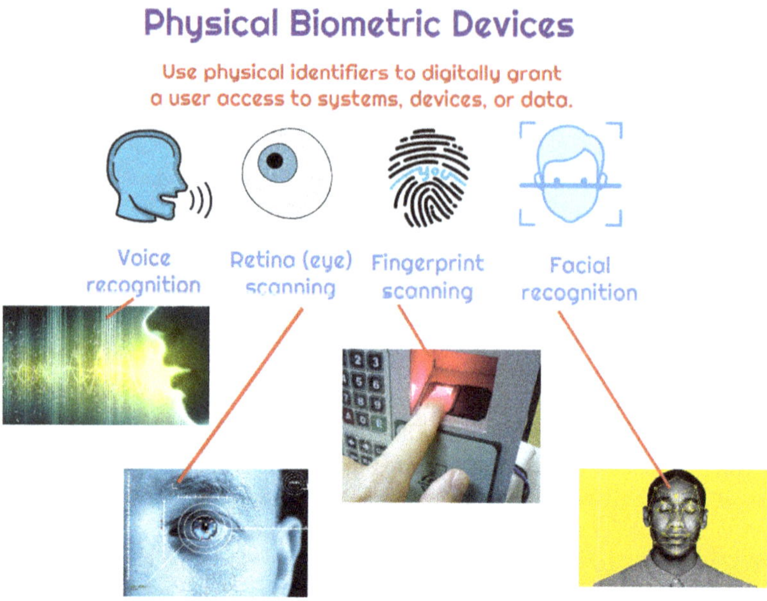

FIGURE 4.16 Montage of Biometrics.

While biometrics can be used to replace credential readers, that is not always the case. In high-security applications, these technologies are often used together. You might combine a keypad with a hand reader or a card reader with an eye scan device; everything depends on your application. Make your decision on the application of which access control devices to use based on the level of threat, the value of the asset and the probability of unwanted human activity.

4.4.7 Smart Phone Credentials

One of the newer forms of credentials today is the smart phone identity. An app is downloaded to a smart phone and a code is programmed into the phone app. Some of the popularity of that approach is based on the notion that people will always have their smart phone with them but they sometimes forget their company ID badge.

In this fast-paced digital world, technological advances have given us many substitutes for previously manual operations. Consequently, it's now impossible to imagine getting through the day without our mobile phones. From waking up to the sound of an alarm clock, to setting up client meetings, to participating in online conferences, mobile phones have become an integral part of our daily existence.

Based on recent trends, it's easy to see why mobile devices are starting to shape the different systems we use not only to connect with people but to manage our lives and businesses. This leads us to the unique innovation in mobile technology – mobile access control. With mobile access control, we are better disposed to access, view and manage critical events by simply installing security software on mobile phones.

While there is some value to this approach it has its own set of problems. Your company security is now reliant on the personal property of each employee and there may be compatibility issues for the app. Moreover, some employees may not have smart phones at all or may want to use a portable phone that cannot load that app. So there are advantages to using a smart phone as a credential but you cannot make that decision arbitrarily.

4.5 DOOR HARDWARE

In addition to electronic devices used for access control, there is also special door hardware that works with this type of system. Your plan must not only include the decision-making devices (cards, readers, control equipment, etc.) but also the electromechanical door equipment that actually controls the door.

4.5.1 Door Locks

The appropriate lock is vital to the proper operation of any access control system that controls an opening. Electronic access control systems are designed to make a decision on admitting an individual through an access opening but what restrains the individual from entering the opening is the door and lock. It is important to choose the appropriate lock for a given door. A well-designed properly installed access control system can be easily defeated if the locking mechanism is not properly selected and installed.

Door locks fall into two broad categories: locks that work with the existing door hardware and locks that are not dependent on the existing door hardware. No one choice is best in all circumstances. An example of a locking device that works with door hardware is an electric strike. The electric strike replaces the "strike plate" on the doorframe. The strike plate is what permits the existing door hardware to hold the door closed (Figure 4.17).

When choosing an electric strike for a door, information is also required about the existing door hardware. Electric strikes are designed to replace door strike plates and not all electric strikes are compatible with all strike plate cutouts. Further, not all electric strikes are compatible with all door handle hardware.

The most appropriate means for determining compatibility between strike and strike plate is to use a cross-reference document published by the electric

FIGURE 4.17 Electric Strikes.

strike manufacturers. However, the exact make and model of door hardware is not always easy to determine by simply examining the outer surface of the door hardware. Perform a tracing of the strike plate that will be replaced by the new electric strike. This will save considerable time in the lock selection.

Using a piece of ordinary paper, title the paper with the name and location of the door. Place the paper over the strike plate, aligning the edge of the paper with the edge of the door jam. Note the side of the paper where the jam is located. Trace the outer edges of the entire strike plate and the inner edges of the cutouts are holes in the plate that accepts the door handle hardware (keeper and bolt). Be sure to indicate on the tracing the location, size and center of the mounting screw holes. This will also be an essential part of making the appropriate electric strike selection. A lock hardware supplier can use this tracing to match an electric strike to the existing strike plate. Share these document with vendors when releasing the bid. It will assist them in preparing their cost proposals.

You can also control other parts of the lock besides the strike plate. There are electric mortise locks. These locks replace the locking and latching mechanisms in the door itself and control the ability to retract the keeper.

However, mortise locks are more expensive and much harder to install (Figure 4.18). They are best used in new construction where doors can be specially ordered to accommodate these locks. The main problem is power … the door must have a hole drilled through the entire width of the door to feed power to the lock. Additionally, an electric hinge (one that permits power to pass through it) must be added to the door. This makes installation difficult and expensive plus

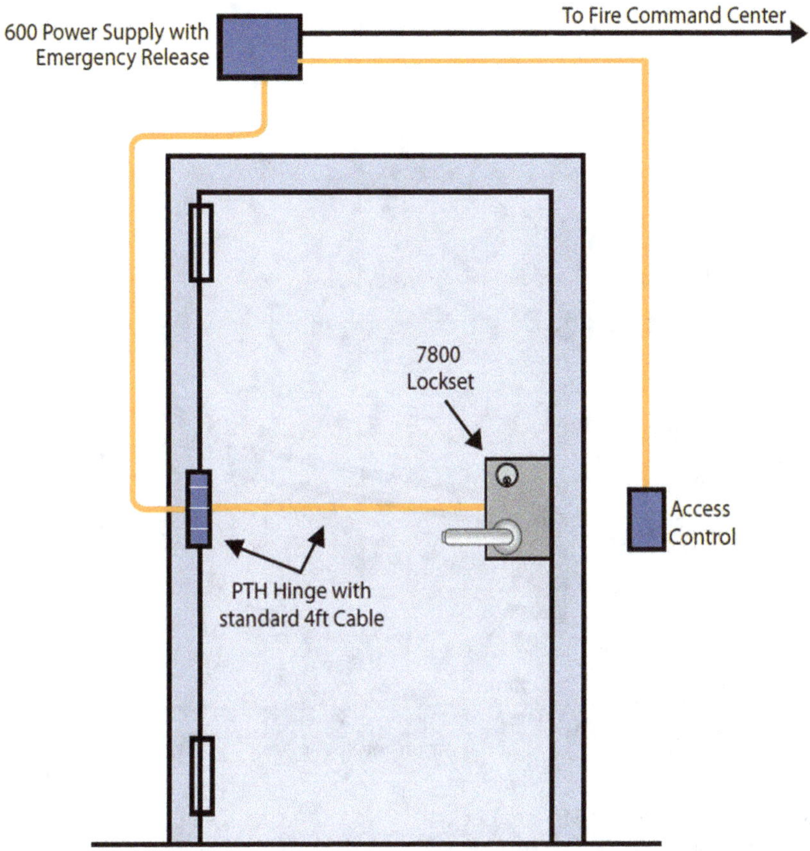

FIGURE 4.18 Mortise Lock.

the risk of irreversibly damaging the door when drilling this core is high. Hence, in most retrofits, the lock of choice is the electric strike.

Other locks are completely independent of the existing door hardware such as power bolts and power magnets. These devices usually have one component installed on the doorframe and another component installed on the door. The relation between these two devices is such that the application (or release) of power will permit the door to open. These products generally hold an opening closed by a mechanical or magnetic means and act independently of any other mechanism on the door. Again, a complete examination of these devices is not necessary at this point; only the designation of a lock and lock type. Each door characteristic has an impact on the lock chosen for the door. Gather as much information as

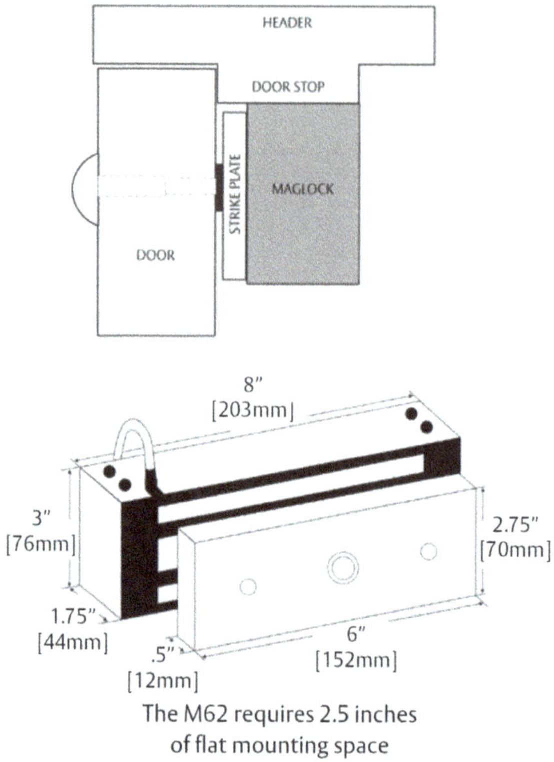

FIGURE 4.19 Power Magnet Locks.

possible about the subject door before deciding on the locking mechanism to use (Figure 4.19).

Consider the following when selecting the lock type for an opening:

1. The nature and construction of the door
2. The door swing (inward swing or outward swing)
3. The height of the door (do not use locks that are installed at the door header on very tall doors. This causes the door to warp).
4. The material the door is made of (in judging the application of electric latches)
5. The ability to bring low-voltage electrical power to various points on the doorframe
6. The type of control devices that will be used on the door (egress control is sometimes necessary in certain application and will dictate the use of special hardware or locks that do not work with existing door hardware)
7. The applicable fire codes that govern the use of the door.

Caution should be used when deciding on a door where the hardware is independent from the lock, the problem is egress. A part of NAPA guidelines under egress control prohibits the use of a dual action when exiting. Most fire jurisdictions interpret that to mean if you have to push a button AND turn a handle that is a two-step process and is therefore in violation of the code. So power magnets and power bolts are effective locking devices on the right size doors when those doors are "hardware free" such as an exterior entrance with door closers.

4.5.2 Exit Button

After locating access control devices, and if egress control devices are used, specify the placement of egress buttons. There are a variety of regulations concerning the placement, use and operation of egress buttons. Refer to the *NFPA Life Safety Handbook* for guidance on the current recommended handling of egress devices (www.nfpa.org/codes-and-standards/all-codes-and-standards/list-of-codes-and-standards/detail?code=101). These are "life safety" issues and carry moral, ethical and legal responsibilities. The state and local fire marshal enforce these regulations and failure to follow them can result in the fire marshal closing the company's facility until the violations are corrected. In this standard you will find:

> 1001.3.1 Workplace exits. Except as specifically provided for in this chapter, no employer or agent of such employer shall lock the doors of or otherwise prohibit exit from any workplace, when by so doing the health or safety of any employee, independent contractor or other individual working in such workplace may become endangered by fire or other hazardous condition. Refer to Article 307 of Title 28 of the Administrative Code.

In addition to egress buttons, the code requires a variety of other means of egress from a protected area. When specifying any form of security system that restrains egress from a protected space, complete familiarity with the entire section of NFPA "Means of Egress" requirements is imperative (Figure 4.20). Some common rules to follow are:

- Place exit buttons (and card readers) at the same height as door handles to comply with ADA requirements.
- On single doors, place the buttons on the same side of the door as the door handle.
- On double doors, place the button on the wall to the right of the double door outside the door swing area where practical.

FIGURE 4.20 Egress Button.

Remember your user base, some uses may require larger buttons, some may need the buttons back lit. Access control can be a little tedious to use but egress must be easy. Always remember that there may be a time when users must exit in a hurry (the building is on fire)!

4.5.3 Door Status Switches (DSS)

Plan to monitor all security perimeter openings. DSS, sometimes called door contacts or alarm contacts, are used to monitoring openings. DSS are simple mechanical sensors that detect the status of an opening. Although the name implies a DSS is for door installations, these switches are also for windows and other types of openings (Figure 4.21).

In general, a DSS consists of two components: a magnet attached to the door leaf and a reed switch that detects the presence of that magnet. Simply put, when the door is closed, the alarm contact is in close proximity to the reed switch and holds it closed. When the door is open, the magnet is away from the reed switch and the switch opens. This provides a signal to an electronic security system that indicates the door is open.

FIGURE 4.21 DSS.

4.5.4 Balanced Magnetic Switch

Balanced magnetic switches are typically used to detect the opening of a door, window, gate, vent, skylight and other openings like a standard door status switch. However, this switch is mounted on the doorframe and the actuating magnet is installed on the door. It has a three-position reed switch and an additional magnet (called the bias magnet) located adjacent to the switch. When the door is closed, the reed switch is held in the balanced or center position by interacting magnetic fields. If the door is opened or an external magnet is brought near the sensor in an attempt to defeat it, the switch becomes unbalanced and generates an alarm (Figure 4.22).

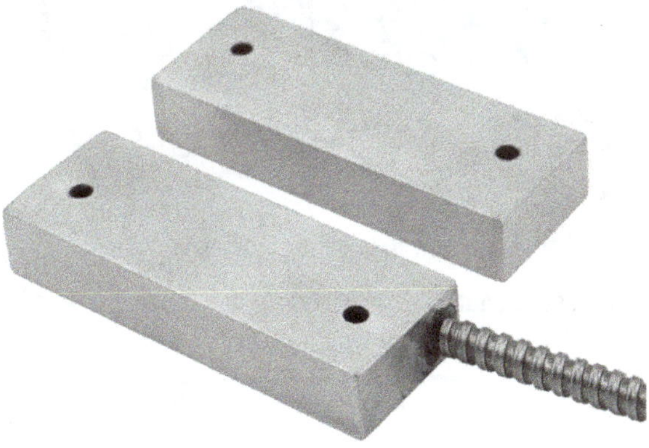

FIGURE 4.22 Balanced Magnetic Switch.

4.5.5 Supervised Door Status Switches

Another in the family of DSS is the "supervised" DSS. Supervised zones use an end of line resistor to maintain a given voltage; if the zone is opened or shorted this voltage will change and activate the control. Unsupervised zones may be normally open or normally closed, normal being the non-alarm state but a supervised switch relies on constant voltage at a given level. If this voltage is changed, such as someone attempting to defeat the alarm by short-circuiting the monitoring line before it reaches the door, the alarm will trigger because the voltage has changed. Use these switches in cases where there is a high-security application and tampering may be suspected.

4.5.6 Pressure Mats

Pressure mats generate an alarm when pressure is applied to any part of the mat's surface. Pressure mats can be used to detect an intruder approaching a protected object, or they can be placed by doors or windows to detect entry. Because pressure mats are easy to defeat, they should be well concealed, such as hidden beneath carpeting (Figure 4.23).

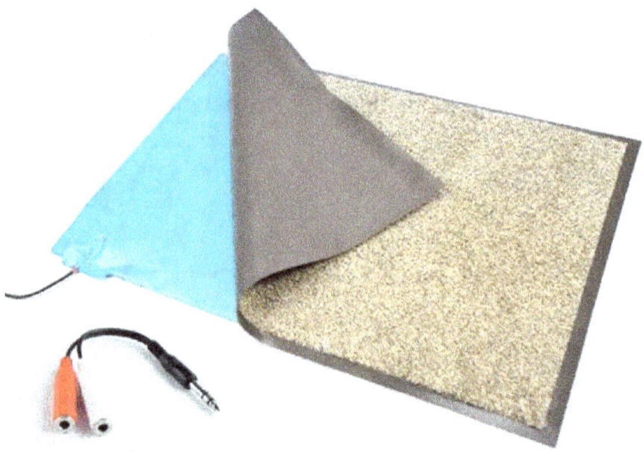

FIGURE 4.23 Pressure Mats.

4.5.7 Pressure Switches

Mechanically activated contact switches can be used as pressure switches. Objects that require protection can be placed on top of the switch, for example, a display item in a museum. When the object is moved the switch generates an alarm. Naturally, the switch must be well concealed. The interface between the switch and the protected object should be designed so that an intruder cannot slide material under the object to override the switch while the object is removed.

4.5.8 Space Protection

If a room requires protection, a passageway or some open area, use a space protection device. These detectors register the presence of individuals in the protected area. Like locks and DSS, there is a wide variety of such devices available in the market. The most widely used technologies are infrared (IR) and ultrasonic (Figure 4.24).

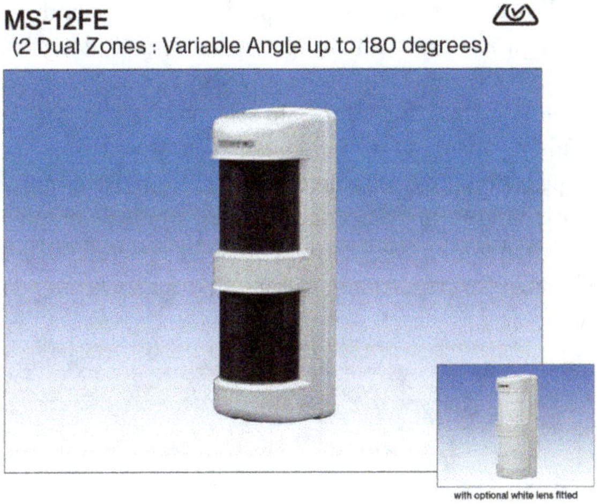

FIGURE 4.24 PIR.

Active IR sensors work with radar technology and they both emit and receive IR radiation. This radiation hits the objects nearby and bounces back to the receiver of the device. Through this technology, the sensor can not only detect movement in an environment but also how far the object is from the device. An IR detector can also be programmed to only respond to larger objects and ignore smaller creatures, making it pet-friendly. IR detectors are quickly becoming popular for motion sensors and cameras. IR detectors use sensors that react to IR radiation. IR waves cannot be seen with the human eye. The eye can see a basic spectrum of color – everything that can be seen in a rainbow of color. However, there are colors that range outside of a rainbow in the electromagnetic spectrum. Humans are called "trichromats," meaning that we can see red, green, and blue and everything in between. Yellow, for example, is simply a shade between green and red. People are, essentially, colorblind compared to some animals who can see a wider range of colors.

Knowing how little our eyes are actually able to comprehend, it's not surprising that we cannot detect IR radiation with our eyes. We can sense it in a way, because infrared also results in heat or a rise in temperature. The IR wavelength is between 0.75 and 1000 µm, while the visible spectrum for humans is between 380 and 740 nm. The spectral range of IR light is separated into three categories: near-IR, mid-IR, and far-IR. Some scientists speculate that, although humans can't directly see IR light, the eye will respond to far-IR.

The second type of sensor is ultrasonic (Figure 4.25). An ultrasonic sensor emits a sound pulse in the ultrasonic range. This sound pulse propagates at the speed of sound through air (about 344 meters per second) until the sound pulse encounters an object. The sound pulse bounces off the object and is returned in reverse to the sensor where this "echo" is received. Temperature has the greatest influence on the speed of sound.

The relationship between temperature and speed of sound is almost linear. Sound travels through air, the medium, at a speed of 344 meters per second at a temperature of 20°F. When it gets warmer, the speed of sound increases. To compensate for this, most microsonic ultrasonic sensors have an internal temperature compensation. This means that those ultrasonic sensors measure the current temperature and compensate for the measured value. This improves the accuracy of the measurement. For an ultrasonic sensor applies that when sound pulses are used at 40 kHz, a distance of approximately 10 meters can be covered. When the ultrasonic sensor uses pulses at 400 kHz, then the maximum distance is only about 65 cm.

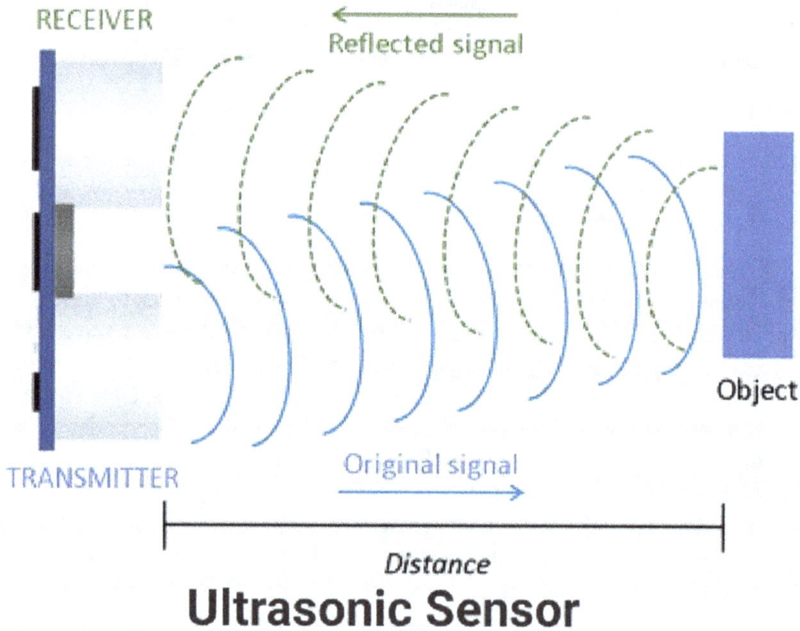

FIGURE 4.25 Ultrasonic.

With an ultrasonic sensor, an accuracy of up to 1% of the set measuring range can be achieved. This means that an object can be detected with an accuracy of 1 mm at a distance of 10 cm. In order for an ultrasonic sensor to work reliably, the sound is emitted at a fixed frequency. The following applies: the lower this frequency of the sensor, the greater the range of the sensor.

While all that science is important for understanding how the sensors work, most of what you will be concerned with is the aiming and range of these sensors. Refer to the manufacturer's specifications when deciding on the most applicable product for your situation.

4.5.9 Glass-Break Sensors

These detect the breaking of glass. The noise from breaking glass occurs at frequencies in both the audible and ultrasonic range. Glass-break sensors use microphones to detect the glass breakage. These sensors are designed to respond to specific frequencies only, thus minimizing false alarms as may be caused by banging on the glass.

4.6 SURVEILLANCE

At this point in your design you have established the protected perimeters, provided sufficient access to the work areas, controlled that access so that no unauthorized person may enter the area and secured all other access points so that access will not be granted at locations that are not controlled without being detected. But you will soon find that employees and otherwise innocent but uninformed visitors violate your perimeter all too frequently to simply respond to every alarm like it was a hostile attack.

The most effective means to investigate all these alarms is to put a guard at every door and along every perimeter and have them respond to every alarm. Obviously, that is impractical, and expensive. The task of managing that size force is huge and the expense puts it out of reach for most organizations. So now we enter the world of remote observations. There are two common ways to monitor your perimeter and your assets – audio and video – and the one most often used is video. Moreover, with the latest advances in artificial intelligence (AI), video surveillance has become something right out of science fiction. So let us begin with video surveillance and the most common application, remote observations.

After the security perimeter is established, assess the video system's needs. Assume a perpetrator has breached the protected perimeter or that attempts are being made to do so and detection has been made by other elements of the security system.

4.6.1 Camera Placement

If you had an unlimited budget you would record everything everywhere all the time because you never know where or when an incident might happen. For most environments that is not the case. Therefore, the placement of cameras is a matter of priority so that the system is affordable as well as effective.

The most important place to start is at the perimeter openings because they are likely points of attack. However, if the perimeter barriers are vulnerable in some way, then the entire perimeter may be subject to surveillance. For example, there was a case in a research lab that handled select agents and experimented on primates. Certain animal rights groups believed that this was unfair to the primates and wanted to release them. The primates were enclosed in a double fence compound with a roadway between the fences for security access. The facility experienced breaches to the 6.2 mile outer fence on multiple occasions but the fence was monitored by a sensor system and cameras were located strategically along the fence line so security could observe the areas in alarm and respond quickly. The second fence was never breached because the response to a breach was rapid and the responding officers had a full description of the perpetrators.

Next consider the corridors leading to the asset. You must assume the perimeters will be breached and the security team will want to know the location of the perpetrators as their officers are responding. When placing cameras in corridors it is usually best to place them in pairs facing each other. The distance between the cameras depends on the lens size selected, the goal is to have the opposite camera and the space below it in full view of the first camera. In that way you can not only monitor the corridor but also monitor the equipment to observe efforts at sabotage (Figure 4.26).

Finally, consider the assets. Place cameras facing the immediate openings to the assets and, where practical, other cameras facing the asset itself.

Place a camera in the location that will afford the optimum view. Consider the physical mounting of the equipment and the availability of power. Judge the value of the "view" in relation to the cost of providing that view to determine the viability of the option. For example, a petrochemical plant with a large perimeter may require mounting poles and long power runs to provide the desired view. This may be financially burdensome. Long lenses are used to offset long viewing distances but they will provide less useful images.

Some of the elements to consider in camera placement are:

1. The range of view (left/right), the angle of view (up/down)
2. The distance from the subject
3. The availability of lighting

When placing cameras remember lighting. In the case of indoor cameras you may need to require additional illumination around the observation area and for outdoor applications lighting will certainly be a requirement. In most

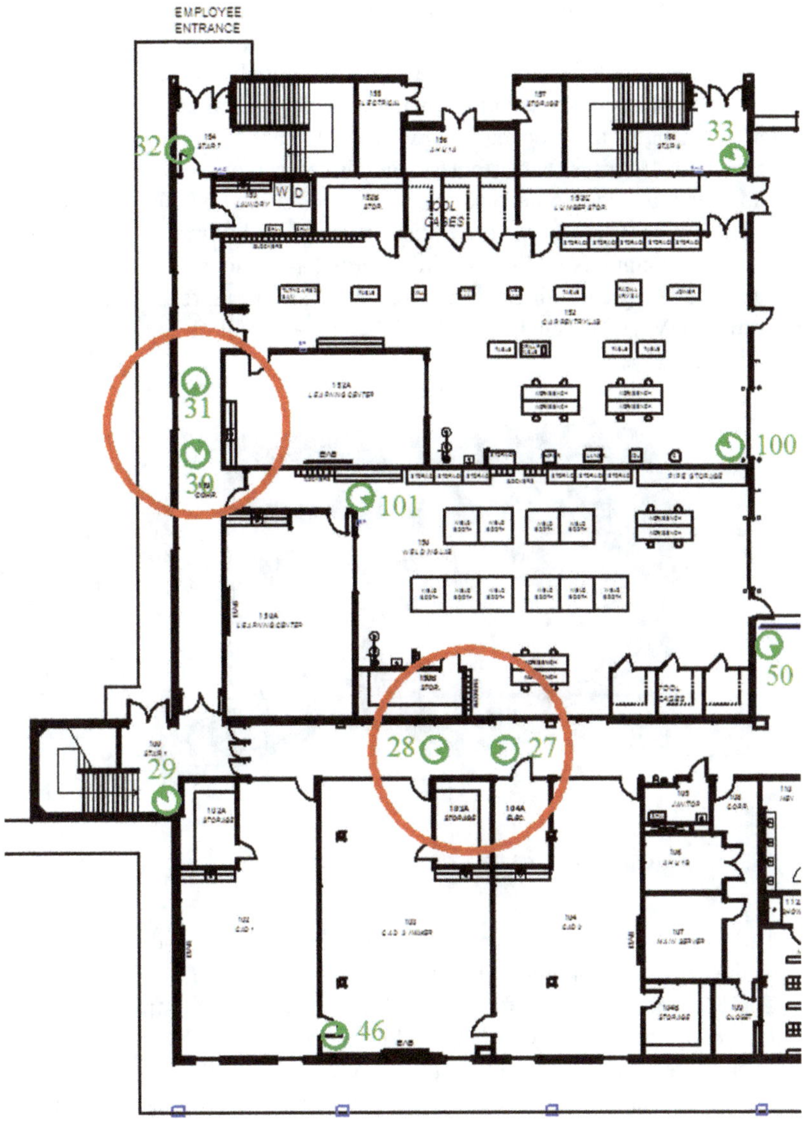

FIGURE 4.26 Double Camera Placement in Hallways.

cases standard illumination methods are adequate plus illuminated areas dissuade unwanted human activity. But in some cases standard white light can pose a problem. For example, in the case described above at the primate research center the adjacent properties were residential communities. Bright white light along the fence lines were offensive to the population and provided clear views of the security equipment in place. Instead of standard lighting, "ultraviolet light" was used.

Ultraviolet (UV) light rays are invisible to most humans. The lens of the human eye blocks most radiation in the wavelength range of 300–400 nm; shorter wavelengths are blocked by the cornea. Humans also lack color receptor adaptations for UV rays. Nevertheless, the photoreceptors of the retina are sensitive to near-UV, and people lacking a lens (a condition known as aphakia) perceive near-UV as whitish-blue or whitish-violet. Near-UV radiation is visible to insects, some mammals and some birds. Birds have a fourth color receptor for UV rays; this, coupled with eye structures that transmit more UV, gives smaller birds "true" UV vision. Nearly all CCTV camera receptors today can see UV light (Figure 4.27).

FIGURE 4.27 Ultraviolet Light.

These lights are manufactured to be used in place of standard flood lights and, to the cameras, look like ordinary white light.

There is another option for camera lighting, IR. IR radiation is generally considered to begin with wavelengths longer than visible by the human eye. However, there is no hard wavelength limit to what is visible, as the eye's sensitivity decreases rapidly but smoothly, for wavelengths exceeding about 700 nm. Therefore, wavelengths just longer than that can be seen if they are sufficiently bright, though they may still be classified as IR according to usual definitions. Light from a near-IR laser may thus appear dim red and can present a hazard since it may actually be quite bright. Cameras also see IR light as white light.

Advances in light emitting diodes (LED) technology had provided a means to manufacture lighting in a variety of sizes and light frequencies. Many mini-dome cameras manufactured today have built-in IR lights, allowing security vendors to install cameras that are complete with their own lighting. You will find these very useful since the camera lights are powered by the same low voltage source that powers the cameras.

4.6.2 Angle of View

The angle of view for your cameras has two dimensions: vertical and horizontal (Figure 4.28).

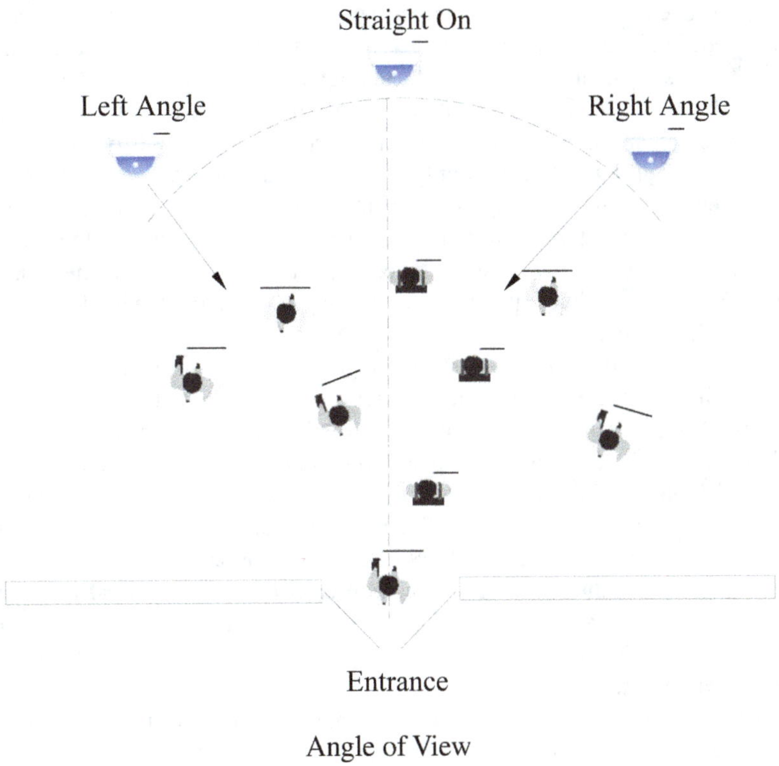

FIGURE 4.28 Angle of View.

The horizontal dimension is usually obvious because the best identification of a subject is a face-on-view. So typically you will want your camera placed in a way that captures the faces of the subjects as they enter the area. This is not always possible but is a goal that should be sought in placement. Sometimes the action of an individual is what is at issue, then profile views may be sufficient. When placing cameras at openings and seeking a face-on-view, the angle may have further complications … backlighting.

Most cameras have either auto irises in the lens that adjust to ambient light automatically or circuitry in the camera that performs the same function with the images gathered by the pickup surface. In both cases the image is automatically adjusted to match ambient light. If you place your camera monitoring an opening in a perimeter and that perimeter separates an outside environment from an inside environment, you will have image problems.

In nearly all auto lighting adjust cameras, regardless of the way the light reception is modified, the camera considers the entire image. The brightest point in the scene take precedence and the camera is adjusted to match that light level. Some improvements to modern cameras permit more of an "averaging" over the entire scene but in the case of an indoor scene with an outdoor opening the camera will self-adjust to the inside light and be temporarily affected by the outdoor light when a door is opened. As a result, your exposure will be adequate for seeing the outdoor environment but the subject entering the door will be silhouetted against the bright light. Often, simply changing your angle of view will correct the problem. Sometimes, changing the location of the camera is preferred so that the scene is more outdoors than indoors or vice versa. Another solution is to add lighting at the interior side of the entrance to compensate for the lighting differences. The solution depends on the scene you want and the angle at which you view the subject.

The vertical dimension is more problematic. Again your goal is a face-on-view but if your camera is mounted too high, all you get are the tops of heads. It is easy to make that mistake in new construction. There was a case of a client building a new building, the floor plans were submitted but not the elevations. A typical lobby ceiling in a commercial building is 8–10 ft. Placing a camera at that height normally yields a sufficient image but in this case, the architect wanted to make a grand entrance and made the lobby an atrium that rose two stories and the building had 12′ ceilings on each floor. The general contractor wired the camera locations at the ceiling as specified but that placed the cameras at 24′ above floor level. Not only was the scene less than acceptable, servicing the cameras was also a nightmare .

The more common environments with standard ceilings usually provide sufficient views and wall-mounted cameras can alleviate the vertical angle problem but now you are approaching another complication … tampering.

The cameras should be mounted at an optimum height to capture a high level of detail while being out of reach for thieves looking to tamper devices. The most common approach is to mount cameras at 8–10 ft from the ground.

Additionally, for this same reason, power sources for cameras should not be located next to the cameras. In new construction, locations are designated for cameras and sometimes contractors believe that the power for these cameras belongs with the camera. That is not the case. For simple low-voltage cameras the installer is required to run cable anyway for the camera signal and it is just as efficient to run two cables as it is to run one. Keeping in mind certain distance limitations of the camera power (from the manufacturer) it is always preferred to run power cable with the camera signal cable back to a central point. This is not only more efficient and secure but also makes servicing the camera easier.

In today's market the buzzword for camera power is Power over the Ethernet (PoE). In that case, the digital signal cable also has conductors for camera power and the power supply comes from the network node.

4.6.3 Camera Type

Consider the light level and the view required. It may be required to also view the location at night to determine the amount of available light. In most cases, a standard camera will permit adequate viewing for most well-illuminated areas. However, your assessment may indicate that the area in question is in close proximity to a vulnerable asset and/or is highly susceptible to intrusion. In these cases, a low light level camera may be needed for night viewing. At this point, it is not important to specify the exact model of camera, instead determine the type of camera needed based on the anticipated available light throughout the observation period.

Dome cameras are the common style for most applications today (Figure 4.29).

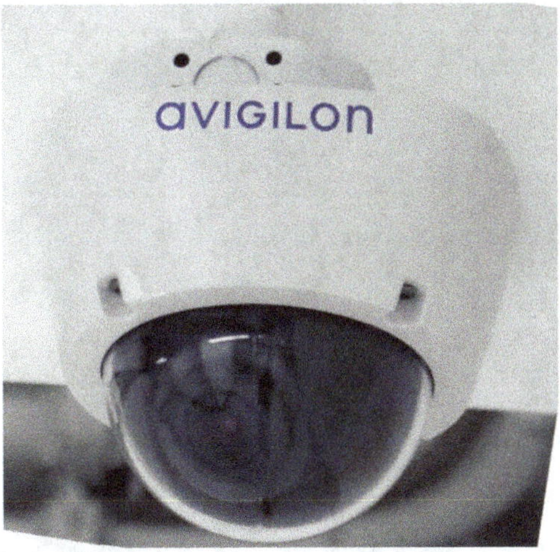

FIGURE 4.29 Dome Cameras.

That is because it is a self-contained unit providing camera, mount, housing and in some cases lighting in a single compact design. Some even have adjustable (manual) zoom lenses so that the scene can be precisely set. More on that is given in the next section.

4.6.4 Lenses

The lens decision provides the "field of view" and determines the size of the subject in the frame. In plain terms it is the width of the scene viewed and the height of the subject seen. The most economical lens type is a fixed lens. Proper selection of lens size is critical to having good images. There are formulas to help you make this determination and camera suppliers provide a handy tool for making this decision. It is a handheld lens that assumes a certain size for the camera pickup element and then allows the user to view what the scene would look like for a given size lens. But you do not have to invest in another tool to lug around when doing your assessments, all you need are rough measurements and tables that are readily available on the Internet. There are many such tools out there and they will tell you for a given imaging surface and a given lens size the height and width of the frame at a certain distance. So, if you know the distance between your camera and the subject you intend to view, these tables and formulas will tell you the lens size to use (Figure 4.30).

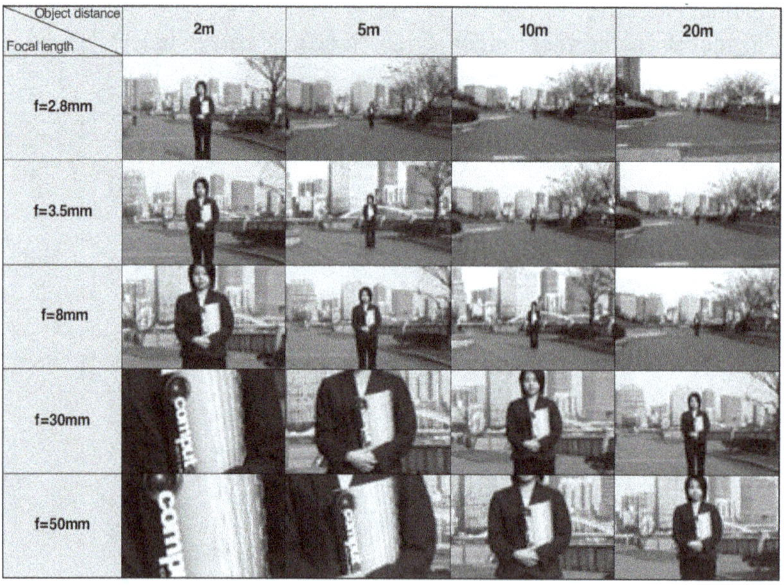

FIGURE 4.30 Field of View.

Here are some goals when making that determination. The scene must be wide enough to cover the subject area and enough of the surrounding area to see an individual approaching it. The height of the scene must be tall enough to cover the subject area but set so that the individual being observed is at least 10%

of the vertical dimension. What does that mean? Assume a person is 6′ tall, then the overall height of the scene must not be more than 60′ high. The shorter the overall height of the scene, the more of the person you will see and the greater the detail for identification. The catch is, as the person is enlarged, the scene area is reduced so there are trade-offs. Finding the optimum height for your scene depends largely on what you are observing and the level of detail you want to see for the subject.

The reason for the 10% minimum is for camera analytics … this is software (explained later) that identifies subjects in the frame. If the subject is less than 10%, the analytics may not recognize it. For a human (security officer) to make a recognition detailed enough to give a description, 20–25% is a better ratio. That means a 6′ person can best be identified in a frame no taller than 24–30 ft.

In some cases, a single focal length lens may not be adequate for obtaining the views needed to make proper identifications in the subject area. In these cases, a "zoom" lens is the correct choice. Again, use the lens tool to determine the minimum and maximum focal lengths for the correct lens. More often as not, you will find that placing fixed cameras throughout the facility is the best choice and, if you have an active command post monitoring those cameras you can provide the command post with a motorized lens and mount combination. This is commonly referred to as a Pan Tilt Zoom (PTZ) arrangement.

Obviously the zoom portion of this arrangement permits the monitoring officer to get a closer view of the subject for identification but you will find that as you zoom in, the scene gets smaller and the camera is not always aimed at exactly the right place to see what is needed for that identification. So the pan and tilt features are used to adjust the aim of the camera. Pan moves from side to side and tilt moves up and down.

As you can imagine, the fixed cameras will provide the overall view and offer multiple scenes, while the PTZ permits close observation of an incident first detected by the fixed cameras.

4.6.5 Digital Zoom

While we are on the subject of zoom lenses we should not forget that even with fixed focal length lenses you can still "zoom in" on a subject. Nearly all CCTV control systems today have a digital zoom feature. That is the ability to magnify certain sections of a live image for better recognition. This is not substitute for a true zoom lens since the recorded image, even if you use a digital zoom, is still recorded in full frame. However, the digital zoom feature will allow a somewhat better recognition of a target. The detail you can see is no greater than the original image though … think of it as using a magnifying glass on a monitor. You will lack the detail you get with a true zoom lens but it could help in presenting a closer image so you can identify the object someone might be carrying.

4.6.6 Camera Housings and Mounts

While many observation points are well served with dome style cameras there are other camera types for unique applications. Usually, when a PTZ arrangement is required, we move from dome to standard style cameras because they are more flexible. You can add a wide variety of lenses to a standard camera (like zoom lenses of various sizes) and condition them with special housings such as explosive proof and bullet proof housings. Cameras require housings to prevent tampering and to provide protection from the elements. Determine if the camera needs an indoor or outdoor housing and if special devices are needed to counter the effects of weather. An example of such devices would be a sun shield in hot climates or wipers in rainy environments.

Housings are attached to structures by means of mounts. A variety of fixed position mounts are available. Record the surface style needed for the subject installation on the Camera Detail Schedule (see Chapter 6). The choices are wall, pedestal, parapet or post mounts. There are also movable mounts called pan and tilt drives. Each type of mount is usually associated with a housing type to provide a complete and working system. Use a general description to establish the basis for system design (Figure 4.31).

FIGURE 4.31 PTZ Camera and Housing.

4.6.7 Camera Monitoring Features

Cameras have two distinct values in a security application: to remotely observe and classify threats and to gather evidentiary data. Gathering evidentiary data is self-evident, all you need to do is watch the 6 o'clock news and see the importance of recorded videos but classifying threats takes a bit more thinking to realize the value. When doing your design try to imagine you are a security officer monitoring a variety of systems in the command center. There are alarms sounding constantly, most of them are from user errors or mistakes made by people who are no threat to the organization … but how would you know the difference. Hence, remote observation.

If you could just see why the alarm happened, you would know if you should send a patrol officer or call for police backup or just ignore it. And the faster you can do this the better. Worse … if you have a large campus you may have hundreds of cameras and the perception of management is a guard is looking at every camera all the time 24/7. For those of us in the business we know that is not possible so along comes camera monitoring features. Today we have enhancements to those features named "Analytics" made possible by what has been termed AI or Artificial Intelligence.

In earlier years, and still prevalent today, is the ability to program devices like digital recorders to observe a scene and signal an alarm when an activity in that scene is detected. For example, a camera can be aimed to watch a perimeter area, as long as the scene does not change abruptly the system continues to monitor the camera images without alarm. But as soon as a person enters the area of the scene designated and the watch area, the alarm is triggered. That alarm can trigger an audio signal to the officer or do a wide variety of other tasks such as turn on lights or other defense mechanisms to assist security in protecting the property. A single large monitor can be designated as the alarm monitor and the alarm image can be sent to that screen. Also, if PTZ cameras are also part of the system they too can be preprogrammed to turn to that area and zoom to a preset level to provide the most useful view to the officer. Consequently, the system helps monitor itself and calls attention to the scenes that require a human decision to determine of the incident is threat or not.

Today we have AI to augment that feature. Companies have incorporated AI into scene analysis and one of the best examples of this is gun detection. This enhancement can be added to a CCTV network to analyze the images and look for certain shapes and configurations of objects. For example, one company offers a system that can recognize a variety of weapons; so if a person in the parking lot takes out a rifle or has a handgun strapped to his side (weapon must be visible) the AI can recognize this and sound an alarm to the monitoring officer. Now the gun may belong to a police officer who just happens to be visiting the business but that is the point. We use the automated systems to show us the things that can be a threat and allow a human to make the decision if it is a threat. That way, the officer is not overwhelmed trying to monitor 150 images all at the same time but instead focuses on those images where threats may exist.

4.6.8 Drones Used in Security

Up to this point we've been discussing cameras that are installed in a fixed location. It is assumed that these cameras are monitored by a human (at some point) and the human has other officers who can be dispatched to personally examine or respond to potential threats that were identified using our remote video cameras. But what if we could not hire enough officers or perhaps the area to observe is too large or having human patrols is just not practical for one reason or another. In the past we simply did the best we could with the limited tools we had. Now we have drones ... flying cameras that can transmit images back to a control station so that a single drone operator can cover a lot of area very quickly, can hover his camera at high altitudes and fly down to view an incident unfolding in real time.

There are companies that make drones that can be placed on roof tops (presumably flat roofs) and other locations of convenience, deployed on an alarm trigger and then returned to the base station for automatic recharging after the mission is ended. For extended observations a second drone can be launched to take over the mission if the first has to return for recharging. There are even tethered drones that can be launched and hover indefinitely for special conditions. The point is that fixed cameras are not the only option today (Figure 4.32).

Admittedly, these circumstances are rare today but as drone technology becomes more sophisticated and reliable it is easy to see how officers can change roles to that of drone operators and those that are still on foot or vehicle patrol can be focused on those incidents that require immediate human intervention.

FIGURE 4.32 Security Drones. https://www.easyaerial.com/sams/

4.6.9 Recording Images

CCTV systems have two distinct functions in security: it provides the ability to remotely observe and classify activity as threat or non-threat and to collect evidentiary data. We've been discussing threat classifications but what about evidentiary data? After an incident is reported, would it be helpful to go back in time and see what happened? Of course it would, it is what we have all come to expect from having a CCTV system.

In a perfect world we would keep all images recorded forever. That was especially difficult in earlier years when all we had were cassette tapes with limited recording capacity but in today's digital world we have high-capacity hard drives and the ability to archive data digitally that take relatively little physical space and can be stored nearly forever. There are two basic ways these images are held: first on a network and second on a stand-alone system usually referred to as a digital video recorder (DVR).

On a network, the hard drives of the computer system store the recorded images, while on a DVR they are stored on a hard drive installed inside the DVR. Network drives have much greater capacity so retention can be much longer. So now the question becomes how much is enough?

At minimum you should keep 30 days of recorded images … but depending on the operation and the nature of the facility longer periods may be needed. The metric is guided by incident reports and periods of investigation. Consider your past security reports, if all incidents were reported within 30 days and it took another 30 days or less to investigate then you have your answer, a 60-day retention is right for you. But you must also consider the odd case, the one that takes a year or more to discover and at least that long to investigate so how do you work that out?

The simple answer is keep as much as you can for as long as you can. If an incident from a year ago is found, then archive all the footage surrounding that period for later investigations. Often times both retention and archiving are routinely used.

The issue is capacity of the recording device. In a network-based system the capacity is limited only by the network capacity to store images. Even though that capacity is large, your information technology (IT) staff will tell you that it is not infinite and video storage takes up a lot of space that must be managed and backed up. This dual retention and archive approach is most often used in stand-alone digital DVRs. Their hard drive capacity is more limited and storage capacity is costly relative to the system price, so a 30-day retention with a 1-year archive is common.

Since digital recording media is reusable, the most prevalent tactic is to hold 30 days on the DVR and then output the 30-day recording every month to a disk or other media to hold on the shelf. This process continues until you reach your time limit, say, 1 year, then reuse the oldest disk for your next monthly segment.

So when designing your system, ensure that you have at least 30 days of active, easily accessible stored images from all cameras and the ability to recall another year of stored images for long-range investigations.

4.6.10 Alarm Monitoring and Panic Alarms

So now you have established perimeters, set control devices on openings and put cameras everywhere to look around the facility for potential threats. That's a really big job for your response team. You will find that whenever there is an incident, the security force is immediately focused on as the weak spot in the defense but it may be that the system they are using is demanding too much of the human elements.

A well-designed system will help the response team focus their attention on the likely incident locations. Earlier we discussed AI and how scenes can be conditioned in the camera system to trigger an alarm when something is viewed that may be a threat but what about intrusions where the activity does not qualify as suspicious as defined in the video system? That is where we use the time-tested technology, alarm monitoring.

The approach is simple, if it is in-house or done by a service, you monitor access points to, and spaces around, all assets and create an alarm if any of these are breached. This is usually done with the DSS and the space detectors discussed earlier in the chapter.

Most sophisticated access control systems today have alarm monitoring. The design goal in the system is to bring together all of the primary elements required for good facility security, access control, alarm monitoring and many have integrated CCTV. In essence, a trespass or intrusions would trigger an alarm, which would show up in the security station as an audible and visual signal from the access control monitoring station. The station would then bring up an image of the area where the alarm is triggered. The monitoring guard then could view the reason for the alarm and decide if it was a threat or non-threat. That is how the system design helps the guard do his job. The guard does not have to hope he stumbles on a perpetrator while looking at the 186 cameras he has to monitor or the 300 doors he must observe, his attention is focused where it needs to be on the potential problem. The simple philosophy is let the machine do what it is best at and let the human do what they are best at.

In addition to monitoring standing alarm points the system can also monitor panic alarms provided to staff so that they can discretely summons help when they see a situation unfolding. Panic alarms are usually small buttons located under a desk top or perhaps a vertical switch in the knee hole of a desk, but regardless of the type of switch used, the function is the same. An alarm is signaled by an employee, the monitoring guard looks at the situation and decides if an action is warranted and what type of action would best be suited for the situation, then responds.

4.6.11 Asset Tags

Alarm monitoring does not just have to be an opening or a panic alarm, it can also be the movement of an asset. You are probably familiar with this type of system in department stores where they tag high-value items to prevent someone surreptitiously leaving the store with this item concealed on their person or carried in a bag or other containers. But these devices have a much wider application.

To provide an extreme example, consider a hospital with a newborn nursery. Newborn babies have a substantial value on the black market, but there are also cases of domestic dispute when a significant other wants to take the baby from the mother shortly after birth. The asset tags are applied to newborn babies in the form of an arm band or leg band. If the band is cut, the alarm is triggered, or if the baby is removed from a confined holding area without proper authorization (such as using a valid access card) the alarm is triggered. The system can go still further in protecting the assets by automatically locking doors when an alarm is signaled.

So if your assets are small portable objects, they can be tagged and their location controlled to a significant degree.

4.6.12 Audio Surveillance

For many years the alarm industry was augmented by a service that was relatively rare, audio surveillance. In a typical alarm monitoring station the equipment was connected to status switches (and similar devices) that detected an unauthorized opening at a door or window and space sensors detecting the presence of an unauthorized individual. To aid in the immediate investigation alarm companies also had listening devices to learn more about the intrusion or incident before dispatching a response team.

That service, while still available, is not widely used since remote CCTV has replaced remote audio but there is a new wrinkle. The introduction of AI has allowed greater ability to distinguish types of sounds and trigger alarms based only on certain sound categories. The most useful of these is gunshot detection. An example of one such device is from a manufacturer called Shooter Detection Systems (Figure 4.33). Here is their product description:

> It's the proven, patented gunshot detection technology that saves lives. By combining purpose-built acoustic and infrared sensors with proprietary detection algorithms, Active Shooter Intelligence takes machine learning to the highest level of accuracy — more accurate than video analytics or acoustics alone. And our gunshot detection technology makes every second — actually half a second — really count.

There are, of course, other manufacturers and other systems that use sound to generate alarms but the point is, if sound is the only or best way for your security team to recognize that an incident is about to unfold, you should consider to add sound-based detection to your security mitigation steps.

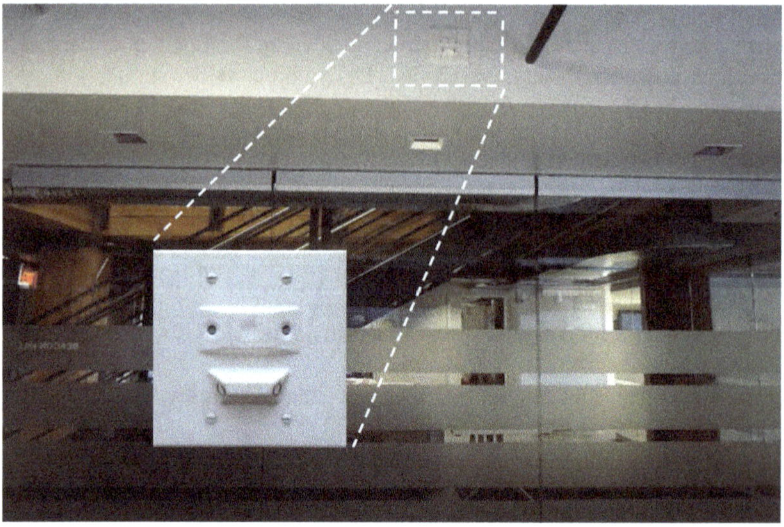

FIGURE 4.33 Shooter Detection System.

4.7 EQUIPMENT LOCATION

In addition to the command center, most large electronic security systems require the installation of control equipment to provide power and communications to end point devices. It is sometimes necessary to have multiple equipment locations to minimize the impact of cable runs to each end point. There are several elements to examine when selecting equipment locations:

- Located within the protected perimeter
- Controlled access to the space by means of secured walls and lockable doors
- Adequate lighting and ventilation
- Cable pathways into the room (a vital consideration)
- (In multi-story buildings) cable pathways between floors
- (In multi-building complexes) access to network and inter-building communications
- Sufficient wall space for mounting equipment control equipment
- Ample access to commercial power and emergency power backup services

Where these facilities are not available, recommend enhancements to the equipment location areas to make them suitable for equipment and cabling.

There are suggestions on how to equip this room, discussed in Chapter 6. For now, you are only concerned with finding and designating this room as your equipment location with permission of the management team on your selection committee.

4.8 KEY MANAGEMENT

Electronic security controls are not always required for every facility door. In many cases, DSS are the only security devices needed. The DSS will indicate to the system operators when improper door openings occur but will not control the door.

Use mechanical locks to control doors in these cases. If you have mechanical locks, you must have keys. Now this is not true in every circumstance, some electric locks as you've seen above are not dependent on door hardware and are completely electrically controlled but in every case some doors are locked mechanically.

It is also useful to note here that you should have some form of mechanical lock in every perimeter. I actually had a case once where the system designer assumed that every electric lock would always work perfectly. Then one day lightning struck the building with such intensity that it set a surge through the building that knocked out all electronic devices (something I have never seen again), but in so doing found its way into the proprietary wiring for the access control system. All of the control panels went off line but the power supplied to the locks remained on. Essentially, all the card programming was lost, not just in the control processor but also in the field panels. None of the doors recognized cards and so they had to "break in" to their own building before a technician could repair the damage. So think of a mechanical lock, even one that can just override an electric strike, as a mechanical safety access.

But back to the keying problem. If you add electric strikes to existing door hardware you should re-key all the doors to prevent someone from overriding the security system using the mechanical lock with an old key. Issue two keys for the new locks on the emergency access door, one to each of two trusted management personnel, in case of emergency. Then secure all the remaining keys for all doors in a key cabinet similar to the one shown in Figure 4.34.

Be sure to label the keys with the door locations and issue keys to the cabinet to the same personnel who received the emergency access keys. Prepare a key management schedule for these locks. This can be an arduous task. One of the reasons electronic security systems are required in a facility is because key management is out of control. Duplicate keys for sensitive areas are frequently given to occupants who do not have an essential need for access.

FIGURE 4.34 Image Key Cabinet.

Documenting the possession of these metal keys will be an essential part of the overall security plan. Use a matrix to document key management. The matrix indicates which doors are keyed and who has possession of those keys. Start with the names of the doors in the left-hand column and "groups" holding keys for these doors are indicated across the top row. Use a symbol such as an "X" to indicate a group has access to and hold a key for a particular door (Figure 4.35).

Other reference sources are available that discuss the ways and means of using master and sub-master keying plans. It is not the intent of this work to address those issues but merely to remind you that such plans exist and need to be studied carefully before a re-keying effort is made. Usually, the implementation of a security system master plan signals the re-evaluation of all security measures in a facility. Instruct the management team to issue only a minimum number of keys under any re-keying process.

Key Management

Client: (Company)
Work Location: (Area)
Project: (Project Description)

Floor	Door Lock	Administration	Maintenance	Clinic Managers	Pharmacy
Basement:	Ampitheater	X		X	
	Tunnel to laundry	X	X		
	Fire exit, west side fron	X	X	X	X
First Floor:	Medical records admin	X		X	X
	Family doctor	X		X	
	Loading dock	X	X		
Third Floor Psyc Ward:	East front fire exit	X	X	X	X
	Ward desk	X		X	
	Central desk	X		X	
Fifth Floor:	East fire exit	X	X	X	X
	West fire exit	X	X	X	X
Sixth Floor Pharmacy:	Pharmacy dispensing	X			X
	Fire exit 1	X	X	X	X
	Fire exit 2	X	X	X	X
Seventh Floor Neurology:	Fire exit 1	X	X	X	X
	Fire exit 2	X	X	X	X

FIGURE 4.35 Key Management Matrix.

4.9 LIGHTING

Adequate lighting has several security benefits, the chief among them is deterring crime before it happens. Potential victims can avoid unsafe situations by seeing danger before it happens and avoiding perpetrators. Criminals also avoid lighted areas where possible to avoid detection and apprehension. Sufficient lighting also provides better images for CCTV systems.

The most severe problem is illuminating the small narrow "corridors" formed by adjacent parked cars. In order to get light into these areas, arrange lighting so that any point in the entire parking lot has illumination from at least two and preferably four lighting locations and with pole lights mounted at a minimum height of 25 ft. The minimum recommended illumination levels for the parking lot proper is 5 Lux (average maintained horizontal to the surface) for self-parking areas and 10 Lux for attendant parking areas (because of liability and potential damage to automobiles). Where additional lighting for business attraction or customer convenience is a consideration, 50 Lux is often used. By contrast, the required light level around a service station gasoline pump is 50 Lux. Now we come to selecting the lights ... this is not a subject for you! The number and styles of lighting available today are huge and knowing what fixtures are best suited for an application or what lighting types are most durable is a subject matter for an entire other book. You should confine yourself to knowing where lighting should be available and the level of illumination required at these environments. You should also be aware of special environmental conditions which may impact the illumination quality (such as smoke or fog) and the factors that will impact maintenance and upkeep such as explosive atmospheres and determined criminals who want to avoid well-lit areas.

The lux is the unit of illuminance, or luminous flux per unit area, in the International System of Units. It is equal to one lumen per square meter. In photometry, this is used as a measure of the intensity, as perceived by the human eye, of light that hits or passes through a surface.

Armed with this information you can set lighting goals and create a lighting specification document, and seek the advice and participation of a lighting professional in your assessment mitigation implementation.

There is one piece of advice worth mentioning … LED. If you have been living under a rock you may not know that the days of the incandescent light are going away. The future of lighting is the LED. No longer is it a novelty to use for accent, it is now the mainstay of the lighting industry. LEDs last longer, burn brighter and use less electricity. As you evaluate your existing lighting consider upgrading to LED style lights.

4.10 SIGNAGE

The purpose of signage on buildings, and directional signage in strategic locations, is to provide first responders an immediate point of reference when responding to a complaint of threats on a premise.

Accomplishing this can be difficult. Start with each area where an incident might occur. Ensure that there are clear and unambiguous names printed on obvious signage. Most might be as simple as a room number but every area where a response might be required should have a designation. This is particularly important in buildings like hotels and schools where there are many rooms and most useful in active shooter situations.

Now consider each entrance to the facility, you never know what route a response team may follow in an emergency situation so it is best to cover all bases. Signage that gives top-level directions at the entrance and then again at each potential intersection will cut down the response time for first responders. The obvious goal is to get the response team to the incident location as quickly as possible. Of course, this is also useful for non-emergency situations such as directing visitors.

Like lighting, signage is a deep subject, another book can also be written on the options available. Aside from correct placement and useful information some considerations for your signage should be font size and type, color and durability of the material used. It is important to be consistent … you will see that people new to a building will quickly orient if you use a medium blue background with large white Arial fonts. This is an example only … the point is once they recognize that type of image as being a directional sign they will look for that type of sign as they continue their path through the building.

While it would seem useful to put directional signs everywhere guiding a visitor to everything, it is not practical. Aside from the expense, too much information can be confusing to a stranger. That is why your directional signs are targeted at the most probable incident locations. A person, like an administrator in a school, can simply use a referenced location when describing the location of an assailant such as an active shooter, "The office to the right of the cafeteria".

4.11 UTILITIES AND EMERGENCY POWER

Examination of utility feeds and backup power is meant to ensure that facilities with critical utility needs will not be shut down by an "on-site" attack at the utility servitudes.

This topic should be covered in the Goal Setting meeting, "What utility services are essential to the business?" In most cases power and communications are the key elements but protecting them can be a problem.

Your responsibility for direct action begins and ends at the property line. Certainly encasing the utility in conduit of some type is the best first step and underground transmission is preferred over aerial but often that does not go far enough in critical situations. If one of the recognized threats to the business is a deliberate attack on the utilities you can encase the underground conduit in concrete reinforced with steel. Obviously that is a mitigation step for extreme situations and even that is not invulnerable. A perpetrator with a bobcat and a chain saw would still be able to breach these measures. So as this book has tried to convey, you must match the mitigation to the threat, if the assets are critical and loss of life may follow, extreme measures may be needed.

4.12 THE FEDERAL GOVERNMENT STANDARDS

If the company is a government entity there may be standards by which their security systems are designed. One such approach is the Physical Security Risk Design Manual for the Department of Veterans Affairs. This document lays out in great detail the expectation of security systems for their facilities.

One could not find fault with the lack of security effort in this document but it may seem like overkill to the commercial environment. These documents seem to have been prepared by engineers who were not budget restricted and so had no motivation to match mitigation efforts to threat levels.

The upshot here is that if your facility falls under the auspices of such criteria, follow it. Set aside those elements of this book which constrain you to reasonable cost controls and do what the manual tells you. It may not seem logical but the management team will have the responsibility of meeting those goals and you should follow their guidance.

4.13 CONCLUSION

This was a lot of planning and analysis and may seem like you have done all that is needed but you're not quite finished. Before moving to the implementation there is still more to design. That will be covered in the next chapter.

CHAPTER 5

Design, the Rest of the Story

CONTENTS

5.1 DESIGN, THE REST OF THE STORY: INTRODUCTION

Wow, that last chapter was a lot of work for you and now you think you are finished planning your security upgrade … not so fast cowboy, you haven't made it to the ranch yet. All you've done up to this point is provide the tools with which your security team will secure the facility. Now you have to put the rest of the picture together. Here is what we have to do now:

- Establish a command center, it will be the nerve hub of the entire system and the point of coordination for the security staff.
- You need to identify or establish a Response Team and then give that team an Incident Reporting method.
- Employee Identification will be important in distinguishing the good guys from the bad guys.
- Visitor Controls will be essential so that your organization can do business in a secure environment.

DOI: 10.4324/9781003490432-6

- You must establish Protocols for proper security conduct and, while you're at it you need to ensure Regulatory Compliance as it applies in your situation.
- Communications cannot be taken for granted … much of how we enforce our security measures is dependent on how well information flows in the organization.
- While it is not your direct responsibility you must confirm that someone is taking charge of cybersecurity.

When all is said and done, your next task will be to convey all this information to the management team and do so in a way that will compel them to act. Security is often thought of as an expense, not an investment. Thus, it is believed to detract from the bottom line, not add to it. To make the argument you must convey the consequence of loss to the management team, both from direct costs and the cost of litigation. All of these matters will be addressed in this chapter.

5.2 ESTABLISH THE COMMAND CENTER

Inspect the existing command center of the facility. If one does not exist, plan a command center for the facility in the recommendation. This establishes the centralized reporting location for alarms and the control point for openings throughout the system.

Usually, some type of security monitoring exists in most organizations. This would be the most obvious place to locate the command center for any new security system. If the company does not have a security command center yet, there may be a control center for elevator and fire alarm reporting. The company's security manager can help to determine where the security command center should be located. Some elements to examine when reviewing a potential command center are:

- Located within the protected perimeter
- Adequate lighting and ventilation
- Easy access to key areas of the facility
- Sufficient room for equipment and security furniture
- Available wall space for mounting equipment (such as access control and closed-circuit television (CCTV) common equipment)
- Sufficient area and distance to mount CCTV displays
  (Note: There are ratios to define the size of a CCTV monitor relative to the distance from the viewer. These are readily available on the Internet and from CCTV manufacturers and dealers.)
- Ample access to commercial power
- Cable pathways into the room
- A containment area with external door locks to hold suspects for the police

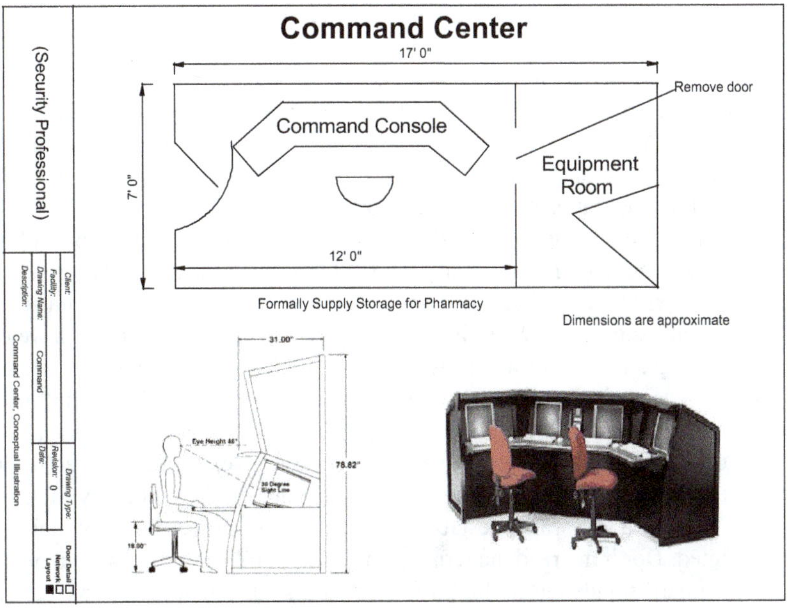

FIGURE 5.1 Ideal Command Center Monitoring Station Layout.

Figure 5.1 provides a basic concept for a command center monitoring station layout. This is a bit idealistic since it assumes security will get all the space it asks for but this is rarely the case. Space in any business is always at a premium, so our job is to do the best we can with what we have. There is more about command center layouts in Chapter 9.

Recommend enhancements to existing command centers to improve the effectiveness of the post and encourage heightened attention by the watch officers operating that post.

Along with the space design there is also furniture design. After all, how often do you sit at a table so you can stare at a TV screen? The point is, common everyday office furniture may not be sufficient to provide comfort and convenience for the security officers who must spend many hours looking a CCTV monitors and remotely controlling doors and gates from a keyboard in the command center. As you lay out your command center be sure to include a review of security furniture to help make the job more efficient. Some of the manufacturers (there are others) of this type of furniture are:

- The Winsted Corporation
- Middle Atlantic Products Inc.
- Legacy Designs
- Panel Built

These companies not only provide furniture for people but also provide racks for mounting equipment that make maintenance easier and equipment more accessible. This results in shorter down time when there is a problem.

5.3 RESPONSE TEAM

A response team is often in-house personnel or other security or law enforcement personnel under contract hired to maintain order and security in a facility. Your report will examine what personnel are on site, how they are used and if they have adequate protocols for their job. Your recommendations may include adding changes in the existing protocols or additional forces.

Presumably the company already has a response team of some type and if it does, it is your job to review the team's capabilities, performance and training criteria. But we will assume that this team does not now exist and so you must recommend establishing one. We will discuss how to do this and the criteria we use for establishing a new team will provide the review criteria for existing teams.

Start by assessing your needs. Certainly you will need at least one officer at the command center at all times … depending on the level of effort needed to monitor the site you may need two, three or more. Next you will need roving patrols; this is largely dependent on the size of your facility. The key metric is response time. You will want to establish a guard post in each area where incidents are suspected. Don't misread the term "post" … it could just be a place or an area where the guard stands during his shift. Part of his/her job is to observe activity in the area but the real advantage comes when the command center observes something outside the guard's field of view and calls her attention to it. So for example, let's say that your facility is large enough to require five roving guards, that plus one at the command center says you need six active guards during a normal business cycle.

But what if there is an incident … do you really want your guard to leave his post to bring a suspect to the command center? When the cat's away, the mice will play! So now you need an investigating officer; one who is stationed at the command center but does not have to stay there. Usually this is a more senior member of the team, one with experience both in private security investigations and a deep knowledge of the facility. So now we are up to 7 active guards during a normal business cycle.

However, these officers are not machines, you can't "set'm and forget'm". They need lunch breaks, bathroom breaks; they have personal needs that go beyond the job so you must be able to substitute other officers during these times. There is no hard and fast rule for this; it is something that will be figured out as you go. The upshot is you need at least one spare. So now we are up to 8.

And while we are at it, remember that in most guard situations it is a long monotonous and often boring watch, punctuated by moments of frenzied activity! How do you keep these individuals "frosty" and engaged? You rotate the shifts. This has several benefits; the scenery changes, you have something to look forward to and you get a rest period. Every one of the eight guards moves to a different post at some interval beginning with the spare officer. He relieves post 1 who then relieves post 2 and so on until they arrive at the command center. In that way, every guard gets to see the entire facility and become familiar with the entire site. The rotation cycle can be every few hours or every day or every week. It depends on the job and the staff. They also come to appreciate what is being seen on the cameras and hear what is on the audio surveillance system. And they get a chance to rest as the "spare" officer during their shift. Your rotation should consider bringing each guard in to the command center at staggered intervals so that all of the outside posts are not stood back to back where possible. Now, of course, this is an ideal scenario, you may not have the budget for this but it is a goal to which you should aspire.

So now you have one complete shift but what are your operating hours … do you need guards 24/7? So your next consideration is the number of shifts to have in a normal work day. Plus, an average work week is ordinarily 40 hours, but some companies want to contain costs by working guards for less hours and relieve the company from the burden of paying benefits. In those situations you will need more shifts.

Next decide which option is most effective in your situation, contract guards or in-house employees. There are benefits and limitations to both. Let's begin with contract guards. This is the less expensive option but the one with least control. To help make that decision consider what activity the guard will be engaged in. You have much less control over contract guards and so they will have the least training and will be less responsive to company policy. If your guards merely observe and report the skill level required is not high but if they intervene and arrest, you will want people who are well trained and knowledgeable on company policy. A guard can get the company into a lot of trouble by a poor or inadequate response, that's how lawsuits happen. Cost is a factor but it is not the only factor.

In-house guards are under your direct control. You can teach them exactly how you want them to behave; while contract guards may change without your notice or permission, in-house guards are always "your people". By the way, if you use contract guards, that does not absolve the company from blame if they misbehave. You hired their company so you are responsible for them.

But now we have another problem, Mary is sick this week, Fred has to go to Boston to attend his daughter's wedding and so on and so on. So your staff of 8 with 2 shifts, for a total of 16 employees, has now grown to 18 or perhaps 20. So in order to ensure that you have adequate staff, you must spend more money. That is a disadvantage of in-house guards. Plus, people quit, misbehave and get fired, personnel is constantly changing. Hence, that is a plus for contract guards, the personnel problems for the number of staff available are theirs, not yours.

But let us assume that you decide to use in-house guards, who do you choose? How do you recruit new talent … and even if you decide on contract guards how do you pick a guard company? These are all very good questions but outside the scope of this work. There are a number of good books out there, some written by members of the International Association of Professional Security Consultants. I recommend reading these and learning about guard personnel management if you want to get deep into that area. For our purposes, you need only identify the needs and provide indications to management on how to find the answers.

That leaves on last topic, training. Training is based on protocols and protocols are based on company policy. Company policy is a function of need. Just like your assessment methodology, you begin with assets, define the threats to those assets and then look for vulnerabilities to the threats. Policy is written around what we want our systems and people to do to prevent the bad guys from causing harm.

This is more fully addressed in the protocol section that follows but for now, accept that a protocol does or will exist. How are the guards trained on this protocol? Are there classes and is there a video that individuals can watch that takes the place of group classes? Are there refresher courses and how often are they scheduled? What tests are done to ensure that officers know what to do in a given situation? These are the questions you should answer to determine if the current staff is implementing the policy decisions of the management team. Your report will confirm or recommend structure for the response team that keeps them well informed on company policy.

5.4 INCIDENT REPORTING

Doing a job is one thing … managing that job is a lot different. You are actually tasked with assessing two things: the results of the enforcement effort and the performance of your security staff. When incident reports are properly structured, they leave no question on what happened and how. Reports should be a clear description of an incident and aid in determining preventative measures to ensure incidents are reduced over time. Let's take the enforcement effort first.

Enforcement begins with company policy. In public law enforcement the police are charged with ensuring that the laws of the land are followed. A security guard, while mindful of public law, has a primary mission to enforce company policy. In Section 5.7 Protocols we will discuss more about company policy but for now assume that the policy exists, the management team expects it to be observed and the security officer is there to respond when it is not. The way that security management and the rest of the management team knows how well employees are adhering to company policy is through periodic security reports.

Every incident requires a report and those reports should be summarized periodically and shared with the management team. Incident reporting should be simple. Your guards must be able to quickly check boxes, record details, mark off critical information needed and then move on. The process is simple enough that they will be able to fill out the information quickly, but thorough enough that you capture the important details. There is no magic formula for what to include in a report but there are some obvious requirements.

- Name of investigating officer
- Date

- Time
- Location of incident
- Names of people involved, age and sex
- Name of witnesses, age, sex and relationship with the victim or perpetrator
- Status of those involved (employee, visitor, and vendor)
- Address and telephone number for non-employees
- Type of incident
- Description
- Damage involved
- Injury to persons
- Action taken (notify police, fire department, etc.)
- Diagrams are helpful in pinpointing where incidents occurred
- Photographs

This is by no means an all-encompassing list; you should discuss the report requirements with your legal department and other management team members. It's important to limit where an officer can input free text. Doing so increases the speed at which reporting is completed and provides for better efficiency.

There are some incident reporting software programs available to help you collect the report information and make conveying this data to the management team. You can also find trends in the data which will be useful in finding new mitigation steps for upgrading your security system in the future.

Managing the guards brings another challenge to the table. The incident reports are helpful but they do not show the entire picture. Incident reports show you what the guards or another employee discovered but not if your guards are making their rounds as prescribed and for that there is another piece of technology that is very useful, guard tour programs (Figure 5.2).

Guard tour programs speak to the rotation suggestion discussed in the previous section on Response Teams. One of the ways bad guys circumvent security efforts is to observe the rounds made by guards and learn their "timing" so that they commit their crime at times they know the guard will not be around to observe their activity. Guard tour programs change that.

A guard tour program provides an identity tag at specific locations, these are sometimes something as simple as a bar code adhesive tag. Each guard carries a "wand" like the one in Figure 5.2 and is required to badge in at certain locations at certain times. However, the program is written so that the path varies periodically (potentially daily) making the guard rounds unpredictable. Moreover, the wand keeps a record of the travel path and times and can be used as a simple reporting tool for minor incidents found. For example, in one system the guard has a small booklet with coded tags, each tag in the book has a specific meaning (wet floor, door open and fire extinguisher missing) and the guard uses the wand to encode what was found. The wand automatically records the date and time and more codes can be read in to describe the action taken. So in one convenient tool the

FIGURE 5.2 Guard Tour Device.

guard records his rounds and that record is uploaded to the system when the guard returns to charge the wand at the end of the shift.

The reports from these systems can help the security manager ensure that the guard staff is making rounds as prescribed and those reports can be shared with the rest of the management team to illustrate how well the security force is implementing the security policy.

5.5 EMPLOYEE IDENTIFICATION

The primary purpose of employee identification is to distinguish between authorized and unauthorized individuals within the facility. In small companies everyone knows everyone else, so identity badges are not often required. But as the company grows, people change, people are added and it becomes harder to distinguish employees from visitors and vendors. That is important because you expect to see employees in certain controlled areas but not visitors and vendors. The way this is usually accomplished is to require all employees to have and wear employee identification badges.

These badges usually have a picture of the employee, their name and, often, the department they work in. That way they can be identified at a glance. Sometimes, the data included with an identity badge can be broad, as in the case of Transportation Worker Identification Credential or TWIC card (Figure 5.3). The TWIC card maintains several overt design features to promote secure use of the credential.

1. Frontal facial photograph of the card holder.
2. Credential Expiration Date: Color-coded background that will update on annual basis.

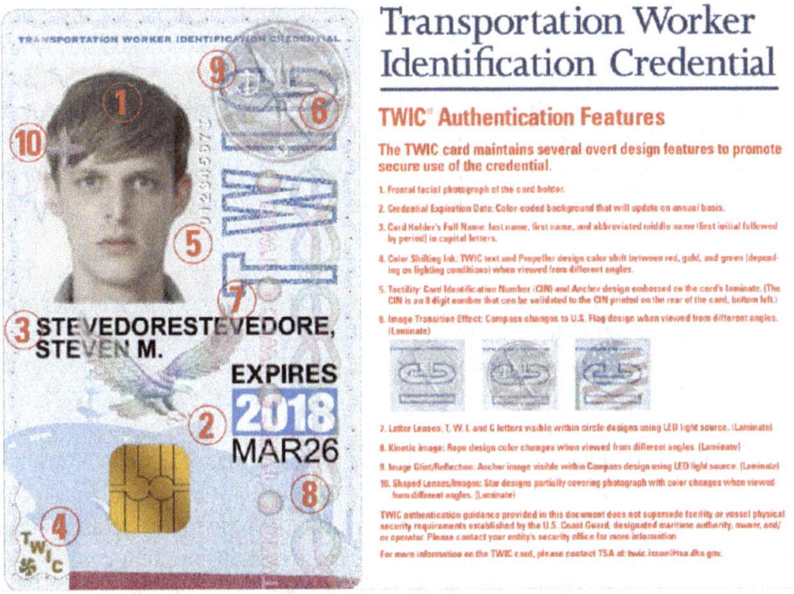

FIGURE 5.3 Sample TWIC Card.

3. Card Holder's Full Name: last name, first name and abbreviated middle name (first initial followed by period) in capital letters.
4. Color Shifting Ink: TWIC text and Propeller design color shift between red, gold and green when viewed from different angles.
5. Tactility: Card Identification Number (CIN) and Anchor design embossed on the card's laminate. (The CIN is an eight-digit number that can be validated to the CIN printed on the rear of the card, bottom left.)
6. Image Transition Effect: Compass changes to US Flag design when viewed from different angles.
7. Letter Lenses: T, W, I, and C letters visible within circle designs using LED light source.
8. Kinetic image: Rope design color changes when viewed from different angles.
9. Image Glint/Reflection: Anchor image visible within Compass design using LED light source.
10. Shaped Lenses/Images: Star designs partially covering photograph with color changes when viewed from different angles.

For more information on the TWIC card, contact TSA at: twic.issue@tsa.dhs.gov.

So, as you can see, an identity card can get complicated but for most commercial applications a simple laminate card with the basic data previously suggested will suffice. One of the elements that the TWIC card focuses on and is recommended here is the ability to avoid duplication. Special images and designs can be included in the card design so that duplicating the card becomes very difficult. Keep duplication in mind when creating your design. Your company may be different, you should discuss ID card requirements with the Personnel Department.

In today's technological world the ID card is not always just for identification. Often it is also the access control card an employee uses to gain access to her work space. Essentially, the ID is laminated to the access card and embedded in the access card is the technology that the access control readers recognize. There are also ways through bar codes and magnetic strip additions to extend the use of the ID card to money handling. For example, I had a case on a college campus where we used the ID card for student and staff identification and the card had an embedded proximity access control technology for access to areas of the campus. But we also added a mag stripe that could be read by the retail facilities on campus like the cafeteria. So the ID card became an all-in-one means to identify all the privileges a staff member or student could have on site. Consider all aspects of your card usage when designing your system.

5.6 VISITOR CONTROLS

The primary purpose of Visitor Control is to permit authorized individuals to access specific areas on site for legitimate reasons but to restrict those same individuals from entering areas for which permission has not been granted. The security management goals for Visitor Control are to be able to:

1. Distinguish authorized visitors from the general public
2. Provide a time limit for visitor permission that automatically expires and notifies the staff that the visitor permission has ended
3. Provide a means for an authorized visitor to access only the areas within which they have permission to enter

Visitor control actually starts with perimeter controls from the last chapter. By controlling your perimeter you limit the number of places someone can enter company grounds. At the designated entry points there must be a way to vet a visitor, why are they here, with whom will they visit, and where do they need to go?

All too often I have seen self-designed "sign in" sheets for visitors when assessing the security arrangements for a client. In those same situations the visitor actually prints their own visitor ID. Sometimes, just to see if someone was paying attention, I would sign in as "Mickey Mouse" and wait for an inquiry. No one has ever challenged me. That should tell you something about how you vet a visitor.

So, since a plain, self-determined "sign in" sheet is insufficient, do we need a strip search, body cavity check, how far do we go? As we have done before, start with the assets, the more valuable/sensitive the asset the greater the screening is for the visitor. Next consider the threats you identified; if one of your concerns is sabotage, does it make sense to allow unescorted visitors into the facility? With all this information before you, assign a security level to each asset area and then based on that security level, establish vetting requirements for a visitor to each area. Thus, the answer to "How far do we go" is "Where is the visitor going?".

At the very least the receptionist must begin by confirming the identity of the visitor. The customary method is to demand a government-issued identity credential such as a driver's license or passport. Company identity is also important but to a lesser degree. Visitors are not always representing a company. Sometimes, to confirm a visitor has left the grounds you can require that the credential be handed over and held by security until the visit leaves. Then you know at the end of the day who is still on site.

The next criterion to consider is "authorized entry". What makes a visitor "authorized"? The thing you do not want to do is make your guard or reception clerk responsible for making those decisions, they should be made by the person who requested the visit. There are two approaches for this verification: first, you can have an authorized visitor process by which the department representative communicates with reception to list all those who are authorized to visit and, second, you can require each time a visitor enters the receptionist must call the department for confirmation.

There are pros and cons to each approach and I favor the visitor list approach. That is simply because if a call is required all too often the department representative is not at their desk or is on another call or for some other reason their phone is not being answered. Hence, the visitor has to wait, reception has to make repeated calls and on and on. That makes the verification call approach more time-consuming and less efficient.

There are lots of visitor control software programs out there and for large companies with a sophisticated network the process becomes very easy. A person's name and company can be entered into a database as a "permanent" visitor and will be fully authorized every time they come to the facility or you can have certain times and days someone is allowed in. Most of these programs are very flexible. The department representative maintains their section of the visitor database and the receptionist simply reads the instructions. The search can be by employee or by visitor name but the concept is the same in all cases (Figure 5.4).

Next you want to certify that a visitor has been properly vetted, this is most often done with a visitor ID. Much like employee IDs, you want to make visitor IDs difficult to duplicate although you need not pay as much attention as with employee IDs. The visitor ID at a minimum should have the following information:

FIGURE 5.4 Visitor Control System.

- Visitor name
- Visitor company name
- Date and time of entry
- A "visit area" code or color that is very obvious
- Frontal facial photograph of the card holder
- Credential expiration date and time
- ID card identification number, this can be a simple sequential numbering so that copied cards can be spotted easily if they appear to be out of sequence.

Essentially, you are making it easy for an employee to spot a visitor who is in an area where they are not supposed to be. Moreover, by requiring the visitor to wear that card (using adhesive backed stickers) a person who has not been vetted can also be easily spotted.

A nice addition to this process is to use Auto Expiring cards (Figure 5.5).

These are chemically treated badges, when the adhesive backing is removed the chemical process begins. The card begins to block itself out by turning black or purple. The longer the card is worn, the darker it gets (worn or not it still gets darker) so that by the end of the expiration period the card is obliterated or expired. So now employees can also see who has overstayed their welcome. These cards come in specific expiration cycles such as 2, 8 and 24 hours.

Now we've addressed the "who" and the "when", let's look at the "where". The printed badge has a designation for an area but employees are not always attentive to these details. Your access control system can help. You can issue

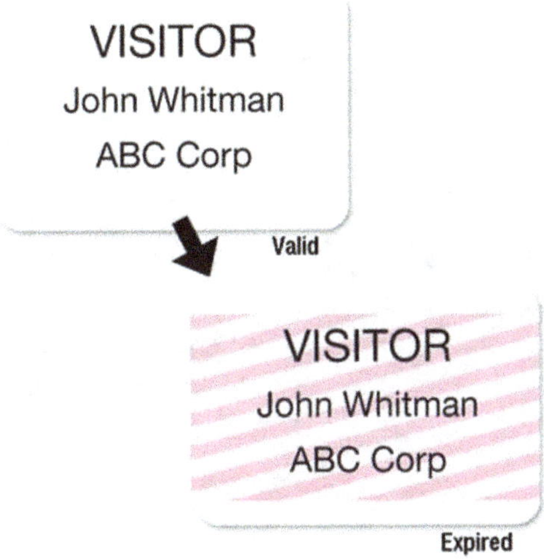

FIGURE 5.5 Expiring Visitor Tags.

temporary cards to visitors that expire at the end of the day and these cards will permit the visit to open doors in a path only to their visit location. Now you needn't be that exacting, in setting up your access control system you can be mindful of visitors vs. employees and grant visitor access to all low level spaces. That decision depends on the assets and threats and more importantly the configuration of your facility. There was one case where the employees carried proximity badges for access and we added card readers that were bar code based (you can mix technologies in the same system) and the access bar code was printed on the visitor badge. The badge was a "wearable" paper badge with a clip strap. Their ID card became their access card and it simply stopped working at the end of the day. These cards were inexpensive and made an effective visitor access tool (Figure 5.6).

Assigning standard access cards to visitors is problematic, the cards are not cheap and if you have a lot of visitors it can be a costly approach. The example above solved that without any compromise of company security and only a small investment in additional card readers.

That brings us to the highest level, the escorted visitor. Again it depends on your assets and threats but company policy may be that no visitor can wander unescorted throughout the facility. In these cases, the approach described earlier is best. The visitor arrives, the receptionist must call the employee they are visiting and the employee must come to the visitor who remains with the employee throughout his stay. The conclusion here is that visitors must be controlled to protect the assets from potential threats.

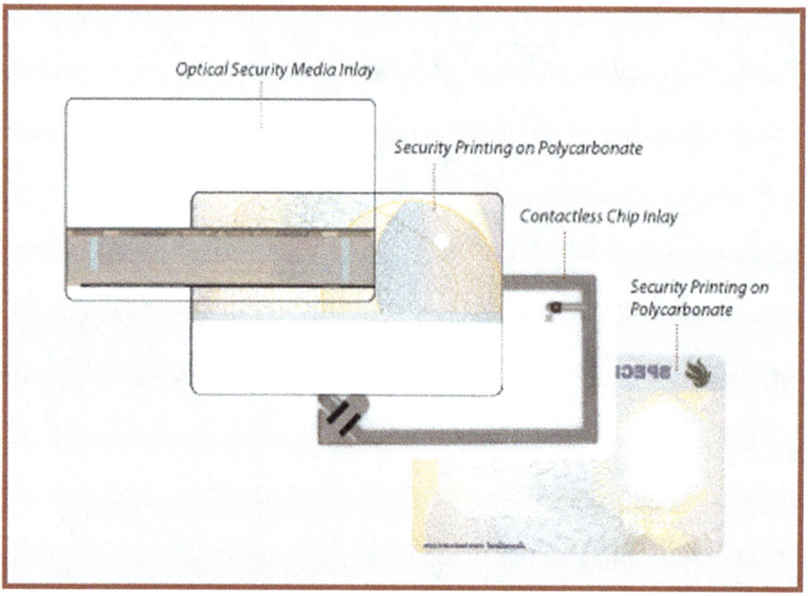

FIGURE 5.6 Multi-Technology Card.

5.7 PROTOCOLS AND REGULATORY COMPLIANCE

Protocols are instructions created for all personnel providing them guidance on how to respond to an incident or the likelihood of an incident unfolding. This may include responses to intrusion, hostile acts and active shooter instructions. The need for protocols should be compared to the assets and threats against the protocols currently in place. This should also include security awareness and recommended steps during an incident such as means of evacuation. This is essentially security planning, training and desk top drills.

We begin with an examination of the company's security policy. Often, that policy is vague or there is no formal policy statements at all. Some of this was addressed in the goal setting meeting but now we must be focused on policy because it sets the standards for all the protocols. If you do not have a formal policy in place, here are suggestions on how to develop one with the help of the management team.

The starting point in your examination must be regulatory compliance. You may be fortunate and not have to abide by outside regulations, but if you are a government contractor or engaged in a highly sensitive work such as handling select agents (bio-toxins) you may be required by law to have certain procedures in place regardless of other considerations. If you are unsure if such rules apply to your company, discuss this with the other members of the management team and especially your legal counsel.

5.7.1 Introduction to Setting a Security Policy

The most important step in the security policy process is the initial goal-setting and policy review meeting. To effectively evaluate threats and vulnerabilities the security professional must know the level of acceptable risk the company will assume. Policy statements determine the risk level. There may be no formal policy statements in place or the current policies do not adequately cover all the elements of risk. Use the following guidelines to prepare or enhance the security policy statement.

5.7.2 Elements of Risk

Some of the common areas of concern are shown below. Consider the risks for the business in light of these considerations:

Employee Identification

- Assigning credentials
- Wearing credentials
- Pictures on credentials
- Biometrics identification on credentials
- The need for other uses for credentials (copy machine)

Visitor Identification and Management

- Collecting visitor data
- What visitor identity data to collect
  - Full name and address
  - Company name
  - Date and time of visit
  - Time departed
  - Purpose of visit and the person visited
- Identification credential used, what are acceptable visitor credentials
- Should visitor credentials be held until departure?
- Should visitors be photographed?
- Will visitors require an escort?
- Will the Response Team be required to search the visitor for restricted items?
- Will the visitor be permitted to drive a vehicle on company property?
- Will the Response Team be required to search visitor vehicles?
- What is considered contraband items?
  - Weapons (even registered firearms)
  - Cameras

- Recorders
- Cell phones

Access and Egress Control Requirements

- For company grounds
- For company buildings (all buildings or selected buildings)
- For selected departments
- Recording authorized access and egress

Perimeter Controls for Intruder Alert

- For company grounds
- For company buildings
- For selected departments or areas

Surveillance (to identify and classify incidents)

- The critical areas of concern
- The ability to do detailed observations
- The ability for automatic event recognition by the video system
- The length of time required to retain video recordings

Response Team

- The need for a centralized watch command
- The need for roving patrols

Decide the levels of acceptable risks or concern for each of these security topics. Write statements that describe the assigned risk levels. An example might be: "All employees are required to obtain and wear their employee identification card at all times while on company property." and another may be: "The identity of all visitors on company property must be verified by company security before a visitor is permitted to enter company facilities."

Incidents

Your policy must anticipate that certain situations will occur and have plans in place to deal with these incidents. Those plans must consider all the employees and visitors and the response team's actions. Start by considering all the threats you identified in your earlier analysis, list them and then decide what action is required if each occurs. Some of the most common incidents to plan for are:

- Perimeter Breach
- Active Shooter

- Hostage
- Mass Gatherings (such as protests, on and around company property)
- Domestic Disturbance (inside the company grounds)
- Workplace Violence (by employees and outside agents)
- Tailgating
- Theft of documents and Other Company Property
- Theft of Personal Property
- Unaccounted Visitors (before and after vetting at reception)
- Stolen or Lost Identification

5.7.3 Drafting the Policy

A policy mandates standards for acceptable conduct. Policies generally contain the following elements:

- Statement of need or rationale
- Statement of purpose
- General principles
- Definitions
- Procedure
- Statement of relationship to existing policies

Policies translate the abstract business values of the operation's mission statement into practical terms to shape the behavior of personnel. The goal is for personnel performance to be consistent with the company's mission statement and values. Properly designed policies will:

- Decrease staff uncertainties about acceptable practices
- Reduce stress and conflict among employees
- Decrease ad hoc procedures and arbitrary decisions
- Increase the involvement of employees in decisions about the operations
- Improve the quality of business decision-making within the company.

A good security policy will promote the activities that safeguard the assets of the company while maintaining compliance with applicable codes for the operation of the company and provide legal protection for company conduct.
The usual steps in drafting the policy include:

1. Examine the institution's mission and values and determine how they apply to the policy.
2. Agreement on general principles by all top management.
3. Obtain copies of policies from other institutions or organizations.

4. Delegate the policy writing to a subcommittee or a standing committee on policy.
5. Circulate the first draft for review.
6. Meet with affected managers to discuss questions about the policy and obtain approval.
7. Revise the policy based on manager input.
8. Have legal counsel review and comment on the revised policy.
9. Revise the draft again based on additional input.
10. Follow the policy through organizational channels until approved.
11. Conduct educational programs so that personnel understand and apply the policy.
12. Evaluate the policy after it is in use and review and revise as needed.

Policy development committees need to understand that a policy is never finished. Even though management approves the policy, it can be improved over time. New situations, new threats and methods of mitigation will necessitate policy revisions. Some strategies for educating company staff about policies include:

- Include the affected staff members in the policy review and revision process.
- Present cases in an educational format that highlights aspects of the policy.
- Distribute summaries of the policy.
- Include summaries of the policy in the company's newsletter.
- Provide copies of the policy in areas where references are needed.

Although it is not part of the assessment process, you should also recommend periodic reviews or "classes" on security policy awareness. It helps to conduct drills at least once per year on major incidents such as active shooter. It is important to keep the assets of the company safe but the highest importance is on protecting the staff. The rational you can provide to the management team is to view such drills in the same light as a fire drill.

5.8 COMMUNICATIONS

Communications examinations are specifically focused on communications tool used by employees and security personnel to notify the response team about an incident or a potential incident about to take place. This may also include two-way radios and mass notifications for situations such as active shooter.

Your responsibility should not include designing and procuring communications systems for everyone's use but it should include verifying that adequate communications exist. Part of that charge is a general assessment for the employee population as a whole and the other part is communications specific to the security staff. So let's begin with the simpler model, communications for the employees.

Your goal in this step is to ensure that employees have a way to quickly and conveniently notify the security station that an incident is unfolding. Some of this was covered in the last chapter under alarm monitoring with the discussion on panic alarms. That situation assumed that an employee was confronted by a hostile actor and they needed to request help discretely (hence the panic alarm buttons). But what if the person engaged with the hostile actor is not near their alarm button, what if another employee observes the situation unfolding and wants to call for help? Equally important is observing a suspicious person appearing to lurk in areas where they do not belong. You really don't want an untrained clerk to confront a potentially dangerous person but rather for them to call for help from security. The obvious solution is to use a standard company telephone to call internally to the security station.

But how often do employees call security? In most cases, almost never. I had one client in a local government office who had that problem and a very large staff. That staff had a substantial turnover and the visitors where often irate citizens who had issues with actions by the government offices. Our solution … we created adhesive stickers with the security phone number (and other information) on it and distributed the stickers to all department for employees to put on their phones.

Most people carry cell phones today and many keep these devices on their person at all times. A simple memo providing the outside number for the security station can be distributed to all employees to encode on a speed dial the security number. That way, if they are away from their desk, perhaps walking to or from their car, they have quick access to the company's security force and can report potential incidents for investigation. Remember, if you planned the CCTV system correctly, the security staff can observe an incident within seconds of a report and your memos to the staff should convey that multiple reports are not an inconvenience for security but their reason for being there.

In some situations there are large campuses and the facility may be open 24/7 such as a college campus. Students often walk across campus and generally feel safe because they are on school grounds. Unfortunately, that sense of safety is not always deserved.

Imagine a young girl walking across campus, she was at the gym and is returning to her dormitory. A person with ill intent is lurking in the darkness and approaches her. OK, so she has security's phone number on her cell phone, perhaps even on a speed dial, how long do you think it will take an officer to reach her? How does the officer know where she is? These campuses are often dark with shadowy coves in which to hide. The crime can be committed and the perpetrator long gone before security arrives.

FIGURE 5.7 Emergency Communications Tower.

One solution is emergency call towers, an example of which is shown in Figure 5.7.

This one was manufactured by Talk-a-Phone and has a single button speed dialer with a speaker phone so the caller can talk hands free and can hear over a speaker mounted on device. When a call is made a light turns on at the top of the tower and there is an auxiliary relay that also triggers when a call is made. That relay can be connected to flood lights to illuminate the area. Obviously the goal here is to scare the perpetrator into believing he/she is about to get caught. Also, you will recall from the CCTV design in the last chapter, PTZ cameras can be programmed so that when an alarm is triggered a PTZ can focus in on the site and security will get a description of the perpetrator on camera. That will make capturing the person and subsequent investigations much easier.

Similar stations can be placed indoors and in all strategic locations where a person might need safe haven. There are wall-mounted units as well as towers and other units with fewer features.

Now that we've addressed initiating communications with security, how about the other way around. Security needs to speak within their own ranks but occasionally needs to speak with the entire employee body.

Communication between officers is usually done using a two-way radio system. It is usually most effective if the entire staff can hear all conversations at the same time. The security staff works as a team, when one is addressing a problem another team member may be close by and can assist. This is especially useful in pursuit situations, you can "Head then off at the pass!". Obviously as the staff grows and the exchanges become more numerous, having everyone hear everything can become a problem but there are radio solutions for this and that discussion is best left to radio experts when the situation (if ever) occurs.

Just keep in mind that these units are battery operated and you must ensure discipline in charging the batteries. Have a 20% spare inventory to allow for units in trouble and encourage all team members to report communications problems.

I recall one client who was deciding on a new radio system. We sat down with a set of plot plans for the entire area and determined where officers might be in the worst possible scenarios. We plotted all the points, obtained test units from the supplier and confirmed the communications quality at all locations. It was a very useful exercise.

But how about communicating with the rest of the staff? Much depends on the business model and the ways in which employees normally communicate to decide on a mass communications method but here are some options:

- Loudspeaker Announcements – Strategically located speakers around the entire facility, including outdoors for emergency broadcasts.
- Integrated telephone paging – Some phone systems have built in paging circuitry and can enable all phones at the same time for an announcement.
- Mass texting — There are services and stand-alone products that permit a text broadcast to be sent with a single step, some of these processes can be automated.
- Auto dialers — Messages generated and multiple lines are used to call everyone on a call list.

With these devices and services security can broadcast a message intended for all employees such as Active Shooter, fire, natural disaster and other events requiring quick action by the staff.

5.9 CYBER SECURITY

The goal of this book is to address "Physical Security" but one cannot ignore cybersecurity. More damage can be done by a bad actor with a computer 1,000 miles away than a perpetrator with a hammer 20 ft away. Your part in cybersecurity is to simply ensure that someone is minding the store. If you want your report to be comprehensive, engage your IT manager and ask for his input, it may help him get funding for his cybersecurity projects. Your direct action is to restrict access to terminals and other means to access the network.

5.10 LITIGATION DEFENSE

There is a dual purpose to your assessment and you must consider both perspectives simultaneously. The first is obvious, protect the company assets from harm; but the second is more subtle but just as consequential, protect the company from liabilities as a result of a successful attack. Lawsuits can cost the company millions in damages and it is much easier to loose in court with a sympathetic jury than you might think.

How will you be judged? I have served the courts as an expert witness for over 10 years. I have testified in depositions and in trials, so here is an insider's view of the kind of scrutiny your company will endure. Assume that a perpetrator enters the facility and in the course of committing whatever crime they intended an employee or visitor was injured. That person can (and usually will) sue the company for not taking sufficient measures to protect them while they are on company grounds.

Your security preparations will be examined under a microscope and the plaintiff's attorney will cast every failure in the worst possible light. Simply put, if the plaintiff can convince a jury that you could or should have foreseen the event, you had a responsibility to prevent it.

Here are some terms which you must be aware of.

5.10.1 Reasonable Care

Reasonable care is the degree of caution and concern an ordinarily prudent and rational person would use in similar circumstances. It is a standard used to determine a legal duty and whether such duty was fulfilled. The criteria for making that determination are to compare the security measures required in a situation against those that are in place. Within reason, differences in needs and performance define achieving reasonable care.

5.10.2 Duty to Perform

We assumed the parties in question have responsibilities, some of which are bound by law. The expert witness does not establish or seek to prove such duty, that is a matter for the respective councils and the court; however, the expert must assume this determination to allow the assessment to move forward. This is not a legal opinion, this is an assumption based on the evidence presented or discovered in research.

5.10.3 Reasonable Anticipation

This is a concept used in security to anticipate unwanted acts; it assumes that a reasonable person would be able to predict or anticipate the ultimately harmful result of actions or a lack of actions given a particular set of circumstances. It further assumes that this average person would have no special knowledge other than what is commonly known by the population of that area.

5.10.4 Expert Witness Assessments

Not all crimes are foreseeable nor is it possible to prevent every crime and still provide a reasonable environment in which people are to live and work – hence the rule of reasonable care.

To determine reasonable care, the approach generally recognized as the most reliable is to view each facility from the perspective of preventing unwanted human activity, while at the same time providing a safe and secure environment that people can occupy without undue concern for the safety or significant inconvenience. It begins by considering the facility without special fore knowledge of the incident currently under examination. That is, given the ordinary day-to-day operation and a historical perspective, what security features should be in place?

After establishing the security requirements, we then compare the required measures with those security measures already in place. The gap between requirements and measures provided guides us in deciding whether the facility managers have exercised reasonable care. This requires evaluating several areas of concern. Those areas are:

- Asset Identification
- Threat Assessment
- Exterior Perimeter
- Building Perimeters
- Access Control
- Remote Investigations
- Alarm Monitoring and Panic Alarms
- Response Team and Incident Reporting
- Employee Identification
- Visitor Controls
- Protocols and Regulatory Compliance
- Related Areas of Concern:
  - Communications
  - Lighting
  - Signage
  - Blast Proximity
  - Utilities and Emergency Power

So as you can probably see, the guidance in this book follows that same pattern. The goal of the book is to help you prepare for such an "audit" and thereby provide a substantial defense for your company should the unthinkable happen.

5.11 CONCLUDING THE SURVEY

At the conclusion of the survey, document all findings and prepare a report for the management team, which will be covered in the next chapter. Base the conclusions of the report on the data gathered and then formulate a recommendation on how best to proceed. A valid recommendation may be to do nothing at all. If the company's existing security measures and the facility's configuration are adequate to protect it from the expected threats, your report can be used as a basis for the company's decision to use resources for other operational requirements. The mission of the security assessment is to determine the company's readiness to counter expected threats.

The report should detail the existing assets, the protected perimeters, the openings in the perimeters and the current methods of controlling those openings. The report should also provide the results of the tests conducted on the effectiveness of existing security systems and the life safety tests. Conclude the report with an explanation of the consequences of loss and a recommendation for improvements or changes needed to meet the company's security goals as defined in their policy statement.

Further interviews with the operations and financial employees of the company may be required to establish this analysis. The goal is to determine the impact of a violation of the security perimeter on the ongoing operation of the company. Make a list of the critical assets of the company and then identify the ways in which a perpetrator could successfully defeat the existing security measures. Next, examine what impact that attack would have on the operation and seek the assistance of company personnel in establishing a cost of that impact. Remember that the cost is not just the loss of the asset but also includes the loss of revenue in removing the asset from service. The conclusions from this analysis will help justify the investment in security equipment and services and provide additional motivation to act. Management awareness of the potential for loss will help to support your recommendation to improve security features.

CHAPTER 6

Documenting the System Design

CONTENTS

6.1 INTRODUCTION TO DESIGN DOCUMENTATION

By now your assessment has identified the assets you must protect, the threats to those assets and the vulnerability in your existing mitigation steps. You've planned new system tools to improve security and considered the other factors like a response team and protocols to operate this new system. BUT … you are the only one who knows all this stuff and your next challenge is to convey your findings first to the management team to gain their support and agreement for the investment needed and, second, to communicate your new system plan to the appropriate vendors so that you can get what you now know you need.

This chapter will discuss documenting the system design and estimate the cost for the equipment selected to accomplish the security system goals. The techniques recommended here will help you describe the recommendation to the management team and bidders and then provide the capital budget for the project.

We will test our plan using the "rule of reason" as we consider the operational value of the asset, the probability of loss and the consequences of loss. It

DOI: 10.4324/9781003490432-7

is important to remember that your job is to evaluate, analyze and recommend the most effective physical security system, company management will decide if the value of mitigating the identified risks is worth the investment in security assets.

6.2 THE SYSTEM DESIGN DOCUMENTATION

To communicate a clear definition of the required system and prepare a budget for management consideration, you must now create the formal system documentation. This will provide the details needed to communicate the system plan and provide enough information to establish a budget for the project. The documents you need to do this are:

- A list of critical assets
- Your Threat Assessment
- Marked plot plans and floor plans showing:
  - Assets
  - Perimeters with blast standoffs
  - Openings
- Mitigation efforts including:
  - Existing and proposed lighting
  - Existing and proposed signage
  - Utility and communications protection
- A Door Detail Schedule (DDS)
- A Camera Detail Schedule (CDS)
- Concept Drawing
- Personnel Security, a text document describing:
  - Response Team and Incident Reporting Program
  - Employee Identification
  - Visitor Controls
  - Protocols and Regulatory Compliance
- Cost Estimate

6.2.1 List of Assets

This is simply a text document listing all of the major assets and their location. Depending on the nature of the asset you may also want to describe why this has special significance. For example, if your facility is a hospital, it is a given to say "All patient areas" or "All staff areas" but may not be as obvious to say drug dispensary and so you might add, "to protect controlled substances from shrinkage or theft".

6.2.2 Threat Assessment

You probably already have a prepared document from your efforts in identifying the threats. So preparation is minimal but that document should be included with your report. To make the overall report easier to read, you could simply summarize the findings in the report and include your threat assessment as an attachment.

6.2.3 Marked Plot Plans and Floor Plans

As you might imagine, the is the "where" component of your report and will probably garner the most attention. I urge you to learn to use a computer-assisted drawing (CAD) system or engage someone who has CAD experience. YOU WILL CHANGE THINGS … erasures and mark outs are difficult to read through but with CAD changes are easy and simple.

Instruct your CAD operator to separate your drawing into layers. I suggest your layer assignments look something like Figure 6.1.

Use a base layer for all existing physical configurations of the building, grounds or whatever other structures exist, do not add exiting or proposed mitigation steps to this layer. The assets are also shown on this layer. If the asset is a protected workspace, such as a lab or other secure area, it should be done in a lighter version of the base color (usually physical structures in black, with the assets in gray).

On layer 2 use something that has been a valuable asset to me, a conceptual perimeter. Remember that a perimeter is a contiguous line of barricades that surround an asset (or an inner perimeter). You simply overlay a line in a different color, thicker than the line used for existing walls, that forms this perimeter. Everywhere there is an opening, the line stops and you add a circle. If there are windows or other openings in the perimeter that are not ordinary passes but could be easily defeated to gain access through the perimeter, you add another circle in a different line style (such as dotted or dashed). That way, you can be sure that your perimeters are well defined and you now know for certain where your openings are and where you must put control points.

On the third layer, again in a different color, show the existing security mitigation steps … what doors are alarm, where the access control devices are and so forth.

The fourth layer has your recommendations, it is also in a different color.

Consistently use symbols for an alarm point or access control device, closed-circuit television (CCTV) camera and so forth. There is a standard symbol set available from the Security Industry Association (SIA). These are Architectural Graphics Standard CAD Symbols for Security System Layout, also known as AG-01, v. 3.1. The standard comes as a joint effort between SIA and the International Association of Professional Security Consultants (IAPSC). It is meant to be used

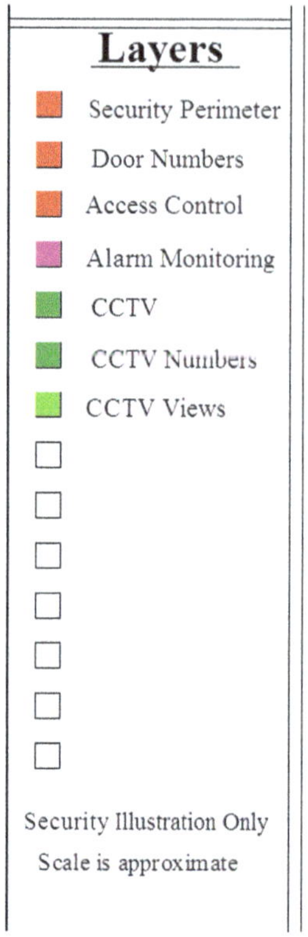

FIGURE 6.1 Sample Drawing Layers.

by architects, engineers, building contractors and security managers to produce planning drawings for building projects. Figure 6.2 is a sample (the full set is presented in Chapter 9).

6.2.4 Door Detail Schedule (DDS)

Now one of the problems you will find in marking your drawings is that there is so much detail needed to adequately address the devices needed at an opening that the drawing becomes cluttered and confusing. You must indicate alarms. Access control devices, special locks and hinges, a whole range of information. Adding symbols for each of these devices can really clutter an illustration. The solution is to use a DDS.

The DDS is a matrix that describes all of the door equipment needed to make the system operational. This document can be prepared in written form and copied to make the work easier. If you are also familiar with spreadsheet

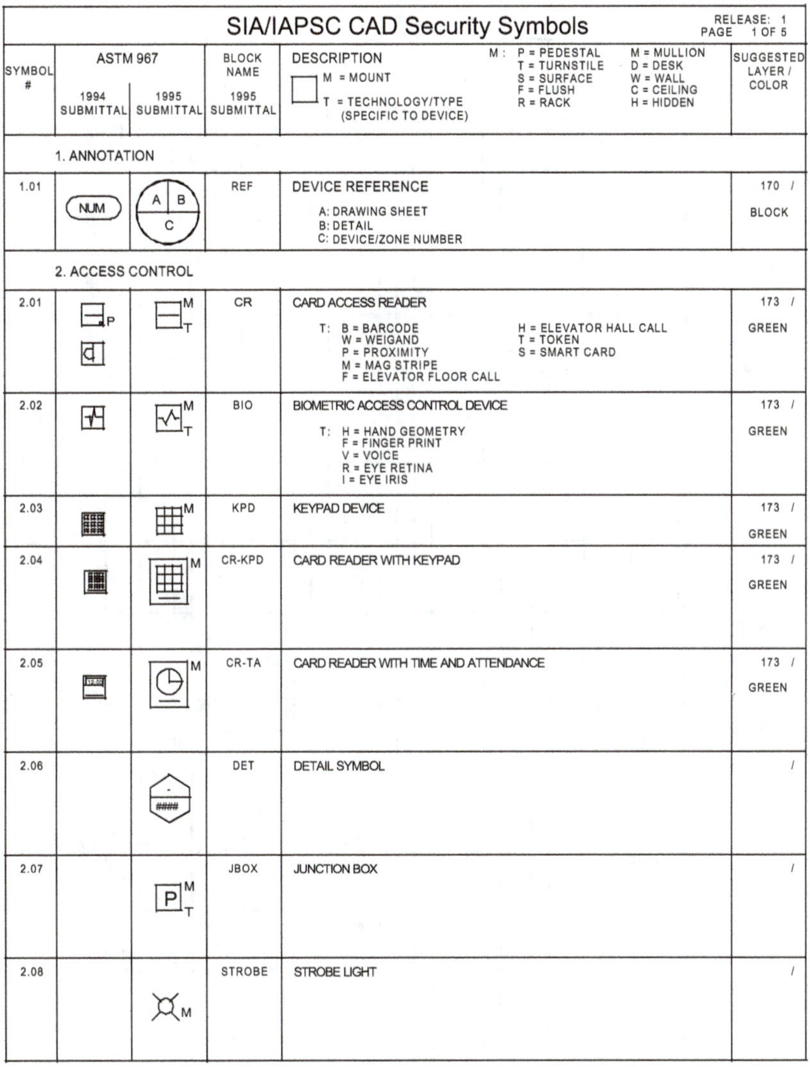

FIGURE 6.2 Sample SIA Symbols.

software, building the DDS using a product like Microsoft Excel will make the job significantly easier. Figure 6.3 shows an example of a DDS.

Begin this matrix by listing the "**Door Name**" in the left-hand column. Frequently, facilities do not use formal names for individual doors. It would be helpful to use the original plans to determine the formal designation for each opening. If facility plans are not available or do not contain formal door names, employees usually have a "local name" for the opening. Facility occupants will

Door Detail Schedule

Client: (Company)
Work Location: (Area)
Project: (Project Name)

By: (Consultant Name)
Revision: 0
Date: (Date)

Door Description	Location Ref on Drwg	Access	Access Special	Lock	Lock Special	Egress	Egress Special	Fire Alarm Interface	Number of DSS Alarms	Number of PIR Monitor	Number of Panic Alarms	Drawing Ref	Remarks
Basement:													
Ampitheater	B-1			PM-D				FAI	1			DD1DY	
Tunnel	B-3								2			DD2NY	
Tunnel to laundry	B-4	CR		2PM		B		FAI	2			DD2PY	Client must replace or modify door
Fire exit, west side front	B-8								1			DD1NY	
First floor:													
Old pediatrics	1-1	CR		PM		B		FAI	1			DD1PY	
Old pediatrics	1-1					PIR						NA	Add exit detector to manual button exit
Lasalle entrance	1-5		Auto Door						2			MCL-CC1	Door will be manned or locked manually always
Front entrance	1-7										2	NA	
West entrance	1-8					PIR			2			MCL-CC2	Door manually locked EGRESS ONLY, Alarmed
Admitting	1-9										8	NA	
Medical records admin	1-11										1	NA	
Walk-in clinic	1-14.1										1	NA	
Walk-in clinic	1-14.2										1	NA	
Family doctor	1-15										4	NA	
Walk-in clinic 2	1-16										1	NA	
East entrance	1-17	CR		2PM		B		FAI	2			DD2PY	
West entrance	1-18	CR		2PM		B		FAI	2			DD2PY	
Fire stair	1-21								1			DD1NY	
Walkway	1-22	CR		2PM		B		FAI	2			DD2PY	Remove door edge seals during installation
Psyc triage	1-24										1	NA	
West rear stair	1-25	CR		2PM		B		FAI	2			DD2PY	Client will repair door before installation.
Loading dock	1-26	CR	Auto Door		Auto Door		Auto Door	FAI	2			AUTODR2	Auto door vendor to provide door lock
Er admit	1-27										4	NA	
Triage station	1-28										3	NA	
Admitting	1-30.1										1	NA	
Admitting	1-30.2										1	NA	
Loading dock freight elevator	1-31	CR	Elevator Control		Elevator Control	B	Elevator Control					MCL-CC3	Connect to elevator floor control buttons
Loading dock passenger elevator	1-32	CR	Elevator Control		Elevator Control	B	Elevator Control					MCL-CC3	Connect to elevator floor control buttons

FIGURE 6.3 Door Detail Schedule.

generally recognize that name when repeated to them. Match the marking of the formal designation on the plan with the common name given to the opening by the employees. Ensure that both names are shown on the DDS and the marked plans.

Often, to reduce confusion I have also numbered the doors. In the next column called "**Location Reference on Drawing**" establish a reference for all openings so that all parties working on the project will have a clear unambiguous key to the opening in question. **"Location Reference"** is an arbitrary numbering plan. Start the numbering plan with the floor number followed by a dash and then a number selected for that opening. If there is only one floor, you can simply omit the floor number character. Start with number 1 and proceed through the number series until all openings have a designation. In a multi-floor environment when changing floors, restart the numbering plan so that the first door identified on the second floor will be designated 2-1 and on the third floor 3-1 and so forth. This numbering plan is not rigid; any numbering system may be used. However, consistency in the numbering plan is essential to make it easier for other professionals in the project to understand the reference notations. This additional designation for the opening will provide a more concise reference when transferring opening identity information to other documents.

Additionally, by using this reference method, there will be certain advantages in unusual situations. For instance, main entryways of office buildings frequently have multiple door leafs. There are door status switches associated with each door leaf and these switches are associated together with the same door input on an access control or alarm monitoring panel, a decimal can indicate multiple leafs. For instance, if the main door to a building has four door leafs and the door designation is 1-1, they can be described as 1-1.1, 1-1.2 and so forth.

The next column is **"Access"**. Under this column, indicate the methods used to gain access through that opening. If a card reader controls the opening, use the text symbol CR. A suggested list of these symbols is presented in Figure 6.4.

The next column in the matrix is **"Access Special"**. Use this designation for other devices installed in conjunction with the primary access control device. For instance, it may be necessary to place a key switch on an entry opening in addition to the card reader to permit facility managers to enter the building if the access control system fails. This key switch can be used to disable one or more locks in the building system for emergency access. Use such auxiliary means of access sparingly.

The next column in the matrix is **"Lock"**. Indicate how that opening will be locked in this column. Refer to Figure 6.4 for a recommended list of symbols to indicate door locks. It would be helpful to other professionals involved in the project to indicate the lock by brand and model. However, during the general system design and budget estimate an exact lock specification is not essential. The symbol shown in Figure 6.4 only designates the "type" of lock to use. This is an important characteristic of the door since the locking type helps determine the egress method used and the manner in which to secure the door.

Definitions	Description
AC	Access Control Device (card reader, keypad, etc. Type defined in bid spec)
BUT	Manual Button
E- PANIC	Electric Panic Hardware (to match the manual panic hardware on other doors)
E-Gate	Electric Gate Latch
HRDWR	Existing Door Hardware
KEY	Metal Key (standard lock and key)
Mag Holder	Magnetic Door Holder to hold door open
MECH	Standard Mechanical Lock
M-PANIC	Manual Panic Hardware (optioned to always be locked)
PM	Power Magnetic Lock
Strike	Electric Strike Lock
ECL	Electrified Cylindrical Lockset

FIGURE 6.4 Recommended List of Door Detail Text Symbols.

The next column in the matrix is **"Lock Special"**. Use this column for additional features of the locking device such as reverse brackets for power magnets and special alarm sensors needed to provide ample security for the opening.

The next column in the matrix is **"Egress"**. The egress features of an opening establish the means to exit the facility. In most applications, egress is unobstructed to comply with life safety codes and so is marked "Hardware", meaning use the existing door hardware as a means of egress. However, in some cases egress control is also required. An example of such situations is when the feature "anti-passback" is desired. In those circumstances, it is important to know when a user has left the facility. Use the same symbols from Figure 6.4 that apply to access control devices to indicate egress control.

The next column in the matrix is **"Egress Special"**. Like the other specialized columns, this one is used to indicate devices that will be applied in alternate use circumstances. For instance, the *NFPA Life Safety Handbook* specifies that egress criteria for power magnet locks include a passive infrared (PIR) detector to provide unimpeded egress from the facility. Indicate the use of a PIR in this column. This would be in addition to egress buttons and other devices used for free egress. By the way, the PIR exit devices are not fire rated, that is, you cannot depend solely on a PIR for a fire egress door, there must be a mechanical means of egress in addition to the convenient PIR approach.

The next column in the matrix is **"Fire Alarm Interface"**. This column is only applicable if the subject door will be locked by a mechanism that does not permit unrestricted mechanical egress. An example of unrestricted mechanical egress is the application of an electric strike with a free passage exit handle. In those cases, there are no constraints to an individual wishing to exit a controlled area and simply turning the door handle will allow egress. Another example of such unrestricted egress is the use of panic hardware. Like the electric strike, panic hardware provides unrestricted egress by simply pushing on the panic device on the door.

But in cases where the locking device is a power magnet or power bolt, it is an essential life safety feature to connect the lock on the subject door to the fire alarm panel. Connect the power supply of the locking device to the fire alarm panel to accomplish this. Arrange the connections so that if the panel goes into an alarm state, power will disconnect from the lock providing unrestricted egress. Indicate "yes" under this column for all door locks that require interface to the fire alarm panel.

The next column in the matrix is **"Number of Door Status Switch Alarms"**, normally abbreviated as DSS alarms. In the case of a single leaf door, this number is always 1; however, some doors have more than one leaf. For instance, in cases where there are two door leafs, the number of DSS alarms is 2. This will indicate to others on the project that two door status switches are required for this door so that both leafs may be monitored. It would also be helpful to remind the vendors in the **Remarks** column that the contacts are to be wired in series.

The next column in the matrix is **"Number of PIR Monitors"**. This is simply a shorthand way to indicate an "area" and not necessarily a door. Use this when area monitoring is required. This alarm point will be included in the overall security plan. In these cases, the door description is actually a room description. Show the number of PIR detectors to protect this space under this column.

Note: The term PIR is used here generically to mean all forms of space sensors. There are devices other than PIR detectors used to monitor areas. Do not assume that this nomenclature means that it applies only to PIR detectors.

The next column in the matrix is "**Number of Panic Buttons**". Again, like space detectors, panic buttons do not relate to particular doors but are included in the overall security plan as indicated here. Panic buttons are generally alarm-signaling devices used by occupants of a facility to indicate that they are in distress. Like the space sensor, list panic alarms in the door description as a "point" and with the name of the location for the alarm. These points are not associated with a particular door.

The next column in the matrix is **"Drawing Reference"**. A drawing reference is a nomenclature that identifies a particular elevation drawing used in association with the devices shown on the rest of the schedule for that door. Elevation drawings will indicate placement of devices so that there can be no misunderstanding as to where to mount the device. Build a library of elevation drawings to use as standard references when compiling a security system implementation plan (Figure 6.5).

The next column in the matrix is **"Remarks"**. In this column, indicate any special considerations for this door not fully described in the other columns. It is always better to over-document than under-document. Remarks may include such items as a requirement to change door hardware or supply special features to the door that are needed to make the security equipment proposed for that door work properly.

The next two columns in the matrix are **"Distance to Panel"** and **"Feet of Conduit"**. None of these columns are an essential part of system design and may be omitted if specific cable estimates are not required in the budget that will be established for the security system. As the names imply, they are an indication of wiring and conduit needed to perform the installation. Often, however, such budgetary information is an essential part of the cost mix. By providing these elements in the DDS when preparing the system design, it will be easier to estimate these cost later. It is usually not necessary to display cabling and conduit descriptions to the management team. Collect this data for budget purposes.

In summary, your plans indicate where the control points are and your DDS indicates what is to be installed at that point.

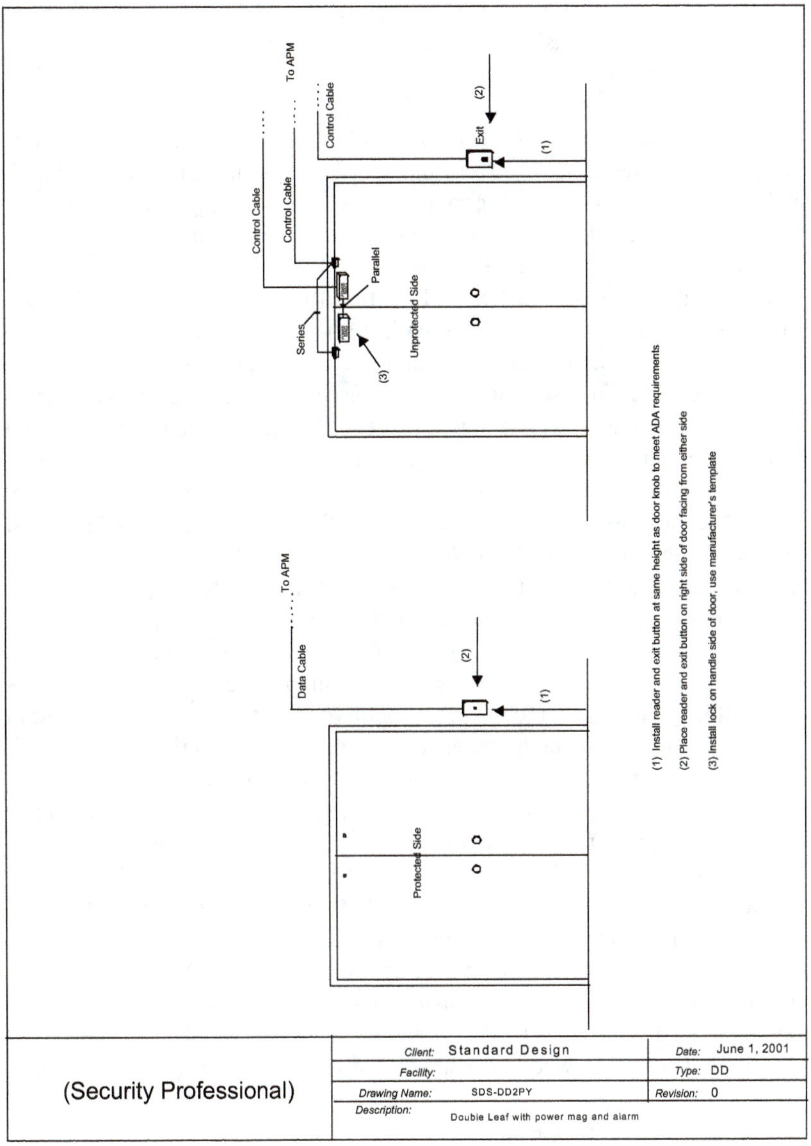

FIGURE 6.5 Sample Door Detail Elevation Drawing.

6.2.5 Camera Detail Schedule (CDS)

The CDS, like the DDS, documents the end point devices on the project and aids in understanding the design of the proposed camera system. It is also used to establish the budget for the project. Like the DDS, the CDS is a matrix that can be more easily developed using a spreadsheet program. An example of the CDS is shown in Figure 6.6.

The first column in the CDS is **"Camera View"**. The camera view or camera location indicates what this camera is looking at or where the camera is located. Often this designation is "rooftop – northeast corner" or "rear hall door". Much like the DDS, use names for camera views easily recognized by company employees. Establish this nomenclature when doing the site survey with the help of the security manager and security staff.

The second column in the CDS is **"Location Reference on Drawing"**. As in the case of DDS, a facility plan is an essential part of communicating where these devices are to be located. It is unlikely that there will be preexisting designations for these camera locations so you must again use a numbering plan to provide a clear and unambiguous reference for the camera. This is important for discussing camera location and features and associating the camera with other equipment. Also, like the DDS, the numbering plan starts with a floor designation followed by a dash and then followed by a numbering system that identifies specific locations.

The next column in the CDS is **"Camera"**. There are two options for camera type: standard and low light. This does not necessarily mean that these are the only two types of cameras available. There are specialized cameras used in special applications. However, it is not wise to develop a preconceived list of exact camera models without a detailed examination of all products on the market. This would artificially limit the choices and competitive aspects of the bid. In the initial steps of system design and budget preparation, that level of detail is not required. Therefore, simply indicating a top-level camera type would be preferable. To aid in the application of the text symbols, Figure 6.7 provides a recommended set.

The next column in the CDS is **"Lenses"**. Again, at this stage in system development it is essential to indicate if the lens is a fixed or zoom lens and the appropriate magnification required for either type. In the case of zoom lenses, indicate the lowest and highest numbers that the lens will zoom and, in the case of fixed lenses, indicate the fixed focal length desired for that lens. Camera manufacturers often provide handy tools that will illustrate the appropriate lens size for a given measurement of distance and field of view. By using such tools you may select the measured distance between the camera and the object you wish to view and the vertical and horizontal field to be included in that view. These shortcut tools will then provide you with the appropriate lens size.

The next column in the CDS is **"Iris"**. There are three designations for iris: automatic, motorized manual and manual. Use an automatic iris in outdoor applications to automatically adjust for varying light conditions. Motorized manual lenses allow the user to remotely change the iris setting based on the

Camera Detail Schedule

Client: (Company)
Work Location: (Area)
Project: (Project Description)

By: (Consultant Name)
Revision: 0
Date: (Date)

Camera View	Location Ref on Drwg	Camera: Standard / Low Light	Lens: Zoom / Fixed= 2.3, 4, 8, Z	Iris: Auto / Manual	Housing Indoor / Outdoor With Fan / Wiper	Special: Hood (H)	Mount: Ceiling / Wall / Pedmt / Post	Mount Duty: Heavy / Medium / Light	Pan / Tilt Control (1)	Alarm Input (1)	Auxiliary Lights (1)	Drawing Ref	Remarks	Distance to Monitor	Feet of Conduit
Main Entrance	E-1	S	F-4	A	O		C	L				CD1		250	25
Freight Dock	E-2	S	F-4	A	O		C	L			1	CD1		275	25
Roof E	E-3	L	Z 75-200	A	O/F/W	H	PED	H	1			CD2		375	150
Roof W	E-4	L	Z 75-200	A	O/F/W	H	PED	H	1			CD2		375	150
Roof N	E-5	L	Z 75-200	A	O/F/W	H	PED	H	1			CD2		375	150
Roof S	E-6	L	Z 75-200	A	O/F/W	H	PED	H	1			CD2		375	150
Water Tower	E-7	L	Z 75-200	A	O/F/W	H	PED	H	1			CD2		375	150
Parking Lot 1	E-8	S	F-2.3	A	O		POST	M				CD3		450	75
Parking Lot 2	E-9	S	F-2.3	A	O		POST	M				CD3		450	75
Parking Lot 3	E-10	S	F-2.3	A	O		POST	M				CD3		450	75
Let Entrance	E-11	S	F-4	A	O		POST	L				CD3		450	75
Lot Exit	E-12	S	F-4	A	O		POST	L				CD3		450	75
Floor 1															
Hall 127	1-1	S	F-8	A	I		W	L				CD4		150	25
Science Lab	1-2	S	F-8	A	I		W	L				CD4		150	25
Fire Exit A	1-3	S	F-8	A	I		W	L		1		CD4		150	25
Fire Exit B	1-4	S	F-8	A	I		W	L		1		CD4		150	25
Fire Exit C	1-5	S	F-8	A	I		W	L		1		CD4		150	25
Fire Exit D	1-6	S	F-8	A	I		W	L		1		CD4		150	25
Floor 2															
Hall 2323	2-1	S	F-8	A	I		W	L				CD4		200	25
Elevator Lobby	2-2	S	F-8	A	I		W	L				CD4		200	25
Hall 2456	2-3	S	F-8	A	I		W	L				CD4		200	25
Floor 3															
Hall 3323	3-1	S	F-8	A	I		W	L				CD4		250	25
Elevator Lobby	3-2	S	F-8	A	I		W	L				CD4		250	25
Hall 3456	3-3	S	F-8	A	I		W	L				CD4		250	25
Floor 4															
Hall 4323	4-1	S	F-8	A	I		W	L				CD4		300	25
Elevator Lobby	4-2	S	F-8	A	I		W	L				CD4		300	25
Hall 4456	4-3	S	F-8	A	I		W	L				CD4		300	25

FIGURE 6.6 Camera Detail Schedule.

6.2.5.2 Recommended List of CCTV System Designations
Camera View
Location Ref on Drwg
Camera: Standard / Low Light
Lens: Zoom / Fixed=2.3, 4, 8, Z
Iris: Auto / Manual
Housing Indoor / Outdoor With Fan / Wiper
Special: Hood (H)
Mount: Ceiling / Wall / Pedmt / Post
Mount Duty: Heavy / Medium / Light
Pan / Tilt Control (1)
Alarm Input (1)
Auxiliary Lights (1)
Drawing Ref
Remarks
Distance to Monitor
Feet of Conduit

FIGURE 6.7 Recommended List of CCTV System Designations.

desired light level needed for a quality image. Use manual lenses for indoor applications where the light source is predictable and fixed. These irises are adjusted during installation and remain at that setting. In the most current version of cameras the iris exposure is built into the camera and is fully automatic; if you have no variations of iris types in your system, this column can be eliminated.

The next column in the CDS is **"Housing"**. Housings may be indoor or outdoor and may have a variety of special features. Some of these features are fans for hot environments and wipers for clearing rain from the outer surface of the housing window to permit a clearer view. Make the appropriate decision for which housing you wish to place at this location and indicate so in this column. But again, in the current technology most cameras come with a housing such as dome cameras. They are easier to install and very reliable. So if you have no variations needed in your system (such as explosive resistant or bulletproof) you may also omit this column.

The next column in the CDS is **"Special"**. This column indicates those features usually associated with a camera housing but is a separate component for the camera location. An example of such a device is a sun hood. A sun hood is a device used to mount above camera housing to keep sunlight from shining on a housing directly, thereby reducing the amount of heat buildup inside the housing and extending the life of the CCTV camera. However, if your system is only dome cameras or pan-tilt-zoom (PTZ) cameras with built-in housings, you can omit this column as well.

The next column in the CDS is **"Mount"**. There is a variety of mounts available for cameras and within each category there is a variety of types of mounts. Again, other professionals on the job will need a specific indication of the type of mount needed for this camera installation. However, as previously stated, it may be impractical to take your specification of this level of detail at this point in system design. Therefore, only indicate if this is a ceiling mount, wall mount, pedestal mount or post mount. This will be helpful in determining the budget for the project.

The next column in the CDS is **"Mount Duty"**. Most manufacturers make several styles of mounts depending on the type of housing used for the camera and the application of the housing. Manufacturers designate these as heavy duty, medium duty and light duty. Again, for the purposes of system design and budget estimates, indicating the strength of the mount should be sufficient to establish pricing. Like previous criteria, if you are not using special housings you will not need special mounts, so this column too can be omitted.

The next column in the CDS is **"Pan/Tilt Control"**. Use a pan/tilt control motor drive for all applications where a zoom lens is used. Attempting to use zoom lenses without pan/tilt control can frequently lead to zooming in on an object and not being able to see the most significant part of that object. Today's technology generally provides complete units for PTZ, so without adding more detail you may simply designate a camera as PTZ and expect to get a fully integrated unit.

The next column in the CDS is **"Alarm Input"**. Although this does not apply in every case, some manufacturers provide control devices for pan/tilt zoom control operations that have alarm input connections that can signal the CCTV system of a potential security violation. Indicate when alarm input can be used in this column. If alarm inputs are used, add alarm detection devices such as a door status switch to the system.

The next column in the CDS is "**Auxiliary Lights**". Use auxiliary lights in situations where additional illumination is required for the camera to properly view an area. Like alarm input, some manufacturers provide control output relays which can switch lights on under circumstances where additional illumination is needed. In other cases, auxiliary lights are used any time the light level of the subject area falls below the required illumination for the camera to view the area properly. Most fixed cameras today have built-in light emitting diode (LED) lights as do many PTZ cameras. However, those lights are sometimes limited in range. Use this column if you find you will need more light than what is normally provided by the built-in LEDs.

The next column in the CDS is **"Drawing Reference"**. Drawing reference for camera detail serves the same function as drawing reference for door detail. These are elevation drawings and indicate the placement of equipment (Figure 6.8).

The next column in the CDS is "**Remarks**". Use the "remarks" column in the same manner as in the DDS. Indicate any special considerations or special alterations that are required to the camera installation site that must be performed before or coincident with the installation of the security equipment.

The next two columns in the CDS are **"Distance to Monitor" and "Feet of Conduit"**. The same rules apply here as applied in the DDS. These are not required fields at this stage of system development however; you will find it most helpful if they indicate an estimate of cable feet in these columns for each camera to prepare budgets quickly and easily. As with door detail, it is not necessary to share these

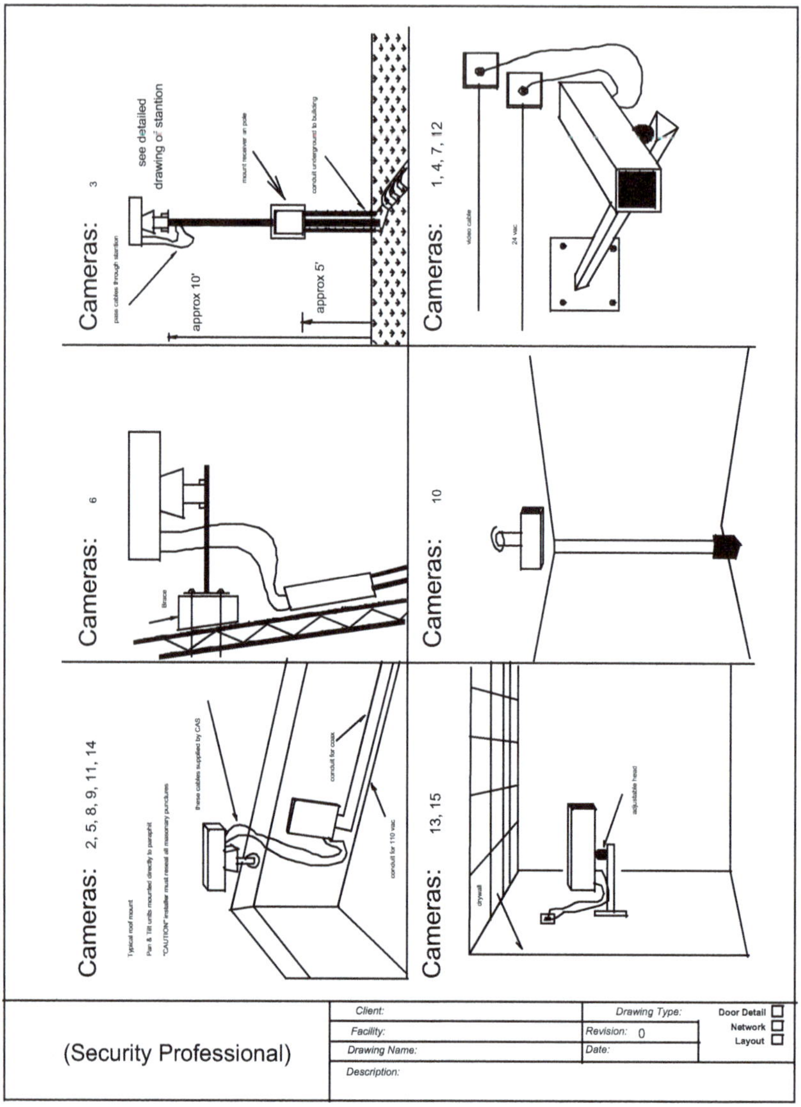

FIGURE 6.8 Sample Camera Elevation Drawing.

columns with the information in these columns with the management team and explaining the proposed recommendation. However, you will find that many of the CCTV systems today are not based on coaxial cable but are digital and use 10base T or similar cable types. So your "Distance to Monitor" will actually be the distance to the digital network interface. Conduit requirements are the same in both cases.

6.3 DRAWINGS

In addition to equipment schedules, it is helpful to graphically illustrate the project design to the company's management team and to the vendors who must perform the work. The drawings to include are:

- Plot Plans with perimeter markings, existing mitigation devices and planned mitigation devices
- Floor Plans with perimeter markings, existing mitigation devices and planned mitigation devices
- Elevation Drawings indicting placement of devices at the device locations

6.3.1 Plot Plans and Floor Plans

You obtained these drawings during the preparation step for the Goal Setting meeting and then marked them during the asset identification and vulnerability assessment. These will be valuable tools when communicating your recommendations to the management team and vendors.

6.3.2 Elevation Drawings

You prepared these drawings, or retrieved them from your library of typical drawings when you were designing the system. These will help the vendors deliver what you are expecting on the project. They will also help the management team understand what you are recommending.

6.3.3 Concept Drawing

A Concept Drawing can best illustrate the overall plan. Such a drawing will convey the interconnection between the devices described in the DDS, CDS, Command Center CCTV Equipment and Command Center Alarm and Access Control Equipment lists. This is a "top level" illustration and is usually a block diagram showing all the major elements of the system (see Figure 6.9 for an example).

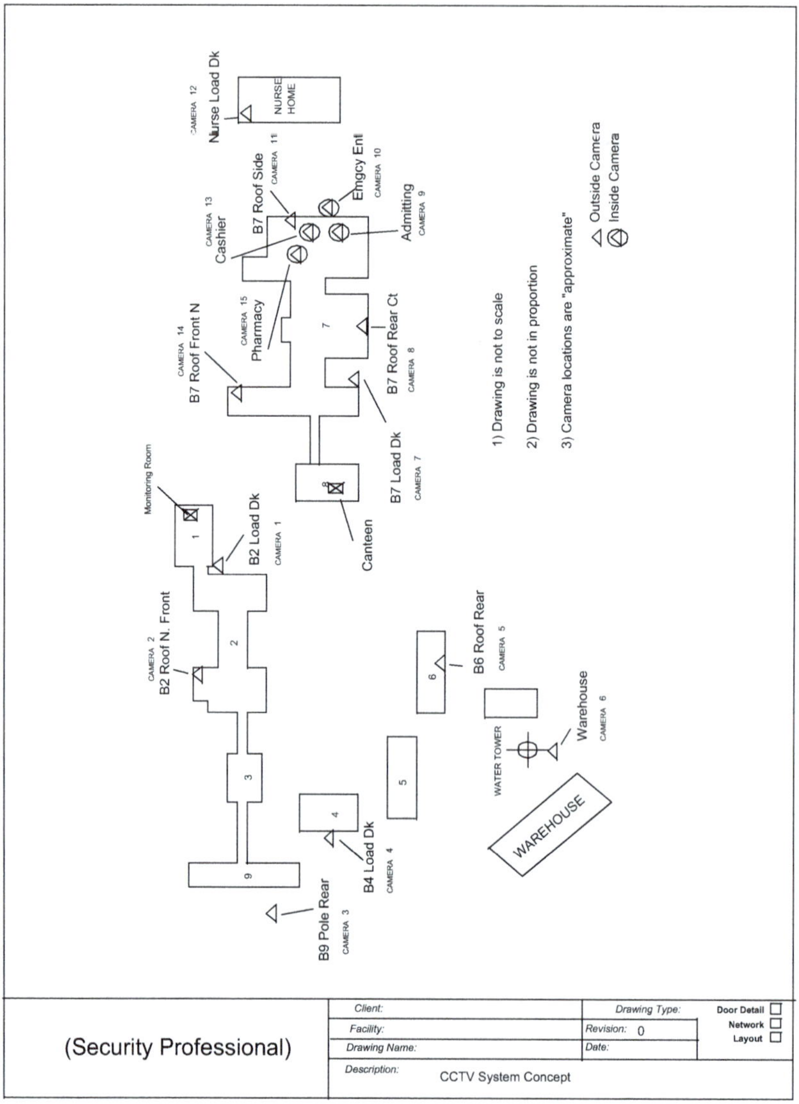

FIGURE 6.9 System Concept Drawing: (a) CCTV and (b) Access Control.

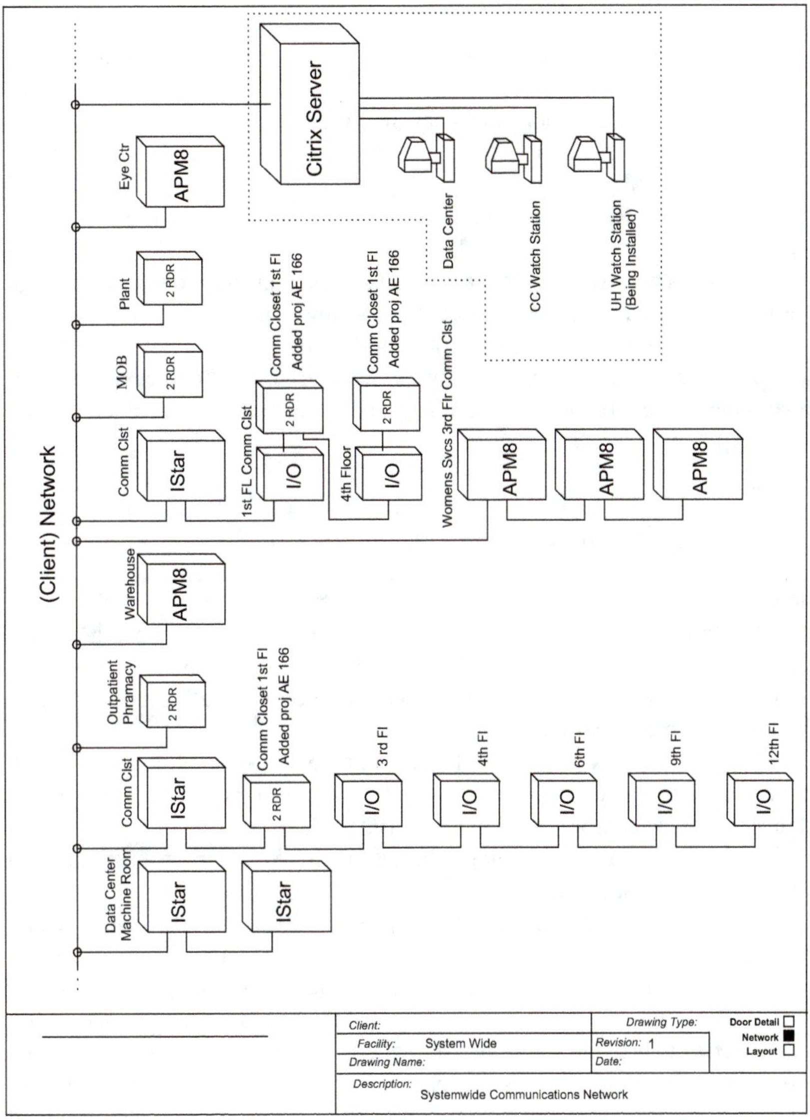

FIGURE 6.9 (Continued)

This is not an essential step but it is very helpful, especially to the installation team, but not terribly valuable to the management team.

6.4 PERSONNEL SECURITY

This is a text document that includes your decisions and recommendations for:

- Response Team and Incident Reporting program
- Employee Identification
- Visitor Controls
- Protocols and Regulatory Compliance

These topics were covered in the previous chapter and as you worked through the process you created documents describing how you would address each of these issues. Much like your approach to reporting the Threat Assessment, it will make your report more readable to simply summarize the findings and recommendation in the report and use your analysis document as an attachment.

6.5 PREPARE A COST ESTIMATE FOR ACCESS CONTROL AND ALARM MONITORING

System design and documentation is only one step in the decision-making process in developing a security plan for a facility. If the cost to implement the plan is prohibitive, the management team will not accept the recommendation. However, the initial budget submitted by you must contain the best overall recommendation without regard to cost-cutting efforts.

The reason for this is simple. If you design a system that considers "cost first" and does not place the security needs of the organization ahead of cost containment, there can be justifiable criticism if the system fails to perform as expected. Establish the initial budget based on the optimum security solution without regard to cost containment.

If there is an established budget and you have been asked to work within that budget, a second proposal which meets the cost objectives set by the company may be generated. This alternate plan includes all of the essential items of the system but makes it clear that this alternate recommendation lacks certain features needed to provide all of the risk reduction elements to secure the facility.

Another alternative is to use a "phased" approach to system implementation. However, priorities change with prevailing business conditions. Good intentions and long-range security plans will sometimes give way to seemingly more important or urgent business priorities. As a result, Phase 1 may be the only step actually implemented. It is therefore important that the essential elements are included in the first step and progressively less important parts of the system are implemented during the succeeding steps. A guiding principle is to design each phase as though the following phases will not take place. In that way, the most urgent and critical elements of the system are implemented first.

The approach I have used successfully in the past is to designate each of my recommendations as A, B or C.

An "A" priority must be done and must be done now.

A "B" priority must be done but the threat is low and can be delayed for later budgets.

A "C" priority includes good ideas, should be done but only when funds are available.

Present all proposals simultaneously to ensure that the optimum recommendation is clear. Highlight the limitations of each choice so that the management team can make informed cost decisions. Remember to consider the indirect costs, such as system maintenance, additions and replacements.

6.5.1 The Access Control and Alarm Monitoring Budget

Before the days of personal computers, it was common to prepare financial models using columned workbooks calculated manually. It is not the author's intent to compel you to become a computer expert; however, detailed cost estimates generally result in extensive arithmetic and can lead to unintentional errors, resulting in wrong conclusions.

The most useful general application software tool available today for such detailed analysis is electronic spreadsheets. The most common electronic spreadsheet tool in use today is from Microsoft called Excel. If you have a working knowledge of Microsoft Excel and can employ this tool effectively in preparing cost estimation, it will save considerable time and effort. This is not a recommendation or endorsement of a particular software product and should be viewed only as a convenient common point of reference when discussing the methods and techniques for doing a cost estimate.

Pricing in a competitive market is highly fluid and can sometimes vary by as much as 20%. At this stage of the process, you are merely establishing a budget for the management team review. The firm fixed price of the system will be determined by competitive bidding. However, budget amounts are necessary to properly fund the project. If doubt exists about the price of a particular item, "overestimate". It is always easier to say to management that the project cost is less than to say the project cost is more.

You must also have marketplace experience and access to vendors that can share approximate prices for security system components. Oftentimes, vendors are encouraged to share such information since they feel it will give them a competitive advantage when the project is released for bid. Additionally, product prices are also available from manufacturer's websites in some cases. If budget information is not readily available, budget prices can sometimes be obtained by calling manufacturers. For instance, door status switch manufacturers and locking system manufacturers will frequently divulge "list price" upon request. Recognize that these are not the best prices, but rather base prices for establishing an overall security system budget.

6.5.2 Primary Material Costs

Begin the cost assessment with the DDS. This document was prepared earlier and provides a detailed list of all the endpoint components needed in a security system. Count the number of devices listed on the schedules by type. The result will be a specific number of card readers, keypads, cameras, locks, etc. In the sample budget (Figure 6.10) the first section is for material used in the project.

Group the DDS into the following categories:

- Electronic controls, such as card readers
- Locking systems
- Exit devices
- Alarm monitoring equipment

Also shown are:

- Network and control material
- Cabling
- Conduit

Show the unit price and extended price for each line item of material. Use caution when establishing the unit price for individual components and, because this is a budget estimate, if in doubt use a higher price to ensure that adequate funding is available for these devices. Multiply the component count by the unit price to obtain the extended price. This is where the cabling estimate on the DDS is most useful.

6.5.3 Labor Costs

The next section shown in the sample budget is for Labor. Base the cost on an anticipated number of hours needed to install each device. The hourly estimate was derived from a table developed for this purpose and is based on historical experience from several sources. You may want to establish a library to compile local historical data based on projects complete. However, the estimates provided in Figure 6.11 are a general guide for approximating the amount of time needed to install a specific component.

Access Control Security System Budget

Client: Client Name
Work Location: Department
Project: (Project Description)

By: (Consultant)
Revision: 0
Date: (Date)

This is a budget estimate for the above captioned project. The amounts shown should be within 10% of the final price of this system, provided the scope of work is not changed. The entire project will be managed by (Consultant), including system acquisition and project management.

Material

		Qty	Cost	Subtotals
Door Devices				
	Card Reader	1	$308	
	Subtotal Door Devices			$308
Systemwide Devices		Qty	Cost	
	Network Panels	4	7200	
	Subtotal Systemwide Devices			7200
Locking Systems		Qty	Cost	
	Power Magnet	1	750	
	Subtotal Locking Systems			750
Exit Devices		Qty	Cost	
	Exit Thumb Button	1	90	
	Subtotal Exit Devices			90
Alarm Monitoring Equipment		Qty	Cost	
	Door Status Switches	20	200	
	Space Sensor	5	550	
	Subtotal Alarm Monitoring Equipment			750
Network and Control Equipment		Qty	Cost	
	Lock Power with FAI	1	800	
	Subtotal Network Control Equipment			800
Cabling			Cost	4201
			Total Material Cost	$14,099

Labor

	Cost	
Design & Project Management Services	2787	
Equipment Delivery & Installation	10,780	
Final Hookup for All Devices	$2,475	
System Testing	Included	
User Training	Not Required	
	Total Labor Cost	$16,042

Summary:
Thank you for allowing (Consultant) to help develop this budget for your new security project. We estimate your project cost to be:

Material	$ 14,099
Labor	16,042
Project Grand Total	$ 30,141
	For Budget Purposes Only

Please contact (Consultant) if you have questions about this estimate.

FIGURE 6.10 The Access Control and Alarm Budget.

Alternately you can use RSMeans Data (www.rsmeans.com/). In the construction industry, RSMeans data is synonymous with detailed costs, and it has been for decades. Robert Snow Means was a Civil Engineer who kept meticulous construction costs in a series of leather-bound books he made at his kitchen table.

By the early 1940s, his peers were so impressed by his tracking of equipment, material and labor costs that they began offering to buy his homemade "cost books".

Today, RSMeans data is offered by Gordian. The database contains more than 92,000 line items and cost engineers spend more than 30,000 hours researching and validating the costs every year. The cost information is still available in books but is also accessible via compact disc and dynamic estimating software. RSMeans can provide an hourly rate for electricians. Use this rate to establish the installation cost based on the number of hours anticipated for a given device.

The Final Hookup Cost is also a part of the labor estimate. Final hookup is the work operations reserved for vendor technicians. The easiest way to define the distinction between installation and final hookup is to view installation as all cable pulls and mounting work up to but excluding the connection of the cable to the end device.

Generally, vendors prefer their employees to terminate all electronic devices to ensure that the person making those connections has been properly trained by the manufacturer and is supervised by the company responsible for the equipment warranty. The estimated number of final hookup hours for most of the commonly used equipment is presented in Figure 6.11 and is a good rule of thumb in estimating Final Hookup cost.

Determine the hourly rate used to calculate the resulting cost of this final hookup by contact with the local security system vendors. Polling three or more vendors should provide a good average hourly rate. Most vendors in a defined geographic market usually have very similar costs.

6.5.4 Estimating Cable

One of the most difficult items to assess in this cost analysis is the cable estimate. These estimates are difficult to develop because cabling is rarely pulled in a straight line. A variety of impediments and limitations to cable paths are usually found in ceilings and walls require alternate cable routes.

A rule of thumb to follow when establishing cable estimates is to pace off the distance between the endpoint device (or simply estimate using your drawings) and the access control panel, adding an additional 20 ft for each end of the cable to allow for passage from the ceiling down to the appropriate device. Multiply that estimate by 1.3 to allow for errors in your calculations and the unavoidable scrap of unusable cable. Again using the electrician's labor rate, and the "feet per hour" amounts shown in Figure 6.11, will provide a guideline to calculate an approximate cost for cable installation. Of course you can use the same method for CCTV.

Cable material costs can vary considerably. There are several factors used to calculate cable cost. Cable type is the first to consider. The simplest way to

Access Control and Alarm Monitoring Installation Estimate of Hours

	Symbol		Hrs to Install
Electronics Controls			
Card Reader	CR		1.00
Key Pad	KY		1.00
Biometric Device	BM		1.00
Locking Systems			
Power Magnet	PM		3.00
2 Power Magnets	2PM		6.00
Electric Strike	S		4.00
Delay Power Magnet	PM-D		8.00
Exit Devices			
Exit Thumb Button	B		0.50
Exit Palm Button	PB		0.50
Emergency Release	ER		0.75
Existing Door Hardware	HDWR		0.00
Exit Sensor	ES		2.00
Touch Sense Bar	TS		4.00
Alarm Monitoring Equipment			
Door Status Switches	DSS		1.00
Space Sensor	PIR		1.00
Panic Alarms	PANIC		1.00
Network & Control Material			
Lock Power with Fire Alarm Interface			1.00
Network APM Panels			1.00
PCs (inc display, kybd etc.)			2.00
Access Control Software			
Cable Estimate			**Feet / Hour**
Reader Cable			100
Control Cable			100
Communications Cable			150
Conduit			NA

FIGURE 6.11 Table of Installation Hours for Access Control.

determine cable types is to select a system that appears to be appropriate for the application at hand. Most manufacturers publish their cable requirements on their website and provide requirements at no charge. Cable requirements are usually expressed in Belden wire number.

The Belden wire cable company is widely recognized as a high-quality manufacturer of communication and control cable. As a result, many manufacturers use Belden wire descriptions as the standard for specifying their cable requirements. Other cable manufacturers will provide what are termed Belden equivalents for the cables they manufacture. You may obtain prices for Belden cable from a variety of sources. This is usually quoted in a cost per foot and sold in lots of 500 and 1,000 ft.

It is important to know if "plenum rated" cable is required in the facility where the system is being proposed. In the 1970s, manufacturers developed plenum cable to reduce the potential for human injury from burning cable insulation in building fires. It is currently a fire code requirement. One case in particular resulted in deaths due to noxious fumes from burned cable insulation and not a direct result of the fire. That incident prompted the code change.

To understand the need for plenum rated cable one must first know that in modern buildings heating ventilation (and) air conditioning (HVAC) systems provide conditioned air to occupied spaces and that air must be returned to the HVAC system for re-heating or re-cooling. The return air "plenum" or airway in these buildings is simply the space between the ceiling tiles and the floor above. This is also the space where installers generally place cables for most retrofit installations. In some cases, the return air is ducted back and plenum cable is not required.

Plenum rated cable is required if the facility in which the system being proposed has these types of return air ceilings. This cable is also referred to as Teflon jacketed cable. The jacket was designed to burn at much higher temperatures than ordinary polyvinyl chloride (PVC) insulation. The cost difference between plenum rated cable and PVC cable can be as much as three times. In older buildings, this problem usually does not exist because the return air was provided through ductwork. Consult with the local facility manager or maintenance engineer to determine if the cable needed in the buildings should be plenum rated. They will usually know the answer.

The plenum jacket requirement applies if standard copper cable is used or if fiber-optic cables are used. Long runs not associated with a Local Area Network (LAN) drop or cable runs that have the potential for signal degradation will sometimes require the use of fiber optics. Although there are cost differences between the application of copper and fiber, using a copper cost for the budget estimate will usually prove adequate. The final decision regarding the choice of fiber or copper cabling will be made after the project is bid and the equipment supplier and vendor are identified. The participation of the providers can be most helpful in making the final cabling decision.

The use of existing LAN services may significantly affect cable costs. Most of the sophisticated systems today can make use of these existing facilities. However, using a company LAN creates other issues such as drop availability, protocol compatibility and bandwidth requirements. Before choosing this option, discuss these requirements with the company's information technology and/or communications group. In either case (whether you use LAN or don't use), some cabling is always required between the access control system network device (sometimes referred to as the Access Point Manager) and the end point devices such as locks, door status switches and egress buttons.

6.5.5 Estimating Incidental Costs

In addition to the direct expenses described above, there are other indirect expenses associated with any project installation. Those indirect expenses are travel, training and project management.

Travel cost estimates are required if the facility is located in areas where local vendors are not available and inter-city travel is anticipated. Make an allowance for the travel costs from the installation and final hookup crews. Estimate travel and per diem cost using the Government Services Administration (GSA) standard cost estimates available on the worldwide web at www.gsa.gov/travel/plan-book/per-diem-rates. These cost tables may also be obtained by contacting the government services administration directly.

Calculate **Training cost** by counting the number of individuals that will administer the system (be sure to consider multiple shifts for security officers). Assume that a single training class will have no more than ten people. In cases when more intense training may be required, reduce the estimated class size to only five individuals. Allow three full business days for each training session estimating six hours per day. Multiply that by the hourly rate established for final hookup services from vendor technicians. This will be the estimated training cost. If manufacturer training is expected as part of the system specification package (as opposed to local vendor personnel), also add the travel and per diem cost necessary to bring this vendor to the facility.

Project management tends to be one of the most difficult elements of the labor cost estimation to assess. This is because the demands on the project manager vary with the experience level of the vendors and other support personnel from the client's facility involved in the process. A number of factors affect how project management is assessed and these calculations can become difficult and tedious. Since this is a budget estimate, the most appropriate shorthand rule to follow is simply to assess project management based on the overall cost of the project. A rule of thumb used for project management in construction with regard to architects and other professionals is 7%–10% of the total cost of the project.

6.6 PREPARE A COST ESTIMATE FOR THE SURVEILLANCE SYSTEM

Use the same rationale in preparing the video system budget as used in preparing the access control system budget. The CDS and Command Center CCTV

Closed-Circuit Television System Budget

Client: **Client Name**	**By: (Consultant)**
Work Location: **Department**	Revision: 0
Project: (Project Description)	Date: (Date)

This is a budget estimate for the above captioned project. The amounts shown should be within 10% of the final price of this system, provided the scope of work is not changed. The entire project will be managed by (Consultant), including system acquisition and project management.

Material

Cameras, Lens, Housings and Mounts	Qty	Cost	Subtotals
Cameras	4	$ 1,400	
Lenses	4	400	
Housings	4	900	
Mounts	4	475	

Subtotal Cameras, Lenses, Housings and Mounts			**$3,175**
Auxiliary Equipment	Qty	Cost	
Auxiliary Lights	3	1875	

Subtotal Auxiliary Equipment			**1875**
Monitoring and Recording Equipment	Qty	Cost	
Monitors	2	750	
Recording Equipment	2	2300	

Subtotal Monitoring and Recording Equipment			**3050**
Cabling		Cost	**293**

		Total Material Cost	**$8,393**

Labor	Cost	
Design & Project Management Services	$ 1,500	
Final Hookup for All Devices	300	
System Testing	Included	
User Training for 2 Users	Not Required	
Equipment Delivery & Installation	$1,459	

	Total Labor Cost	**$3,259**

Special Contract Cost Items	Cost	
Intercom system	$350	

	Total Special Contract Cost	**$350**

Summary:
Thank you for allowing (Consultant) to help develop this budget for your new security project. We estimate your project cost to be:

Material	$ 8,393	
Labor	3,259	
Special	350	

Project Grand Total	$ 12,002	For Budget Purposes Only

Please contact (Consultant) if you have questions about this estimate.

FIGURE 6.12 Sample CCTV Budget.

Equipment list provides the component count for the CCTV budget. Figure 6.12 provides an example of a video system budget.

6.6.1 Primary Material Cost

The first element of the budget is material. Within material the first subcategory is a combined cost for cameras, lenses, housings and mounts. Group all of these items (cameras, lenses, housings and mounts) as a single-line item. In Figure 6.12, each item is broken out individually. Use this method if the management team wants to examine equipment at a detailed level.

The set of costs in the sample budget is auxiliary equipment. Auxiliary equipment includes alarm input modules, auxiliary lights and similar devices. Auxiliary equipment usually refers to devices installed at the controlled points or perimeter observation points.

The next group in the sample video budget is monitoring and recording equipment. Once again, if management does not prefer a substantial level of detail, you may group all of these components into a single-line item budget. However, the first step in the roll up is to group all the monitoring equipment into a single-line item and then group the recording equipment into a separate line item. In Figure 6.12, all of these items are separated into even lower groups defined as switchers, monitors, recording equipment, lens and position control equipment. This format assumes that the management team would be interested in that level of detail.

6.6.2 Estimating Cable

The last item in the material estimate is cabling and conduit. Take cable lengths for this estimate directly from the CDS that was prepared during the system design survey or estimated in the same fashion used for access control cable estimates. This cabling estimate will include at a minimum low-voltage video cable, power and control cable (along with connections to commercial power supplies) and conduit. A discussion of cable and conduit estimating is presented in the next section on preparing an access control budget.

6.6.3 Estimating Labor

After estimating material, estimate the labor. Figure 6.13 provides a recommended breakdown of the labor cost line items.

As in access control, equipment delivery and installation represents that portion of the work involving cable, conduit, camera mounts and housings installation. Generally, this is a basic estimate of man-hours at a given rate expected from a security installation company.

Likewise, final hookup for all devices is an estimate of hours for a technician from a local vendor at the vendor's anticipated rate (see the access control budget for a discussion of establishing these rates).

System testing and user training are both generally a part of the vendor's responsibility and again was addressed in the access control budget estimate. Refer to the next section for a discussion of estimating these costs. Also refer to the access control budget discussion for design and project management services.

Surveillance System Installatio
Estimate of Hours

	Symbol	Hrs to Install
Cameras		
Standard Cameras	S	1.00
Low Light Cameras	L	1.00
Lenses		
Fixed 2.3 / Auto	2.3/A	0.25
Fixed 4 / Auto	4/A	0.25
Fixed 8 / Auto	8/A	0.25
Zoom / Auto	Z/A	0.25
Fixed 2.3 / Manual	2.3/M	0.25
Fixed 4 / Manual	4/M	0.25
Fixed 8 / Manual	8/M	0.25
Zoom / Manual	Z/M	0.25
Housings		
Indoor	I	0.50
Outdoor	O	1.00
Outdoor / Fan	OF	1.00
Outdoor / Wiper	OW	1.00
Outdoor Fan / Wiper	OFW	1.00
Outdoor Hood	H	1.00
Camera Mounts		
Ceiling / Light Duty	CL	3.00
Ceiling / Medium Duty	CM	3.00
Ceiling / Heavy Duty	CH	4.00
Wall / Light Duty	WL	2.00
Wall / Meduim Duty	WM	2.00
Wall / Heavy Duty	WH	3.00
Pediment / Light Duty	PL	3.00
Pediment / Medium Duty	PM	3.00
Pediment / Heavy Duty	PH	4.00
Post / Light Duty	POL	3.00
Post / Medium Duty	POM	3.00
Post / Heavy Duty	POH	4.00
0	0	
Pan and Tilt Motor Drive	1	2.00
Control Receivers	RT	2.00
Specials		
Alarm Input	1	1.00
Auxiliary Lights	1	3.00
Cable Estimate		**Feet / Hour**
Coax		100
Power and Control Cable		100
Conduit		20

FIGURE 6.13 Table of Installation Hours for CCTV Equipment.

Special contract cost items are a result of unique circumstances in an installation that requires the material and labor from specialized companies. An example of this in a CCTV installation environment might be the installation of cameras, mounts and other system components in a location that requires special lift equipment. Add the cost of rental for the lift equipment and operator to the CCTV budget.

6.7 FORECAST EXPENSE BUDGETS

The above calculations establish only the capital investment required to institute the proposed system, there are other costs involved. In addition to the capital budget, provide an expense budget for the ongoing maintenance of the system. That expense budget includes an estimate of annual service cost and an estimate of identity card purchase for systems that are card reader based.

Security cards are consumed at a fairly regular rate. Cards are lost or stolen, and in some cases, cards are discarded because employees are terminated. In systems where photo IDs or other unique cosmetic identifiers are imprinted on the card, the turnover rate in the authorized population will have a significant impact on the quantity of cards used. Estimate card cost as an expense item with ongoing system maintenance and include it in the expense budget.

Extending the project costs still further you may also want to consider recommending that the company stock their own spares for a quicker response time and lower overall costs. The value of this decision can only be measured in light of the annual maintenance costs from the selected vendor (after receipt of bids) and a careful comparison of the options.

Another consideration is "planned obsolescence" and system replacement. Even if the system is still operational after 5 years, the state of technology may render the recommended equipment obsolete and some consideration should be given to investment allowance for future replacements. However, looking that far into the future may overstep the point of diminishing returns. That is, the cost of finding the right answer may exceed the savings of early planning. The most prudent choice is to advise the management team that such long-range planning requires attention and allow them to decide how far to take the analysis. Sometimes taking such a long-range view in companies that normally see a much shorter forecast can confuse the primary objective of providing for today's needs.

Do not overwhelm the management team with detailed costs for individual components. In most cases, the "bottom line" is what's most important. Some level of detail is certainly required but all the detail previously described is usually not shared in the primary recommendation. It is usually better to include detail level information on attachments.

6.8 HUMAN RESOURCE REQUIREMENTS

A cost estimate would be incomplete without some review of the personnel needed to operate the system. In most circumstances, existing on-site personnel will be used as system operators; however, this must be verified.

If it is company management's intention to operate this system with new personnel, there will be hiring and training costs that must also be addressed in the system recommendation. The human resources department is the best place to obtain personnel cost information.

Begin by first estimating how many individuals will be needed to operate and monitor the proposed system. Some of that was covered in the preceding chapter on establishing a security force. Establish broad definitions of job responsibilities and job titles and then share these expectations with the company's security manager. Develop an outline for the use of existing personnel and help the security manager determine if the current force can do the work.

From these discussions develop a profile of the force needed to operate and manage the proposed system and the personnel required to supplement the existing force. Conduct an interview with the human resources manager to determine cost for additional resources.

6.9 COST ANALYSIS

After compiling the cost data on the preliminary system, further analyze the investment in the project. The anticipated cost for the recommended security system should not exceed the value of the assets being protected. When the best efforts are made to contain costs but the investment exceeds the value of the potential loss of physical assets and there are no human assets to consider, the recommendation will usually be to use insurance or other risk aversion approaches.

The value of the security survey will be the knowledge that the facility had been thoroughly reviewed and it was determined that the cost of preventing anticipated losses exceed the losses themselves. A valid recommendation in such a circumstance may be to use the security survey and budget as a decision-making tool to justify the purchase of additional insurance or duplicate resources to ensure business continuity if the asset being protected is stolen or damaged.

Assistance from company personnel is essential for this step. You must learn which assets are considered critical to the operation and establish a value for those assets. The company accounting can be a useful resource for this information. However, management perception cannot be overemphasized. The raw cost of the asset may not be as significant as the ability to replace the asset if it is lost or the business income loss that will result if the asset is taken out of service.

The preliminary system design should include a cost comparison of potential loss of revenue and the cost of replacing assets if the anticipated threats are realized. This will guide management in making an informed decision for investing in new security measures.

6.10 LEGAL ISSUES

A recommendation for security systems can have broad-reaching implications for you and the company. In today's litigious-minded society, companies must guard against legal exposure as a result of perceived or implied negligence. One of the frequently used phrases in legal environments with regard to security is the application of "reasonable care".

An excellent example of this perspective can be found in the healthcare industry. In addition to liabilities from medical malpractice, healthcare practitioners also have many of the same exposures of major hotels. Likewise, because of their high visibility, healthcare institutions are often exposed to "slip and fall" claims.

One of the most compelling arguments for investing in security, with regard to litigation in a healthcare institution, is the protection of children and newborn infants. Consider the case of a newborn infant disappearing from a healthcare facility. Juries find it very difficult to place a value on human life and the life of a child is especially significant. Jury awards in such cases are usually extremely high. If the institution that is being protected by you is a healthcare institution that provides care to newborn infants, it follows that a single lawsuit awarded to a claimant can offset the expense of most physical security systems.

The central question in such cases is usually: "has the institution taken reasonable care to protect the lives and property of their employees, visitors and patrons?" The definition of reasonable care tends to change with each legal jurisdiction and, within those jurisdictions, opinions change over time. So you and the company must be diligent in their efforts to constantly assess the physical security requirements and, where necessary, improve the devices, procedures and manpower to demonstrate the application of reasonable care.

You must therefore consider the "implied" potential for loss if reasonable care is not taken and illustrate the comparison of costs for company management. At the conclusion of this analysis, you must present the assessment to the management team. The next chapter deals with how best to make this presentation.

CHAPTER 7

Presenting the Solutions

CONTENTS

7.1 CONVEYING THE BENEFITS OF YOUR SOLUTIONS

After completing the assessment and documenting your findings you must present it to the management team so that they can make an informed decision to proceed. The management team decides if additional investments are worth improvements in physical security, but it is your role to present the facts and opinions upon which those decisions will be made.

The goal in presenting the recommendation is to clearly convey the benefits of the security solution and the investment required to obtain those benefits. The recommendation may also conclude that the current level of security measures is adequate and that the company need not take further action. The recommendation may also conclude that the investment to implement the system may exceed the cost of simply replacing the protected assets following an incident. The recommendation will help the management team make the right decision. The company is relying on you to guide them through the decision process.

7.2 WHAT MANAGEMENT WANTS TO KNOW

The management team must ensure the successful ongoing operation of the company. To accomplish this they must provide a safe and secure work environment for their employees, customers and visitors. The management team must also protect the assets of a company from individuals with deliberation and intent to cause harm. They are relying on you for answers on how best to ensure continued operation. Some of the more urgent questions the security profession must answer are:

DOI: 10.4324/9781003490432-8

1. Why would I want to do this?
2. What would happen if I didn't do this?
3. Who needs to be involved to implement and operate the system?
4. When should I act?
5. How long will it take to implement the recommended solutions?
6. How much will it cost?

7.2.1 Why Would I Want to Do This?

The physical threat assessment and vulnerability assessment explain the most compelling reasons to act. Include a summarization of these reports in the system recommendation. These reports identified the threats that the company is (or should be) concerned about and how susceptible the company is to suffer loss from these threats.

The recommendation must make the extent to which human lives are at risk clear and the value of the assets protected by the proposed solutions. A review of the concerns expressed by employees during interviews would be also helpful in creating a well-rounded description of the situation. Focus attention in the recommendation on the loss of business income resulting from damage or loss of the protected assets.

7.2.2 What Would Happen If I Didn't Do What Is Recommended?

Address the consequences of not acting on the recommendation. The physical threat assessment and vulnerability assessment will provide the basis for the conclusions and the recommendation must remind the management team of what is at risk.

Direct the management team's attention to the loss of protected assets. Help them imagine what the conditions would be like if each of the threats suggested by the physical threat assessment were realized. Emphasize the catastrophic business losses that could result if deaths or serious injury were to occur to key personnel.

Present a review of losses due to indirect cost. Examine the potential for losses due to lawsuits in the recommendation. If a litigant can show an injury resulted because the company failed to take "reasonable care" in a security matter identified by the physical threat assessment or vulnerability assessment, explain if and how the company could sustain substantial costs.

Another indirect cost is "public image". It is difficult to quantify the losses from negative publicity but easy to imagine. Help the management team envision their company's name on the six o'clock news associated with words like "negligence, apathy, carelessness and mismanagement". These indirect costs can have as much an impact on business results as the loss of a critical asset.

7.2.3 Who Needs to Be Involved to Implement and Operate the System?

Aside from capital investment, the company is also concerned with the human resource investment in implementing any proposed system and the ongoing personnel cost in operating the system. Address the human resource needed initially and what is needed to serve the ongoing operation of the recommended solutions. The most likely candidates are the existing security force. Use the information gathered during the assessment about force management. Incorporate that data into an outline of the human resource operations plan.

Review the security force utilization by describing what the new post orders for the security officer will be and how the plan will reallocate the force. Assess the "savings" expected when labor is replaced by automated systems. Those savings can be re-employed in other areas of the company having the effect of "adding security officers to the staff".

For example, when an officer stands an 8-hour post at a primary entrance door simply to screen individuals entering and leaving a building, an electronic security system can replace the officer. This substitution can result in a savings of eight man-hours. These savings can also be in dollars but that assumes that the company would dismiss the officer. The more likely (and recommended) outcome is to utilize the officer in other more productive ways.

System implementation will also require the participation of Risk Management, Purchasing, Legal, Facilities and Information Technology to name a few. Provide an overview of the implementation process and how each of these groups will contribute to the overall success of the implementation in the presentation.

7.2.4 When Should I Act?

If the assets to protect are substantial and the probability of loss is moderate or high, the answer to this question is always "now". Justify the timing of the implementing the recommended solutions by showing the management team what a delay would mean. If there is a delay in the decision to implement the solutions, illustrate how that delay will affect the recommendation and what additional risks would result. Will equipment or labor prices rise? Will the threat of litigation grow? What are the downside risks of inaction?

In earlier chapters, we discussed a phased approach to implementation. If the company is not ready to move immediately because of budget considerations, have an alternate plan ready for discussion that builds the proposed solutions over time.

7.2.5 How Long Will It Take to Implement?

This is usually a difficult question to answer and especially when multiple disciplines are involved and multiple vendors implement the recommended solutions. The larger the project the greater the installation time, but installation time is not the only factor. In addition to equipment installation, estimate a time line for the entire process. This time line includes at least the following tasks:

- Final system design
- Preparing the request for proposal (following by an approval process)
- Bid solicitation and vendor response to the request for a proposal
- Evaluating the bid responses
- Examining the equipment (including vendor presentations)
- Visiting installation references
- Final contract negotiations and award
- The equipment delivery interval (1)
- The installation time (1)
- The final hookup time, including testing and troubleshooting
- User training
- Staff announcements
- Issuing credentials (in card-based populations)
- Enrollment processes (in biometric applications)

These estimates are generally expressed in "months". The recommended solutions may take up to a year to implement. A good reference source is the local vendors that would ordinarily have an opportunity to serve the company for this project.

7.2.6 How Much Will It Cost?

Cost is always an issue for discussion, but there is a relationship between time and budgets. The company may find the cost reasonable but simply cannot assign the capital to the project yet. It is likely that you were called in at this time to help establish a budget.

Display costs as fully and objectively as possible. Usually top management is not interested in the fine details of the cost computation, so omit them from the body of the recommendation. This cost presentation is broad and top level but also have an "appendix of details" that will address the most rigorous examination.

7.3 METHODS OF PRESENTING THE RECOMMENDATION

There are two components of the security solutions presentation: a written proposal and an oral/visual presentation. The written proposal outlines in detail the rational behind the recommendation and describes the proposed solutions. The oral presentation is a less detailed "concept presentation", usually supported by visual aids. In some cases, the management team will simply not have time to read the written recommendations; therefore, the oral presentation carries a tremendous responsibility to accurately and briefly convey the entire concept and focus on key issues that will provide sufficient information for a decision.

7.3.1 The Written Presentation

The written presentation contains all of the details necessary for the management team to make the decision to authorize funding and grant permission to implement the proposed system. It should be a "stand-alone" document, that is, a reader should have all the information before them to understand the justification for the recommendation without having anyone explain the information. That is a steep hill to climb, you must take the perspective of your reader, realize that they do not know what you know, have not examined the site and need "proof of concept". Conversely, if the studies conclude that no action is required, clearly describe the justification for these conclusions.

Written proposals usually begin with an "Executive Summary". These opening remarks summarize the main points of the proposal and permit the reader to understand the proposed solutions without having to read all the detail. To be effective, the Executive Summary will be well spaced (that is to say, wide margins and ample vertical distance between paragraphs), speak in broad terms and address only key decision points. The details supporting these arguments and conclusions are in the body of the proposal. Assume that the reader will accept the judgment and conclusions in the Executive Summary and do not offer details that prove the point. If details are needed for further justification, the reader can simply read the rest of the written package.

Following the Executive Summary, prepare a table of contents. Numbering the pages is helpful for all written presentations but especially for large ones. Group information together behind tabs allowing the reader to find what they want within a defined section.

If you have not done a written presentation before, obtain copies of other proposals done for other types of projects for the management team. This will provide a good guide as to how management in this company is accustomed to seeing such recommendations. Use this proposal as a guide to the organization and structure of the written package

Section 1: Project Objectives and Scope of Work

Fully describe the objectives of the study in this section and the benefits expected if the recommendation is accepted. This section is also the appropriate place to limit the Scope of Work addressed by this project. Both definitions are an essential part of the introduction. For example:

> **Set the Stage**
> The company created this project to review the current level security that exists facility wide. The purpose of this project is to establish an improved level of security through a joint effort of all departments by using the combined technical resources and cooperation across departmental lines.
>
> **Identify the Goals**
> The goal of this project is to create a centralized command and control system with maximum flexibility while permitting individual customization for all users. In conceiving the system the company intends to take advantage of the most technologically advanced features available in the electronic security industry and integrate the chosen system features into existing communication facilities and data control practices.
>
> **Limit the Scope**
> The application of this system is limited to meeting the needs identified in the physical threat assessment and vulnerability assessment. The solutions recommended shall also result in a proposed realignment of security watch stations and new procedures for alarm response. It is not the intent of this project to investigate internal security matters regarding personnel or prepare the company for threats from "natural" catastrophes. This project addresses man-made threats from perpetrators with intention and deliberation to do harm to company personnel or assets.

This definition of Scope of Work also provides management an opportunity to expand the scope of the project in cases where items are not included, and are of principal concern. A clear definition of the Scope of Work will ensure that your efforts meet the results expected by the company.

Section 2: Threats and Countermeasures

Summarize the physical threat assessment, identifying the key assets and personnel at high risk. Using the data gathered in the physical threat assessment, explain what those threats are and how likely each will occur.

Define what, if any, systems are presently employed to address the threats identified in the physical threat assessment and the gaps found in that mitigation effort. The present method of operation includes a detailed listing of all existing security systems and resources used to secure the company's facility.

Describe where the company is vulnerable to these threats from information gathered during the vulnerability assessment. Be specific in the description of the areas of exposure; emphasize the reasons for implementing the proposed solutions and the rationale for proceeding with the proposed solutions.

This would be the best place to include your threat assessment analysis from Chapter 2. Using the assessment worksheets MEVA, CARVER and MSHARPP, provide the conclusions in your report and attach the entire analysis to the report.

Again, you do not have to do this unless you feel it will support your case. The management team will want to know why you are spending money in some areas and not in others. If other aspects of your proposal do not clearly demonstrate this or if you feel additional justification is needed to clearly demonstrate that attention should be paid to one area and not another, these reports will help. Additionally, you may not get all the funds you require to do the complete system and so you must prioritize your decisions. You will recall that we ranked our decisions as A, B or C, the threat analysis worksheets provide the justification for that ranking.

Sometimes it is not just protection of company assets from direct threats that must be considered but also indirect threats – in particular, lawsuits from a lack of reasonable care. So your justification should also consider the company's legal exposure when setting spending priorities. I have been involved in legal cases where the defendant (a company) knew of a security issue but failed to take action because they felt the solution was too expensive at the time. Had they simply identified the problem and solution, and designated a budget for implementation but delayed the implementation based on a solid analysis of their spending priorities, they would have shown reasonable care.

Section 3: Benefits of the Recommended Solution

Explain what the proposed methods of securing operation will do to benefit the company. Emphasize how the proposed systems and other recommendations will satisfy the needs of the physical threat assessment and vulnerability assessment. For example:

> The current method for perimeter access control is to use the security force at the building's reception desk to control visitor access to the facility. However, other doors leading into the facility that are intended for emergency egress only are frequently jammed open to allow convenient access to the parking lot.
>
> As a result, a perpetrator may enter the building through one of these uncontrolled and unmonitored doors thereby gaining access to the entire facility without the knowledge or permission of the security staff. One of the identified threats in our physical threat assessment is access to the

> data center by unauthorized personnel. The failure to prevent unauthorized access may result in sabotage of the data communications network resulting in lost data and delays in the operation that can cost the company $ XXX per day.

By comparing each method of operation against the threats identified in the physical threat assessment and vulnerability assessment the proposed solutions will convey the need for improved security procedures and additional security monitoring equipment.

Section 4: Recommendation

Begin with a description of what the company should do and when they should do it. Specific details of the recommended system, such as how many card readers, how many alarm contacts or the recommendation location for command posts, will be listed on attachments. The recommendation section is reserved for summary conclusions, giving only as much detail as needed to clearly illustrate what is to be done to solve the identified problems.

Focus attention on the involvement of security personnel in the operation of the new security system. If the plan recommends using existing security personnel to respond to the threats detected by the proposed systems, describe how the system will employ them. For instance, the recommendation may say:

> This system will require the security force to monitor the alarm terminals and closed circuit television screens 24 hours a day, 7 days a week. This will result in a three shift watch, with each shift standing an 8 hour tour. We recommend that the officers in each watch rotate through the command post alternately serving as roving patrol and command center watch station personnel.

By defining the recommendation in this way, the management team will recognize the total investment required for implementing the recommended solutions.

Section 5: Investment Required

Explain the cost of using the recommended systems. Cost details are not an essential part of this section and are to be included on an attachment to the recommendation. The recommendation will provide a cost comparison of all the potential solutions.

To establish these comparisons, begin with the statement of proposed capital investment. Include the investment of labor and material needed to install the recommended systems and the anticipated human resource cost for implementation. Summarize the details of this investment option in a single-line item. The second line item is the anticipated expense for additional personnel to operate or monitor this system. The third line item is the annual maintenance anticipated for the recommended system. This cost was calculated when the system design was created. Estimate annual maintenance using approximately 10% of the material cost of all equipment on the project. Estimate annual labor maintenance by using approximately 15% of the final hookup costs established in the system budget.

Next, show the cost of additional personnel, if any, or the resulting savings in redeployment of personnel that will be possible if the recommended solutions are accepted. Then examine other options to address the identified risks. Compare the cost of these options against the recommended solution. The first comparison is the investment in the recommended solution versus the cost of doing nothing. Assess the potential loss from a perpetrator successfully causing damage to the assets of the company. Add the cost of lost income resulting from damaged property when making this assessment.

Next, compare the cost of using business insurance to offset the loss in income and assets to mitigate the identified risks. Remember that these are "rough order of magnitude" estimates and the substantial investment time to arrive at exact numbers is not necessary.

Examine the phased approach to implementing the recommended solutions. A phased approach will scale back the principal recommendation giving cost containment first priority (see Chapter 6). If the recommendation uses this approach, explain repeatedly and deliberately that this is not the primary recommendation but a "stop gap" measure of only the most critical elements of the recommendation. Always present the best solution to the company first, regardless of the cost.

Type the recommendation on standard 8-1/2 x 11 white paper and bound in some convenient manner so that the reader may examine the proposal quickly and easily. Avoid fancy binders or covers that detract from the content of the presentation. It would be helpful to also produce this document in an Adobe PDF version for those who are more oriented to electronic media.

7.3.2 The Oral Presentation

After the written proposal is finished, prepare an outline for the oral presentation based on the written package. The face-to-face meeting is usually a "dialog" not a monolog and questions will be raised by the audience. The outline will help to keep the presentation on track and ensure that all of the important elements of the presentation are covered.

Practice the oral presentation before the meeting. Sometimes, a passage sounds good when written out but sounds awkward when spoken aloud. This exchange of information should be free and relaxed. Do not "read" from a script. You are there to convey knowledge, not recite a speech. Be intimately familiar with all the details of the recommended solutions.

Prepare visual aids based on the oral presentation. A useful tool for visual aids is a computer program from Microsoft called "PowerPoint". PowerPoint allows the user to create a slide show from other programs. This slide show uses a personal computer and a digital projector for the presentation. Ask the company's media center what equipment is available for use in the presentation. One note of caution … computers and other electronic devices can fail. Have a backup! Copy the presentation material to a disk so that another computer can be used. In complex presentations, create a printed copy of the slide show to distribute to illustrate important points if the electronics devices fail. For mission-critical information, one may even prepare easel boards that duplicate the electronic visual aids.

When constructing the visual presentation it is often helpful to use charts, graphs, images or other images that do not involve the written word. It is frequently easier to convey a concept with an image than it is to write it on a screen and compel the audience to read and imagine what the message should be.

Some techniques I have found effective include capturing an image of a drawing from a CAD program and then pasting that image on the PowerPoint slide. You can also capture photographs and other illustrations in the same way, thus conveying in images the points you are making verbally (Figures 7.1 and 7.2).

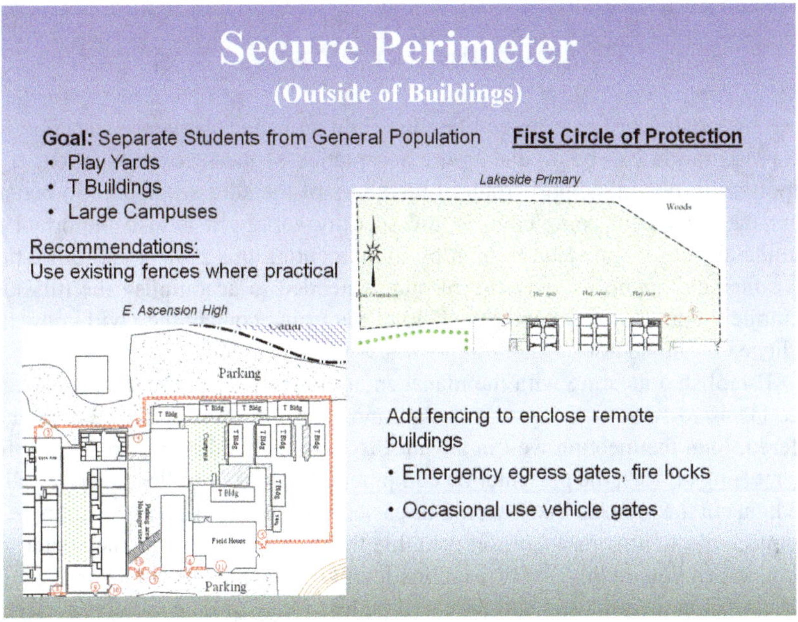

FIGURE 7.1 PowerPoint with Drawing.

FIGURE 7.2 PowerPoint with Picture.

7.4 DELIVERING THE PRESENTATION

Here comes the hard part, assembling the right audience. Audience selection for the presentation can be crucial to the acceptance of the recommendation. It is important to obtain support from all members of the staff who stand to benefit from the successful completion of the security survey. It is also important to include all those who stand to gain by implementing this project and those that have financial authority over the resources needed to accomplish the mission. Compile the invitation list with the help of the prime contact they will know the audience if you do not.

Establish a meeting with the management team. Explain the purpose of the meeting is to review the system design and to make decisions on the choices offered. Plan the meeting well in advance to ensure attendance. Arrive early for the meeting and test the presentation equipment. Before the audience arrives, dim the lights in the room so that it would be easier to view the visual presentation. *Do not* place the written packages on the table for the audience when they enter the room. When you do this, the first inclination of most attendees is to immediately begin reading the proposal and they will be less likely to give the oral presentation their full attention.

Begin the presentation with a brief description of who you are (for those who don't know you) and why this subject has surfaced at this time. Describe the agenda and how long the meeting will last. Note if there will be breaks during the meeting. This will allow the audience to pay more attention to the presentation, knowing that time has been set aside to tend to other company business.

Early in the presentation, be sure to express appreciation for the support of the individuals who have assisted you in the collection of information and it is always helpful to indicate them by name. Restate the objectives of the project. Explain the techniques used to achieve those objectives. It is best to keep the discussions at a relatively high level.

Present the information gathered and the conclusions reached. Answer all questions as quickly as possible, do not tell attendees to hold questions to the end. If you force them to wait, you will lose their attention because they are stuck on the question. However, if that question will be answered shortly in the presentation, say so. The questioner will then be anxious to hear what you have to say and pay attention to your presentation. If you do not know an answer, DO NOT GUESS! It is better to say you do not know and commit to finding the answer after the meeting and responding. Write these questions down and answer by memo after the meeting.

7.5 GAINING ACCEPTANCE FOR THE SOLUTIONS

This step is the most important one in the entire presentation process. It is not difficult to do but anyone who has ever had to convince an audience to take a particular course of action will understand the effort needed to "ask for the decision". After describing the conclusions, what must be done, how to do it and when to act, a decision is needed to move to the next step. Turn to your audience and ask, "Do I have your support in implementing this recommendation?" You have been doing all the talking up to this point, now it is time for audience feedback.

The presentation builds a business case that helps the company management team decide if improvement needed in company security measures justifies the cost. It is your responsibility to identify and clearly define the options available to the management team and make an appropriate recommendation for the correct course of action. "Gaining Acceptance" means presenting the recommendation in such a way that is clear and meaningful to the company and helping the company reach a decision.

One of the roles you must play is that of a "motivator". Large organizations are especially sensitive to major decisions. Managers are reluctant to take chances by making decisions that have a major impact on the company when there are substantial areas of uncertainty. They are placing their reputation on the line and you can help them decide with a solid, well-supported recommendation. You will take the risk of the decision and will guide the management team to the right conclusions that support an informed choice.

Seeking acceptance is an uncomfortable situation for most people nevertheless; it is an essential step in moving the project forward. It is the moment of rejection and most people have a tough time dealing with rejection. It is helpful to remember that a lack of acceptance simply means that the audience may be rejecting the conclusions, not the work done or you. "No" sometimes means they do not know enough and a revision of the presentation is required to make the choices clearer.

Frequently in decisions involving large complex systems, the management team is usually not prepared to make an immediate decision following the presentation. That is one reason why the written package is an essential part of this entire process.

Oftentimes, there is "sticker shock" when the investment cost of the project is revealed. Everything you have presented may be justified and is completely logical but the funds are simply not available to act on the proposed recommendation at this time. Do not be discouraged. Make every effort to work with the management team to arrive at an appropriate decision.

In cases where an immediate acceptance is not forthcoming and additional discussions between the decision-makers are necessary, the written package will stand in place of the oral presentation. Expect delays. After the oral presentation, distribute the written package so that further review and discussions can take place in light of all the information at hand.

The overriding thought to keep in mind is your job is to assess, analyze and recommend, not decide.

7.6 THE POLITICS OF CHANGE

Very often people resist change simply because it is a change. That change may impact them personally or professionally and they are not certain how that change will alter their current position. Your job is to explain how that change will impact each decision-maker. It may be better to discuss these matters with those decision-makers that are most impacted before the presentation meeting. You may even want to alter your recommendation to gain acceptance from this person if it does not substantially affect the level of security you need to protect company assets. Consider your actions before you make your formal presentation and "grease the skids" to make acceptance more desirable.

Then there is "corporate culture". Companies are driven by the management team and that team has an expectation of what is it like (or should be) to work in that company. Sometimes people chafe at security constraints, they prefer a more open and relaxed environment. The challenge here is to emphasize the down side of failure to act. If the threats you are attempting to mitigate can stop the company's operation or do significant harm to its ability to do business, your job is to emphasize those points.

7.7 FOLLOW UP

Stay in constant communication with the management team after the presentation. Answer all questions quickly and accurately and help the team arrive at the most useful decision for the situation.

When the management team grants approval to the project, draft a confirming letter. Address this correspondence to all those invited to the presentation. Include a detailed description of the scope of the project, the resources needed and the schedule for completion with the expected results. Conclude the memorandum with a brief description of the reports expected on the progress of implementing the recommended solutions.

Remember that you are there to guide the company to an informed decision. When a decision is made to move forward with the project, begin the system acquisition phase.

CHAPTER 8

How to Buy Your New Security System

CONTENTS

8.1 INTRODUCTION TO THE ACQUISITION PROCESS

Congratulations! Your recommendation was accepted by the management team and you have budget approval to move forward with the project. Now you must translate the design into a solicitation describing the products and services needed to meet the design objectives. This process is usually referred to as a "Bid" and is released to the market to obtain actual pricing and availability on the specified products and services.

In this chapter, we will examine some of the ways competitive bids are constructed and the reasons for selecting a type of bid for a particular situation. We will review how to create a "Request for Proposal (RFP)" and the benefits of each type of bid process for system bids. You should know that this is not the first thing the company has ever bought … there are people in the company who specialize in acquiring products and services and you must work with this group (usually referred to as the Purchasing Department) to understand and follow all the rules that the management team has set forth for buying goods and services.

 DOI: 10.4324/9781003490432-9

In this working relationship, you know the needs and the technology involved but Purchasing knows the buying rules, plus they have a wealth of experience in dealing with vendors. The dilemma is that you must learn everything they know OR you need to teach them what you know to get the job done. This usually works out by you writing the technical description of the purchase and leave all the business matters to Purchasing.

8.2 CHOSE THE BID TYPE

There are several types of bid specifications commonly used to describe a physical security system acquisition. The complexity of the project, the need for specificity in matching the system requirements to the products and services and the company's purchasing policies determine the type of bid to use. The bid types described below represent some of the more commonly used bid types but by no means represent a comprehensive list of all types of bids. Furthermore, a specification may combine the elements of several types of bids. These common bid types are as follows:

- The Request for Information (RFI)
- The Request for Quotation (RFQ)
- The Request for Proposal (RFP)

8.2.1 The Request for Information

An RFI is used to gather information to develop an RFP or an RFQ. The RFI usually does not require the vendor to reveal prices but may ask for budget estimates based on the broad parameters of the RFI.

The RFI is a useful tool when the needs defined by the security survey are so unusual that the writer cannot adequately develop an RFQ or RFP. The RFI will not be specific in what the company wishes to buy but instead will provide a broad definition of the mission and functions that are needed in the system to be acquired. The RFI may address performance requirements to some degree but is usually not specific in the details of how to achieve those requirements. The RFI explains the overall goals of system performance and requires the respondent to describe how to accomplish the mission and the performance results expected.

In this way, the company can gather expertise from the industry and allow the marketplace to share in problem solving. It provides a broad reach of participation and substantial creative input from the manufacturers. Use the RFI for situations where there are unusual environmental circumstances and it is not possible to develop a system design.

Use the RFI sparingly. Because it is "non-specific", it opens the design to wide variation and makes competitive comparisons very difficult. The RFI lacks design detail, so the results may not address all of the problems. Vendors will tend to recommend only products that they sell and not necessarily the best fit.

RFIs are usually very good in situations where a completely new product is being engineered but in most security applications the products already exist to solve the problems and it is your role to define the problem and establish the components of the recommended solution.

8.2.2 The Request for Quotation

Use the RFQ to solicit costs from the market when the equipment make and model has been predetermined. It is the most straightforward method for soliciting competitive offers and comparing bids. Use the RFQ when you do not want to open the bid to a wide variety of alternatives. The RFQ describes the required components and then solicits a price on the equipment and other bid elements needed for delivery. Some of the other elements of the RFQ are:

- Project Management
- Scheduling and Cost Controls
- Project Administration
- Fabrication and Factory Testing
- System Demonstration
- Disassembly, Storage, Freight and Insurance
- Installation
- System Testing and Start Up
- User Training
- Warranty
- Post Installation Support

Use the RFQ, to compare bids when all bidders are making offers on the same product. The RFQ can provide competitive pricing on pre-selected systems. Assuming all bidders meet the bid conditions equally, the company with the lowest overall price generally wins.

Prewritten specifications will often form the basis of constructing RFQs. These prewritten specifications, commonly referred to as "Boilerplate Specifications", are hardware specifications that describe a particular product. Equipment manufacturers that have boilerplate specifications will readily supply them, then you amend these specifications to fit the circumstance. This is a useful approach and saves considerable time in preparing systems specifications. In addition, this approach is useful when an *internal standard* exists for system installations and the intent is to be consistent in acquiring new systems and system additions.

However, when specifying a new system and there is no internal standard established and the products for the system have not been pre-identified, the RFQ can create some unwanted situations. Because the RFQ describes the system in specific product terms, it requires system selection before the bid is released to the market. The "Catch 22" is that reviewing all available systems before each bid to determine the "one best fit" is not an economical use of your time or the company's consulting fees (in the case of a professional consultant). Additionally, if you are not a qualified consultant with years of experience and possess at minimum a Physical Security Professional (PSP) certification from ASIS International, doing an evaluation of the market can be arduous and overwhelming. Inexperience in interpreting features can lead to false conclusions.

A valid argument can be made that you should be the expert in system design and, as such, should specify the exact system components for the proposed solutions. This argument does not consider the commercial aspects of the system acquisition but focuses entirely on the technical capabilities of the equipment under analysis.

As of 2023 there are 94 manufacturers of access control products (not counting locking systems and related products) and 121 manufacturers of closed-circuit television (CCTV) equipment. Having full knowledge of all of the features of all of the manufactures is nearly impossible, even for a trained professional. Further, even if the research identifies the one best system, there is no guarantee that there will be a vendor willing to assume the responsibilities of installation and maintenance on the chosen system. System support is an essential part of the process. In this instance, the definition of support is technical assistance before the sale, qualified installation labor after the sale and user training and system maintenance after implementation. Establishing bona fide offers from interested vendors first reduces the number of systems to review. The RFQ would preclude this advantage.

This is not a recommended approach for most new installations. The exposure to the company and you is great since the full responsibility of system selection falls on the writer of the RFQ. The vendors have no obligation to "perform" to specifications but rather must only provide the equipment specified. If the system does not perform as expected (except in cases of faulty material or installation), the vendor is not liable. System integrators and engineering firms that have full-time professional engineers (PEs) and technical staffs also find it extremely difficult to keep up with product improvements, many of which occur on a monthly basis, particularly in software development.

Complicating the process even more are the variations in network configuration for the various access control and CCTV systems on the market today. The manufacturers of these systems do not always use the same method for network design or component pricing. The criteria used in system design and included with the RFQ may inadvertently impose mechanical or technical requirements that have little value in system performance. These unintended requirements limit which vendors may participate in the bid process by virtue of the design elements chosen. This artificially reduces competition and may unintentionally exclude a "best fit" system.

Another consideration to pre-selecting an equipment type is open competition. To obtain the best product for the system design at competitive prices, allow the marketplace to vie for the business on a level playing field. Selecting a manufacturer beforehand removes a large element of competition from the marketplace and restricts bidders to only those products identified by the RFQ. In bids using public funds, such restrictions can open the door for complicated protests that delay system implementation unnecessarily and create a strained relationship between the buyers and the sellers. This also does a disservice to the company by artificially eliminating a competitor that may have a superior system to the one specified in the RFQ.

However, the RFQ should not be dismissed and ineffective. In many cases there are compelling reasons to specify a unique system type. Some examples of this are system expansions where an existing system is in place and the task is to add to that system. In addition, some companies have set internal standards for their security system based on technical criteria developed to meet certain compatibility issues or minimum performance standards. Competition in such bids would be legitimately limited to vendors that provide products designed to work within certain technical parameters. In these cases, RFQs are most useful and provide an opportunity to obtain competitive prices on products that meet specific compatibility criteria.

If in doubt, add the services of a certified PSP security consultant to the team. To find a qualified consultant, contact the International Association of Professional Security Consultants (IAPSC) at www.iapsc.org/.

8.2.3 The Request for Proposal

The RFP is the most inclusive method for obtaining costs and establishing project criteria. An RFP contains all the elements of an RFQ but replaces equipment descriptions with performance criteria. This means that the specification describes what the system is supposed to accomplish, not what equipment to use. Base performance criteria on the needs identified in the system design. There are several forms of RFP. The most commonly used types for security projects are:

- Firm Fixed Price
- Fixed Price with Economic Adjustment
- Fixed Price with Incentive
- Fixed Ceiling Price with Retroactive Adjustments
- Cost Plus
- Cost Sharing
- Cost Plus Incentive
- Cost Plus Fixed Fee

We will only discuss the Firm Fixed Price option in this book. Many conditions accompany each type of proposal contract. For a comprehensive listing of contract types and conditions usually found in these contracts, consult the National Contract Management Association (NCMA). Information about NCMA is available at www.ncmahq.org/.

The RFP takes a top-down approach to limit the field of possible systems. It begins with a call for all interested vendors and then examines the broad parameters of system capabilities to exclude the ones that do not meet the stated criteria. By calling for offers instead of specifically asking for certain pieces of equipment, the market defines who is willing to assume the responsibilities for meeting system criteria. A detailed examination of the offers reduces the field further to the most likely candidates that will meet the established needs. The examination process continues until there is only one (or sometimes several) offers that accomplish the required goals. Much more about this is covered in Chapter 10. A review of the bidder's business plan rounds out the analysis to focus on the overall best response.

The preceding chapters assumed that we are dealing with a new installation. We will therefore confine our discussions here to the RFP for a new system and examine the elements of this approach.

8.3 PREPARING THE RFP WITH PERFORMANCE SPECIFICATIONS

An RFP with performance specifications does not refer to brand or model for the components required in system acquisition. RFPs with performance specifications tend to be the most difficult and lengthy type of bid to prepare. The performance specification identifies the needs established in the system design and then describes specific outcomes expected from the system offered. Use RFPs with performance specifications when developing a new physical security system and there are no established standards for equipment compatibility. RFPs with performance specifications are the best way to obtain a broad reach of competitive bids.

By using an RFP with performance specifications for new installations, you can describe the function that must be performed by the required physical security system and then require the vendors to explain how their systems will meet the performance criteria. Of course, this method requires considerably more time on your part in evaluating the vendor's bid responses. It also requires the greatest commitment on the part of the vendor. Apply this approach in larger, complex installations. Vendors will be reluctant to invest this much effort in relatively small projects. A general rule of thumb is that larger systems have a budget of more than $100,000.

RFPs with performance specifications will allow you to engage the vendors in a discourse about the optimum solutions defined in the system design as compared to the products available from all potential vendors. It is the recommended approach to obtain the broadest response in the marketplace and an examination of all competitive options. This approach also shares the burden of system description and system performance with the vendor, thereby allowing you to evaluate all the company's choices without introducing a bias in the evaluation process.

Using the RFP approach requires you to be intimately familiar with the value and limitations of certain product features to determine if these features may be useful to the company when investing in a physical security system. Conducting this process should be done by a systems expert, well qualified in the technical aspects of system design and be certified by ASIS International as a PSP. A novice should not attempt to use the RFP approach without support and guidance. Evaluating RFPs requires years of experience in system design and a strong background in the nuances of security system installation techniques. If you are not a systems expert, add the services of a PSP certified consultant to the project team.

Using the RFP approach makes comparing prices on an item-by-item basis very difficult. This is because the manufacturers do not build or price their systems the same way. However, the "bottom line" is the most important pricing element, regardless of individual component pricing. Even though it is difficult to make price comparisons on individual components, you can compare the total cost of the proposals to determine the best value. Again, more on this is presented in Chapter 10.

Use major subtotals for additional comparisons to help provide a more detailed analysis of the offers made in RFP responses. For instance, separate labor from material and break down final hookup and installation. Further, subdivide materials into network equipment and field equipment. This subdivision gives a clearer picture of the cost for devices proposed to control openings and the common equipment used to support those devices. These price breakdowns can give an indication of the future costs of system additions.

One of the techniques I have used successfully in the past is to include in my RFP a future forecast. By that I mean project how many endpoint devices will be added in the next 5–7 years. The period selected is the anticipated life expectancy of the system under consideration. All electronic systems have a "site life". Certainly you may expect wear and tear but the real issue is technological advancement. After 5 years on site, with products constantly being enhanced, your system could be relegated to the status of bear skins and stone knives! The forecast can help with some of that. By projecting the future use you anticipate AND asking for long-term pricing on maintenance and upgrades, you will get to peer into the future of the products you are considering. More on this will be discussed later.

Regardless of how the analysis subdivides the numbers, the "bottom line" is what matters in a price comparison. Evaluate the proposals in other areas. Some of these are:

- Product hardware
- Product software
- Installation methods
- Technical skills (of the support staff)
- Business experience
- Technical Experience
- Licensing
- Stability of the firm (both the vendor and the manufacturer)
- Documentation provided with the system
- Training
- User support after the sale

8.4 THE SINGLE STEP RFP

The single step RFP requires that the bidders supply all the information needed in their response for the final selection process. This means that all the technical considerations and the financial considerations will be lumped together in a single response document – therefore providing you all the information needed to choose the appropriate vendor. This approach has the advantage of saving time and minimizing the bid cost when soliciting vendors for a new project. An RFP tends to be more useful in situations where the technical aspect of the system design is relatively simple, but use a two-phase RFP for more complex installations.

8.5 THE TWO-PHASE RFP

The two-phase approach allows more opportunities to examine product features closely and not compel vendors to disclose price information and other competitive data early in the process. The two-phase RFP begins with a technical evaluation of the offers in Phase 1 and then limits the bidders who are allowed to participate in Phase 2 to only those companies that can meet the technical criteria.

The two-phase RFP process assumes that the bid will occur in two steps or phases. The first phase is "Discovery" and defines the technical parameters of the security needs of the company and other considerations required by the company's management team. In Phase 1, the vendors have an opportunity to specifically address how they would solve the company's problems using their system. This may reveal new, important features to use in the proposed security solutions. This step brings the vendors in partnership with you and the company. The analysis of Phase 1 will also help identify "deal breakers" or features that may not be available in some manufacturers' products.

For instance, if the management team determines that the solution must include component communications on the company's Local Area Network

(LAN), Phase 1 will eliminate all manufacturers who do not have this capability. This reduces the number of offers to review and only those companies that can meet these criteria will participate in Phase 2. This saves time, effort and expense for all.

The second stage of a two-phase RFP provides the business deal and solicits financial offers and terms from the vendors. The evaluation of both submittals is necessary to arrive at a valid recommendation for the most responsive bidder. In nearly all cases, the single phase RFP is used; therefore, we will confine our further discussion here to that method.

8.6 ORGANIZING THE RFP

It is important to organize information in a bid to allow quick and easy comparisons and justify recommendations. This helps the bidders and you to focus on the comparison of solutions.

To accomplish this, the RFP must be well organized and indexed. Borrowing from the techniques used in Federal Government contracting is an organization pattern called the "Work Breakdown Structure" or WBS. A WBS separates the component parts of the project into clearly definable tasks and features so that the reader can verify that all the elements of the work are included and so that bid responses can be easily compared. Anyone who has ever tried to compare two or more reports from writers with substantially different points of view will be able to appreciate the value of a WBS.

In the case of security system RFPs, the process has been modified somewhat and focuses more on system capabilities than work steps, but the concept is still the same. The WBS separates the features and capabilities identified in the system design. The WBS identifies each feature individually by section and the vendors are required to respond to each section. It is then easier to compare proposals because all respondents record their answers in the same place.

For instance, if anti-passback is a required feature and the RFP calls for a description of how this feature works in the offered system, the feature question would be labeled with an index number, like, "4.3". All vendors will be required to describe their system's anti-passback capabilities in section "4.3". If this is not done, the description of the feature may be anywhere in the bid and the bid could be many pages long. By using an index, comparing features side by side will be much easier. When evaluating the RFP, it will be also be easier to question the vendors by referring to specific sections of their response to ensure complete understanding.

The evaluation can rank RFP responses if using weighted measures (more on this is presented in Chapter 9, "Getting Approval for the RFP"). Ranking allows the evaluation to assess each feature based on the stated outcome as it relates to the specification. Ranking assigns a numeric value to each feature for objective comparisons. It will be easier to support the recommendation using this objective ranking system and will help justify the conclusions reached when selecting the recommended vendor.

8.7 PREPARING THE RFP, DOING IT ON YOUR OWN

Earlier the discussion suggested partnering with the Purchasing Department for the acquisition and drew a line between the technical aspects of the bid and the business aspects. In most cases, a purchasing department will have ready-made bid document business sections that were preapproved by the management team. Use these for your bid's business section. In the next chapter we will discuss the technical portion of the bid but here we are going to assume you either do not have a ready-made bid document or for some reason you are not at liberty to use it. So if you are constructing your own "from scratch", here are some suggestions.

8.7.1 Cover Page

The RFP will have a cover page that provides the name of the project, the company soliciting the bid and some unique reference that will permit this project to be clearly distinguished from other bid requests from the company. This is typically a "project number" consisting of alphanumeric characters. The company will usually have a project numbering plan in place and you should discuss this designation with the company's purchasing office. If the company does not

Request for Proposal

By
(Company and Company Address)

For

Project: (Project Number)
Entrance Gate Surveillance System

Prepared by

(Security Professional)

Pre-Bid Conference (Date, Time and Location)

BIDS DUE: (Date and Time)

All bids must be submitted on or before the Bid Date at the time specified in a sealed envelope or package as described in the specifications to:

(Company Purchasing Office Address and Contact Person)

Bids may be hand delivered, or mailed. Early submission is recommended.

(Release Date)
Release (Issue Number)

FIGURE 8.1 Example of RFP Cover Page.

have a project numbering plan, you will use a unique project name. This will reduce confusion in discussing this project with others. Contact information for you is also required and will include your name, firm name, address, telephone, fax and e-mail address. The project date and "issue number" will also be on the cover page.

Issue number (or revision number) is helpful when there are multiple versions of the RFP. The issue number will help distinguish the most current version. Also include the "Bid Due Date" and "Bid Time" to ensure that the vendors are fully aware of submittal deadlines. Figure 8.1 is an example of an RFP cover page.

The second page is a "Table of Contents" to help the reader find information quickly and easily. Each section will be number as described above. The numbering plan is flexible but the recommended approach is to separate the information into top-level numbered sections and then arrange the subtopics under each section. Within each subtopic, number the individual features or components of each section. Include the page number beside the description of the topic.

8.7.2 The Bid Sections

Part of the objective in preparing the bid is to help the company build a good business relationship with the bidder that will provide and service the proposed solutions. Two of the cornerstones of a solid business relationship are communications and agreement. The bid is more than a simple price request; it is the "contract" between the company and the bidder. Constructing a good contract means considering all the aspects of a business relationship and making provisions for each aspect that is fair and reasonable. Your bid request represents the company in this transaction and must provide for the company's needs at the lowest overall cost. However, a one-sided business deal is not the bargain it may seem. Bidders who become trapped into delivering products and services at a price below fair market value or who are compelled to render unreasonable levels of service without adequate compensation will not approach the project with enthusiasm.

Sometimes, the bidder makes an error in price calculations or the true nature of the obligation is not clear before the agreement is accepted. There exists a legal obligation to fulfill the contract so the bidder will make efforts to comply. However, one may expect the bidder in such circumstances to take every avenue allowed to reduce cost and minimize labor effort. Thus, the focus of the project from the bidder's perspective changes from doing the best job possible to doing a job that meets minimal acceptance standards so they may be discharged from the obligation.

You can help avoid such difficult situations by making the business plan as clear and forthcoming as possible. If the RFP fully explains all of the expectations and limitations of the agreement, bidders will have a greater opportunity to understand what is expected of them and what constitutes outstanding performance. The bid establishes the agreement for the initial installation and sets the stage for the subsequent agreements for system additions and maintenance. Construct each section of the agreement with the understanding that this document will endure far beyond the initial installation. The bid represents a bilateral agreement between the company and the bidder. The purchase order resulting from the bid will most likely be referred to the bid document as the basis for agreement. It is important that this document be complete and accurate. The subsections below provide examples for constructing the bid.

8.7.3 Scope of Work

The scope of work defines the limits within which this system will be acquired. Adding a phrase that would set the stage for system acquisition is:

> The vendor shall provide a complete and working system in every respect to meet the objectives set forth in this RFP.

But broad, sweeping definitions like this can sometimes be confusing to vendors if the limits of the terms are not fully described. The RFP scope of work will explain how far the vendor must go to make the system complete. For instance, it is usually a better idea to require company personnel to enter cardholder information into new systems. This approach has the benefits of establishing familiarity with the system by in-house personnel and permits the individual doing the data entry to customize system programming to more closely match with internal nomenclature.

An example of this might be how to enter an employee card authorization in the system. Also, vendors are reluctant to assume responsibility for such labor-intensive tasks where little technical expertise is required. Vendors will not want to use high-cost skill resources for simple data entry functions. This will increase the overall project cost without a corresponding benefit. The scope of work will then continue:

> The vendor shall be required to provide a complete and working system as described in this RFP. The vendor's work shall be limited to providing all locks, card readers, alarm contacts and other endpoint devices to provide input to the security system network. The vendor shall also be required to provide all labor, tools and material necessary to install, test and fully implement this system except for certain programming features as defined herein. The vendor shall establish all tables, access control parameters and other system programming features but will not be required to enter the data that establishes the parameters of these features. The company shall provide the labor resources necessary to enter cardholder information, alarm information and access control information with the assistance of the vendor. The vendor shall supervise

> this data input ensuring that company personnel are performing system programming as required.

By clearly delineating responsibilities and scope of work, the RFP shall avoid some potential conflicts during system implementation. This will help to enhance the relationship with the vendor and ensure proper installation and implementation of the acquired system.

In addition to this primary objective, explain other goals that help provide a more complete picture of the intention of the RFP. For instance, the secondary objective may be:

> In addition to providing an access control and alarm monitoring system for this facility, it is the intention of the company to integrate this new electronic physical security system into the existing company data network. This system is to make use of existing LAN network where possible and take full advantage of the security and communication protocols already established for the company's management information system.

The RFP may have as many secondary objectives as needed to fully describe the company's intention in preparing this RFP. Remember that the purpose of the RFP is to establish a complete and comprehensive set of objectives for the bidders.

8.7.4 Invitation to Bid

The invitation to bid describes the intent of the offer. Some of the usual and customary paragraphs included in this section make these points:

1. State that this is a request for bid and describe the criteria for participation.
2. State your name, firm name and contact information.
3. Show the company's name, purchasing department, purchasing contact and bid address for receipt of bid.
4. Provide the date and time the bid is due.
5. State that this is a sealed bid.
6. Provide an overall description of the system and where the system will be located.
7. Refer to the bid for the equipment description and quantities. This section may also contain amendments or adjustments to the initial system configuration that alter the original scope of work or technical parameters.
8. If this is to be a "turn-key" installation, state so in the RFP. Use the phrase, "a working system, complete in every way" to make clear that the bidders must supply all that the labor and material required for full functionality.

"Turnkey" is a common term used in various technology industries. As the name implies, the buyer simply has to "turn the key" to make the system work.

9. Provide a general statement that describes default conditions when elements of this RFP conflict with any of the general terms and conditions of the company or applicable laws. The possibility for conflict exists even in carefully written documents. Most RFP writers are not both security professionals and lawyers, so provisions should be made when the RFP conflicts with previously established rules. State that where such conflicts exist the general terms and conditions of the company's purchasing policies, the company's rules will apply.
10. State that any or all bids may be rejected without reason and include a statement that informality or irregularity in bids may be waived at the owner's discretion.
11. Require the bidders to attend a mandatory pre-bid conference and, the date and time of that meeting. As in, this is a face-to-face meeting to clarify requirements.
12. In cases where the installation requires turn-key performance, state that this is a "all or none" opportunity. This says that labor is an integral part of this offer and that the company will not accept "material only" bids. Add, "this does not preclude bidders from subcontracting some portion of the work to others but overall project responsibility must be borne by the bidder".

8.7.5 Bidder Qualifications

Bidder qualifications describe the minimum requirements a vendor must meet to be able to compete for this business. This also limits the number of competitors that may bid on the proposed system. Some of the most frequently used qualifications are:

1. Minimum number of years in a business
2. Minimum number of years as a dealer for the system proposed
3. Number of technicians trained to install and service the proposed system
4. Authorized dealer for the proposed system
5. Minimum number of installations of the proposed system done
6. Location of a service office within "X" miles from the company location
7. 24/365 service operation
8. Centralized service dispatch

This list by no means comprises all of the bidder qualifications. Determine bidder qualifications by the task and the circumstance for the acquisition of the new or upgraded system.

For instance, in installations where there is an existing electronic physical security system, add another criterion requiring the vendor to be an authorized dealer and service company for the existing electronic physical security system. Obviously, this is true only in cases where the RFP intends to add components to the existing system and not replace it.

8.7.6 Additional Bidder Qualifications

You will want to establish a criteria for a company's ability to bid on your project. The basic criteria might include:

- Authorized distributor for the product offered (certificate of authorization).
- Authorized service provider for the product offered (certificate of authorization).
- Must have a local service office.
- Minimum service response time is 2 hours.
- Equipment must be UL approved (provided by a UL registration number).

Also there are similar criteria that have an applicable bearing on the decision to accept this vendor. Some other less obvious criteria might be a minimum number of service technicians or minimum stock of spare parts. There are circumstances where it will be necessary to amend the qualification list in the RFP if you discover something meaningful that limits the market. The evaluation of bids will reveal if the RFP requires more qualifications to improve the standards used for vendor selection. For instance, if the analysis reveals that it is desirable to use the company's LAN for system communications and that was not part of the original design, the selected vendor should also be LAN certified.

Do not change the Vendor Qualifications indiscriminately. If such changes do not appear to have a legitimate basis or seem designed to exclude one or more of the bidders without good cause, there will be protests. In extreme cases, lawsuits will be filed that will delay and may even cause cancellation of the project.

8.7.7 Submittals

RFPs for large complex projects usually result in requirements for extensive vendor information submittals. The amount of information required can be confusing to vendors and omissions may occur. Include a submittal page with each RFP to provide a simple comprehensive list of items that the vendor must supply.

The Proposal Submittal page is a valuable tool that helps the vendor understand what is required in a proposal response and avoid omissions that can disqualify them from the bidding process. It provides a clear and unambiguous list of documents that are required from the vendor to bid on the project. Your submittal requirements may look like this:

1. Bidder Qualifications: The bidder shall provide a complete response to each item listed in the Bidder Qualification section of this RFP.
2. Material List to meet system design specifications, including:
   a. Description and quantity of products proposed
   b. Names of manufacturers and model numbers.
3. Technical specifications and sales literature on each product proposed.
4. A complete operations manual for the primary systems proposed.
5. One line block diagram of proposed system.
6. A copy of this RFQ, signed by an OFFICER of the bidder's company indicating acknowledgment of the RFP and all subsequent amendments. List amendments by number on the signature page. The RFP signature page (usually the last page of the RFP) must be signed by an "officer" of the bidder's company indicating acknowledgment of the terms and conditions contained in the RFP and an acknowledgment of all addendums described by Addendum Number.
7. Submit a complete response to all item listed in "Additional Vendor Qualifications".
8. Submit a list of products or services (except commercial power) that the company must furnish to make this a complete and working system.
9. Submit a bid bond equal to X% of the purchase price of the contract (this is usually 5%).
10. A X% (usually 100%) performance bond will be required with this contract.
11. Submit the following insurance certificates:
    - Workman's Compensation
    - Liability
    - Material Loss (see Equipment Storage).
12. Submit prices for the proposed system in accordance with the Pricing Requirements section of this RFP that includes all the elements in the block diagram.
13. Submit a letter from the manufacturer of the proposed system stating that the bidder is an authorized distributor or dealer and how long that dealer has represented that manufacturer.
14. Submit a training syllabus as required in Post-Installation Support.
15. Submit the warranty description required in Post-Installation Support.
16. Submit a Dun and Bradstreet identification number for the bidder and the primary equipment manufacturer.

17. Submit a list of at least five other similar systems sold and installed by the bidder. Include in this list the name and address of the company, the contact person, and title and their telephone number.

Require the vendor to submit all documents described with one original and "X" copies (the number of copies should include one for each member of the system selection committee and one for you. The purchasing manager will hold the original.) The above list may include items you do not feel are necessary for your buying decision. Every case is different so only choose the criteria that will aid in your decision process.

Require the vendor to submit the bid typewritten on 8 ½ X 11 plain white paper using a font not smaller than 10 pitch or not larger than 14 pitch. Specify that the bid must have a cover page showing the project description as provided on the cover of the RFP and list the vendor's company name, address, telephone and fax numbers (and web site if applicable). Require the cover page to indicate the name and telephone number (if different) of the contact person and his/her e-mail address.

The RFP should require the vendor to assemble the entire package in a suitable binder (the exact type of binding is not important) and stipulate that the binder include an index as the first page with tabs or similar stationary supplies showing the start of each indexed section. Allow the bidder to include other documents at the bidder's discretion that would clarify their bid. But add: "The indexing and sections described in the RFP should be strictly adhered to and other documents that are not called for in the RFP are to be added at the end of the bidder's submittal package."

Instruct the bidder on how to package the bid. The purpose of this regimented organization is to make reviewing and evaluating the bidder's submittal easier for the company and you. This is more than just a matter of convenience, if bid information is difficult to find, the review may miss important details.

8.7.8 Electronic Submittal

However, in today's world of technology, paper submittals are more tedious to manage than what is necessary. A technique that has been effective for me is to require a single paper copy so that the company has original documents with original signatures in case there are disputes, but then to also require an electronic version submitted on suitable media included with the package in lieu of multiple copies. The electronic version of the bid can then be shared and reviewed more easily, especially if there are multiple evaluators.

Now, of course, this assumes a major project with sealed bids; but if you have a small project, there is no "sealed bid" requirement from Purchasing and you are evaluating the bids on your own, the commonly accepted technique is to request offers by e-mail and usually in an Adobe PDF format.

But now back to assuming this is a major project …Most US Federal Government contracts require electronic submittals for large RFPs.

Specify the acceptable programs and use common electronic tools such as MS Word, and Adobe Acrobat . This will help when sharing and discussing the bids. This will also reduce the paper burden in the process. The most useful format is Adobe PDF. This file format can represent all other programs that can print to an ordinary computer printer. Adobe PDF simply takes the output that would normally go to a paper printer and converts it to a readable image that looks just like paper. If an electronic submittal is used, it can save considerable time and effort.

8.7.9 Bid Requirements

Bid requirements provide "boundaries" for the bid process. Sometimes there are unique aspects to an environment or installation that require clarification. In other cases, clarity is not the issue but latitude for the bidder. Well-written RFPs will help produce good purchase agreements, minimize contract disputes and increase mutual understanding. Add terms and conditions in the RFP that clarify vendor performance and expectations.

The "rule of thumb" is that if you do not specify something, bidders are open to select the option that suits them best. There is nothing wrong with giving bidders some leeway, as far as it does not affect the quality of the product or service delivered.

8.7.10 Basic Definitions

Explain terms used in the RFP that may cause confusion by the bidders. This section is not essential unless certain nonstandard terms are used.

8.7.11 Verifying Conditions

State that certain preexisting conditions may exist that could have a bearing on the price quoted. Advise the bidders that they are responsible for informing themselves of any preexisting condition. Make clear that the bidder shall be responsible for any additional costs for system modifications resulting from preexisting conditions after award of contract. Of course, this also means that you must afford all bidders a chance to view all conditions before rendering a bid. That is addressed in part later in the discussion on the Pre-Bid Meeting.

8.7.12 Owner Requirements

Require the bidder to specify facilities or services required by the owner to provide a complete and working system. An example is as follows: The RFP requires the bidder to use the company's LAN for system communication. This interface requires communications devices that are compatible with the LAN. Company network managers usually want full control over any devices connected to their network. The bidder would require the company to furnish these devices.

Require the bidder to clearly describe all devices or services the company must furnish. If the requirement contains technical devices to work with bidder-provided equipment, like personal computers, the bidder must provide a full technical description of the required equipment. Also, state in this section that if the bidder fails to describe these devices, the bidder will be responsible for providing these products or services at their expense.

8.7.13 Life Safety Considerations

In some installations, state fire marshal's (SFM) approval is required for the interface of any locking system to a fire alarm system. State that the bidder must create these submittals for the state fire marshal and submit them to the company for presentation to the SFM. State that approval from the SFM is required before making connections to the fire alarm panel.

A catchall phrase also helps to include the bidder in the burden of compliance, "The bidder shall comply with all applicable local, state and federal regulations concerning life safety. Failure to comply will be at the bidder's peril. Costs associated with compliance after system installation will be borne by the bidder". The company cannot relieve themselves of life safety responsibilities in this way, but including the bidder's responsibility in the RFP adds bidder liability and provides the company with recourse if the bidder violates life safety rules.

8.7.14 Prior Approvals

The RFP should require the bidders to install the same system described in their bid. However, since the bid process may take several months and system manufacturers change or substitute system components, such changes place bidders in technical violation of the RFP. Describe the conditions under which a bidder may receive prior approval in the RFP. State the timeframes allotted for substituting or changing system components and the terms and conditions for changes. Describe the submittals required for making a technical comparison. If the substitute products have equal or greater capabilities, grant prior approvals to the bidders.

8.7.15 Insurance

Most state laws require companies to provide Workman's Compensation Insurance. Require these certificates in the RFP. To protect the company from liability exposure, require the bidders to provide Liability Insurance in the RFP. Discuss this requirement with company Purchasing, there may be pre-established limits for this insurance. If such limits exist, add them to the RFP.

In either case, add to the RFP a "Hold Harmless Clause". This requires the bidder/vendor to relieve the company of any liability burden for faults created by the bidder/vendor in the course of fulfilling the contract. These protection clauses provide another modest layer of protection for the company. The insurance company, upon request from the bidder, will issue a certificate protecting the company.

> Note:
>
> This submittal should be required after a letter of intent is received by the most responsive bidder but before the purchase order is issued. The purpose of putting it in the RFP is that there will be no surprises when it is time to award the contract.

8.7.16 Bid Bond and Performance Bond

Bid bonds are usually required in construction jobs to ensure that the bidder will honor the bid price submitted. The bid bond provides this guarantee by allowing the bondholder to file a claim against the bid bond if the bidder fails to honor the price offered in the bid. The claim permits the bondholder to recover the difference between the bid price and the price paid by the bondholder to engage another contractor if the bidder defaults on delivery.

Bid bonds help to establish the financial stability of bidders. In order to obtain a bid bond, a company must also be able to obtain performance bonds. Financial companies issue performance bonds after a review of a bidder's business. They must fund the completion of work should the bidder fail to finish the project. Therefore, requesting a bid bond ensures that the bidder has the wherewithal to obtain a performance bond. Bid bonds are a good indication of a bidder's financial stability.

In most situations involving the installation of a new physical security system, a performance bond does not substantially enhance the company's position in the award of contract. Usually, withholding payments will serve as sufficient motivation to guaranty that the bidder finishes what they start. Moreover, a well-crafted payment schedule (earned value schedule) will encourage quick substantial completion. Performance bonds serve little purpose in these circumstances and are usually not recommended. This item was included so that the reader would be aware of the tool.

There are costs associated with bid and performance bonds but these costs provide certain benefits to the outcome of the project. Use bid bonds on all major installations to confirm that a financial professional reviewed the bidders' performance history and found them a capable provider. Performance bonds are substantially more expensive than bid bonds and, as explained above, do not usually provide additional value in these installations. Do not plan to use performance bonds but discuss the option with the company's purchasing agent. There is often a standing policy in most company purchasing offices on the use of these financial instruments.

8.7.17 Pricing Requirements

In most cases, the bid process results in a turnkey installation by the selected bidder. There are several ways to arrange these contracts but the one used most often in these situations is the firm fixed price agreement.

Firm fixed price agreements require the bidder to submit a single price that includes all of the labor and material necessary to complete the work. Other information required in the RFP, such as material inventory and block diagrams, serve to confirm that the firm fixed price quoted covers all of the areas that are to be included in the system design.

Use a "Pricing Form" or at least specify a format. You may allow the bidder to also submit pricing in their format but make response to your format mandatory. Figure 8.2 is an example of a pricing form.

The reason for this should be obvious but in case it isn't, remember that you have to compare these bids. Bidders use substantially different pricing formats that are usually based on their particular kind of system design. Sometimes they are easy to compare, but usually they are not. If you try to interpret their pricing and "normalize" their format into a consistent structure that you can easily compare, you could be mistaken and wind up making decisions on bad data. So by compelling the bidders to structure their pricing to meet your requirements your comparison job becomes much easier.

Page 1 of 3

Access Control System Request for Proposal
ATTACHMENT 5: PRICING FORM

Date: 710/16/17
Revision: 0

1. Configuration

Please provide a list of components with a "one-line" connection diagram for your offer that would make a complete and working, stand alone system. This sample system should include the maximum number of card readers available to a network panel and any supporting equipment your product needs for communications, alarm input boards and relay output boards to meet the specification in our statement of work. You may exclude locks, lock power and alarm point devices but please include every device necessary for a complete and working system.

We will use your prices and diagram to assess your billing for each facility if you are awarded the contract. The illustration should be attachment to the Pricing Form. Below is am EXAMPLE of the illustration required.

As necessary you may attached pages to your submittal to explain your pricing or cite special conditions of cost.

Typical School

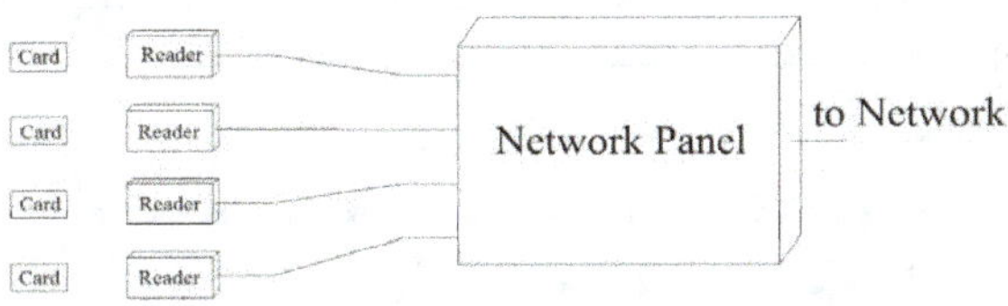

2. Pricing Form, Access Control

Please insert your prices for the products and services itemized below:

	Material		Labor	
Access Control Devices:	**Your Product Number**	**Unit Price**	**Equipment Mounting (2)**	**Termination and Testing (1)**
cards				
card reader				
Network Panels				
OPTIONAL Host Processor, see Attachment 1, para 1.4.18				
Host Processor Software				
Other Products Required in your System but not Shown Above				

	Material		Labor	
Optional Products:	**Your Product Number**	**Unit Price**	**Equipment Mounting (2)**	**Termination and Testing (1)**
Photo ID Software and Camera				
Hole Punch (for ID cards)				
Laminator (for ID cards)				
Visitor Management System				
CCTV Control and Management				

FIGURE 8.2 Pricing Form.

Ascension Parish School System
Access Control System Request for Proposal
ATTACHMENT 5: PRICING FORM

Print Date: 10/16/17
Revision: 0

3. Cabling:	Material Cost per Foot	Installation Cost per Foot (2)	Wire Brand	Wire Number
IP Terminal to Network Panel				
Network Panel to Reader				
Network Panel to Door Lock				
Network Panel to Alarm Input Point				
Network Panel to Output Point				
Rigid Metal Conduit				

4. Pricing Form, Auxiliary Systems

By adding prices to this section the proposer agrees to perform the installations required

	Material Costs Unit Price	Labor: Equipment Mounting (2)	Labor: Final Termination and Testing (1)
Potter Hold up Switch, HUB-M			
NEMA 1 Type enclosure			
12 position barrier strip			
Altronix RBSN isolation relays (3)			
Edwards trivolt transformers (3)			
Altronix RB7 isolation relay boards (3)			
Altronix AL300ULPD8 power module (3)			
Designed Security, Inc Switch Bank (4)			
Strobe Lights LED625H-X (5)			

Notes:

(1) If final termination is not included in equipment mounting, show as a separate price here.
(2) Must include misc hardware as needed for installation.
(3) (1) Other manufacturer's products may be substituted if they are exact equivalents.
(4) See Attachment 1A for product details and contact information for the manufacturer.
(5) Other products may be substituted, criteria: wall . Ceiling mount, 4" - 6" tall, 2" - 4" wide, red dome, 12 / 24 VDC, flashing

FIGURE 8.2 (Continued)

Page 3 of 3

Access Control System Request for Proposal
ATTACHMENT 5: PRICING FORM

Date:
Revision: 0

5.

	Year 1	**Year 2**	**Year 3**
ONSITE Maintenance Agreement (*) Full coverage for all labor and material	________	________	________
ONSITE Maintenance Agreement (*) OPTIONAL Labor Only	________	________	________

* Commences with the expiration of the 12 month warranty

6. Signature

The signature below was provided by an officer of our company or an individual authorized to legally bind the company for contract offers.

We acknowledge that all cost associated with this installation are itemized here Any labor or material required but not shown above were documented on the attached itemization that also bears my signature

We hereby certify that these prices will be valid for 30 days following bid opening and if we are awarded the order these prices will be valid for 2 years from the date of award

Company Name ____________________

Name of Officer or Authorized Representative ____________________

Signature ____________________

Date ____________________

Number of pages attached (1) ________

(1) must be filled in put 0 (zero) if none

FIGURE 8.2 (Continued)

8.7.18 Recommended Spares

In addition to the firm fixed price, ask the bidder to provide a list of recommended spare parts. The company will maintain these parts for use with the installed system. This approach helps to guarantee that parts are readily available for service calls. Require the bidder to include unit prices for each part.

8.7.19 Projected Cost for Major System Components

In addition to the list of recommended spares, request the bidder to submit a price schedule that illustrates the unit cost of each of the major system components. Require this schedule to be valid for at least 1 year. This will permit you to establish a cost forecast for system additions and assist in determining the system with the best value. This approach also places a ceiling on prices for the period chosen. Extend this forecast and price ceiling in large installations to 3 years. The intent of these requirements is to prevent a bidder from offering a low initial price to receive the contract and then substantially increase the price for system additions.

8.7.20 Anticipated Future Work

Although this section is not generally required in RFPs, it is usually a good idea to provide the vendors with an expectation of other works that will follow the installation of the proposed system. There are two key reasons for describing the anticipated work to be done at the conclusion of the current project.

The first is to illustrate the potential income for the vendor if awarded the contract is for this project. By providing realistic expectations of other works that will follow, the vendor will have an overall appreciation for the revenue potential available, thus encouraging them to bid the job. This perspective generally encourages more competitive pricing since there are usually substantially greater profits in a long-term relationship with the company.

The second is to provide the vendors with a forecast of upcoming projects to allow for technical considerations in the initial purchase. There are circumstances where purchasing larger system capacities on the initial order can reduce expenses in future years to expand the proposed system. The vendors know how future equipment additions affect their system price. Providing a forecast of future expectations allows the vendor to assist the company in the planning process.

If the company expects security needs to grow rapidly in the first few years, request a long-term price forecast from the bidders. Provide the bidders with a purchase forecast of system additions and require that they submit price projections for known system elements. This could be tedious if taken to extremes. Limit these long-range projections to the provision of major equipment components and technical labor. Exclude installation and end piece devices such as locks, alarm contacts and exit push buttons to make bidding and evaluation easier.

8.7.21 Annual Hardware Maintenance

Require the bidder to state the anticipated annual hardware maintenance cost for the proposed system and state when the maintenance contract begins and ends.

8.7.22 Maintenance Forecast

Require maintenance costs for 3 years following the expiration of the system warranty. This forward looking cost projection prevents the bidder from providing an initial low price only to recover these lost profits at the conclusion of the initial contract. Bidders do not want to be in a money losing or break-even position for 3 years. This forecast will provide clues about the bidder's pricing strategy.

8.7.23 Annual Software Maintenance

Software is the fastest change item in most manufacturers' catalog. Be sure that software maintenance is included in the offer. This may be a separate contract with the system manufacturer but the bidder will administer it. Request the bidder to provide software license and maintenance fees for a period of 3 years following expiration of system warranty.

8.8 EXECUTING THE CONTRACT

The execution of contract section provides general terms and conditions under which the work shall take place. In this section, explain how the bidder is to perform while on-site and add any unique conditions to avoid or give special attention.

8.8.1 Requirements after Acceptance of Bid

Determine if there are special conditions that require the bidder's attention or action before starting the work. Add such actions to the RFP. Always include a requirement for the following:

1. Completions Schedule (firm installation schedule)
2. Schedule of Earned Values (when will payments be requested for each billable item)

An example of another requirement is registering the contract with local authorities. Contract registrations simply means that the agreement between the company and the bidder becomes a matter of public record and follows certain rules and guidelines. The company's purchasing office will usually have a policy regarding contract registration and the RFP should reflect that policy.

8.8.2 Equipment Substitutions

Stipulate in the RFP that written prior approval is required for equipment substitutions (see Section 8.7.14 Prior Approvals, preceding).

8.8.3 Scheduling

Require the bidders to submit a commitment for the earliest installation start date. In some cases, the ability to start a project quickly will have a bearing on the award of contract. In those cases, advise the bidder of the desired installation interval.

Require the bidder to provide an installation schedule expressed in "man days" for each set of tasks. This completion schedule is the man-time needed for the installation, not calendar dates for completion of work. In comparing offers, there may be situations where several bidders would propose the same equipment and have near identical prices. Completion time may be a deciding factor in these circumstances.

8.8.4 Equipment Storage

Define how the bidder intends to store the equipment before the installation in the RFP. This can vary in importance based on where and when "delivery" will actually take place. Put another way, define the point in the process at which the company owns the equipment. This is not a minor detail. It is important to specify the point of ownership because equipment may be lost or damaged before installation due to unforeseen events. Contract disputes may arise regarding the replacement of this equipment if the point of ownership is not clearly established.

The term Freight on Board (FOB) is generally used to indicate the place for accepting equipment. The FOB point is usually the company's receiving area. However, the RFP must define what constitutes delivery. What complicates the issue is equipment staging and testing. The RFP will require the vendor to stage the system (see below) but the vendor will want to effect delivery so that they may bill for the hardware.

Equally important is "when" the system equipment is accepted. Regardless of the physical location of the equipment acceptance, the RFP must define the point in the process where the company will accept ownership of the system equipment. Stipulate in the RFP that the company will accept equipment at the vendor's place of business, under the following conditions:

1. All equipment for the entire system installation is on hand (minus cable and connectors).
2. The bidder must provide an inventory of the equipment delivered before the inventory inspection (matching the equipment list required in bid submittal. The inventory must include the serial numbers of all major items of equipment.
3. The bidder will submit to a physical inspection of the equipment and verification of the inventory by you. (The RFP will permit the bidder to bill for the equipment after this initial inventory).

4. The bidder will provide adequate insurance to protect the equipment against all forms of loss until the system is installed on the company's premises. Insurance certificates may be required in the RFP.
5. At physical delivery (FOB), the bidder will again allow a physical inventory of the equipment for verification. A clerk in the Receiving Department usually does this. The clerk will verify that the equipment arrived at the company's loading dock and the serial numbers of that equipment. This requirement allows a cross-check against the inventory at the bidder's place of business versus the inventory of delivered goods. This second inventory is important because some of the equipment will be installed above ceilings or in other areas that are difficult to access for verification.

8.8.5 System Staging

One of the most troubling aspects of a new installation is "infant mortality". This term refers to the failure of a system device shortly after installation. To minimize these failings, require the bidder to "stage" the system before installation. Staging means to connect all major system devices together in the bidder's workshop and test the system for at least 72 hours. This burn-in period can usually identify borderline components that the bidder must replace before system delivery.

Usually, endpoint devices such as locks or alarm contacts are not subject to staging. This test identifies critical components that require data communication to operate properly. Require the bidder to assemble the major component parts, power up those parts and then demonstrate the use of the entire system.

Require the bidder to electrically test the end point devices in the RFP. Require the bidder to power up electrical devices and verify operation. Require the bidder to meter non-power devices (e.g., door status switches) for proper signaling operation.

8.8.6 Job Site Rules and Regulations for Vendors

Describe the conduct expended of vendor employees in this section of the RFP. In some cases, there are time constraints that prohibit the bidder from working after normal working hours. Describe the times of the day and days of the week the bidder may perform work on the premises and any special access permissions the workmen need.

An example of this may be requiring the bidder's workmen to wear identification badges and to check in with the company's security force upon arrival at the job site. Also, include general conditions for workmen conduct. For instance, prohibit the use of profane language or loud speech. Also, prohibit the workmen from playing music or any other conduct that is disruptive to company employees.

Include in this section of the RFP a description of cleanup responsibilities. Most electronic systems have protective packaging for shipment to job sites. Make it clear that the vendor is to dispose of this material and any recommended methods for that disposal.

8.8.7 Supervision of Work (Project Management)

Require the vendor to provide a project manager to interface with you and supervise the vendor's employees while on the company's premises. Direct the vendor to channel all questions that arise during the installation through the project manager to you. This will reduce confusion and foster good communications.

You will act as the company's representative in all circumstances. This does not mean that you must have all the answers but must be the first person to receive the question. You will direct the vendor's project manager to the company employee who can properly answer the question.

Require the vendor to hold periodic meetings to review the progress of the installation. On very large, complex installations, hold these meetings weekly. For smaller installations, require these meetings at installation milestones. Those milestones are:

1. All equipment on site
2. Completion of cabling
3. Completion of equipment mounting
4. Completion of final hook up
5. Preliminary test
6. Final test

Invite selected company employees to coordination meetings when there are issues concerning their department. The Information Technologies department plays an important role in the implementation of security systems and is usually involved early in the process.

8.8.8 Split Contracts

A split contract is a circumstance in which the company elects to provide some portion of the labor or material themselves while requiring the vendor to provide the remainder for a complete and working system. Cost containment is the usual motive or to take advantage of existing facilities or personnel that are available to the company and not utilized for other functions. Although there is a certain value to the cost savings in this approach, it is fraught with problems and even under the best circumstances can result in conflicts between the vendor and the company and a potentially dysfunctional system.

For example, the company may have a staff of electricians who routinely do work in the facility. In an effort to fully employ these electricians and to reduce the cost of the security system installation, the management team may suggest that company personnel provide the cabling and equipment-mounting portion of the work.

On the surface, this sounds like a desirable outcome but the results are usually not as beneficial as it would initially seem. This is especially true if the personnel elected to do the installation have never performed this type of work in the past. If in-house personnel installed devices improperly and damage occurs, serious equipment liability issues can arise. This can lead to contract disputes and ill will between the company and the vendor.

Avoid split contracts whenever possible to minimize company and vendor frustration. Coordination in these situations is often difficult and it can be nearly impossible to clearly delineate lines of responsibility for correcting system anomalies. The savings in dollars do not always warrant the risks associated with split contracts. If you must use a split contract, the best approach is to limit company employees to cable pulls and equipment mounting but specifically exclude connecting cabling to equipment. This is a vendor exclusive task.

8.8.9 Change Orders

"The best laid plans of mice and men may sometimes go astray". Although you will endeavor to be thorough and accurate in the creation of system performance specifications, company circumstances may change or the environment may change, thereby requiring alternative approaches. In such cases, the RFP must provide for ways to change the existing plan. Those changes may also cause changes in the price quoted. Explain in detail the conditions for a change order. Describe how to document and submit these changes and who will receive these change orders (almost always you).

8.8.10 Default Considerations

Indicate in the RFP what constitutes default of the agreement and what action will result if vendor is in default. Define the conditions for default. This includes the inability of the system to perform as promised, the failure of the vendor to deliver in a timely manner and other conditions the company finds unacceptable.

Promised delivery intervals are part of the decision in award contract. The vendor must be permitted time to correct system anomalies but if the system fails to perform as expected in a reasonable period of time, the RFP must provide recourse for the company.

The RFP will provide what actions the company will take if the vendor is in default. This could include a demand for a full refund of all monies paid, the substitution of another system at the vendor's expense and on-site correction of anomalies by the system manufacturer.

This section will also describe the "escalation" procedures taken in the event of potential default conditions. For example, the first recourse would not be demanding a full refund. State the steps taken, in the order taken to correct problems. The progressive order provides the vendor with a specific interval to bring the system to expected standards. Failure to do so requires the next step of escalation. The next step is to require the manufacturer of the system to participate in the correction process. State a specific interval for the manufacturer to correct system deficiencies. If they cannot correct the system deficiencies, then the bidder is in default of the agreement. The vendor is then required to remove the noncompliant parts of the installed system and refund payments for labor and material used for that part of the installation. Proper planning and thorough investigations will prevent installations from arriving at this point. You are responsible for the success of the installation.

This section should also deal with the company's obligation for default. The purchasing department will be a good guide for these terms. A suggested approach is as follows:

> The (company) has the right to cancel this agreement at anytime, without cause. Said cancellation shall obligate the company to pay for all labor and material, calculated at cost, expended for the installation of this system up to the stop work notification. The company shall not be required to provide a profit to the vendor but only make the vendor whole with regard to expenditures for this project.

8.8.11 Basis of Payment

The RFP must stipulate how and when the vendor will be paid. Contract disputes occur when payment terms are not clear. Avoid such disputes by clearly describing when the vendor should invoice for payments, where to send the invoices and what can be included in each payment request.

Instruct the vendor how to request payments. Vendors have invoicing procedures and the company has payment procedures. The RFP establishes the payment terms so these two methods merge successfully. Discuss payment terms with the company's purchasing manager. They will describe considerations expected before releasing funds. Add these considerations to the RFP. In some cases, waivers against liens are required with each invoice or the use of special payment request forms.

Work closely with the company's purchasing manager to ensure that payment demands are properly structured and submitted in a timely manner for prompt payment. Require the vendor to submit a duplicate copy of all invoices to you for approval. This will permit you to verify delivery before payment is authorized.

8.9 POST-INSTALLATION SUPPORT

Even after the system is installed and working, you are not done! No security system is valuable until it is put into service. By that I mean it is being used. It is a big mistake to assume everyone will know how to use this new tool and turning it on will go smoothly … that can happen but it takes more work. Everyone in the organization must be trained on their part of using the system, including those who are just card holders and require access.

8.9.1 Personnel Training

In addition to the delivery of the installed system, the bidder must provide training for system administrators and system operators. The RFP establishes the criteria for training.

System training is a small part of the overall training the users need to fully implement the recommended solutions. The RFP should specify the vendor's portion of user training.

Require the vendor to describe in detail what system training will be provided. The extent of vendor training provides another comparison of the offers. Training is an essential part of system performance and vendor participation is essential for a successful installation. This part of the training is more for the operators of the system.

8.9.2 Warranty and Service Agreements

Require the bidder to provide a complete statement of warranty terms including a detailed description of the milestone that signals the start of this warranty and the period for which the warranty will be valid.

Warranties usually begin at system acceptance and last for 12 months. However, in business negotiations such as these, assume nothing. If the company has preestablished criteria for warranty, state these requirements for the bidders and add that these conditions nullify any contrary terms in the bidder's offer. However, it is usually prudent to simply require the bidder to state the conditions of their warranty so as not to provide too many barriers to bidder participation. Warranty descriptions include:

1. Which components are covered.
2. The length of time the coverage will exist.
3. What elements are included in the warranty (labor and/or material).
4. The milestone at which the warranty shall commence.
5. Any special conditions which may adversely affect the warranty.

Require the vendor to state the milestone for starting the warranty. Warranties sometimes begin upon delivery of equipment and sometimes when the equipment is turned on. The RFP will require the warranty to start when the System Acceptance Test is finished and when all parts of the system work as expected. The milestone for this is usually the Final Delivery Walkdown (see Chapter 11, Implementation).

The RFP will also state the duration of the warranty. Manufacturers usually provide a 12-month warranty on hardware and installing dealers offer a corresponding 12-month warranty under installation work. Do not leave the warranty terms to chance. State that the warranty should apply to all devices for at least 12 months.

Also state that the warranty must include all devices provided by the vendor (there are some cases where the company provides a portion of the equipment). Stipulate the time expected for device replacement when reported to the vendor.

Require the vendor to state how company representatives place a warranty service call. The vendor must include the contact number and, if applicable, the person to contact when placing service calls.

Add the expected response time to the RFP. Usually a 24-hour response is satisfactory but certain portions of the system may require shorter intervals. State all intervals expected.

Sometimes, warranties are "at factory", meaning that the vendor is not responsible for the expense of removing the defective equipment and sending that equipment for repair. The RFP will require 'in-field" service that sets the service point at the company's premises.

8.10 WRAP UP

This completes the Business Plan section of your requirement, next we will turn to the technical bid. As a reminder, your purchasing department may have a pre-approved and ready-made bid document for the business plan, which is always the better choice. That document may have all or some of the material covered here but it has the advantage of being "pre-approved". So your best course of action is to review the prewritten bid, compare it with what you have seen here and if something is missing and is important to you, suggest adding it to the base document. That way you get the best of both perspectives.

CHAPTER 9

Prepare the Technical Specifications

CONTENTS

9.1 INTRODUCTION TO TECHNICAL SPECIFICATIONS

In the last chapter we reviewed the means by which you would acquire your new security system. We discussed partnering with the Purchasing Department because they understand and usually control the purchasing process for the company. We learned that in this joint process the most effective division of tasks is for you to handle the technical aspects and for purchasing to handle the business arrangements. We also discussed how you would handle the business portion of the project if you did not have a formal purchasing department to rely on. Now it is time to focus on your portion of the work, the technical document.

The role of Purchasing is to tell you how to buy your new system but your role is to tell purchasing, and the market, what you want to buy. So let's get going!

9.2 PERFORMANCE SPECIFICATIONS

This will be a Request for Proposal (RFP) and, as such, must contain a performance specification. This document explains the job you are trying to accomplish

DOI: 10.4324/9781003490432-10

without necessarily telling the market "how" to accomplish this. For example, if your assessment revealed you need an access control system you will want to say you need card readers at certain doors, which side of the door the card reader will be on and what other door features may be needed … such as an electric lock, door status monitor and so forth. What you will not say is "I need 10, BR350 card readers from the ABC Company". That approach is used in a Request for Quotation (RFQ) where you have a standard and the equipment must meet the standard. The reason you do not specify equipment is to permit the market to make their best offer to meet your needs, and that way you open the door to multiple competitive offers and can choose from the best one for your situation.

9.3 DESIGN PARAMETERS

So your RFP begins with design parameters. Design parameters provide the vendor with unique technical requirements for the systems. This establishes an overview of special technical considerations within which the system must perform. The vendors should be given as much information as possible about all the goals intended for the proposed system so that adequate consideration may be given to all elements of the design criteria. For example, you may be placing your security equipment in an outdoor environment and whatever is used must be weather resistant. That would be part of the design parameters.

I had a case where that exact situation occurred, access control readers at exterior fence openings. The specification I provided the client and their engineer specifically called for exterior rated hardware. The engineer overlooked that requirement and did not include it in his technical specifications to the bidders. Thus, the bidders choose the less expensive indoor rated panic hardware for the opening. It was discovered during the final acceptance and an exception noted for the client. Somewhere along the line someone failed to follow up on the exception and I was called out a year later to investigate why those openings failed to lock properly. The interior rated panic hardware had rusted over and the latching mechanism was failing to operate. So as you can see, design parameters can have a serious impact on the long-term application of the products used.

Performance specifications are usually the lengthiest section in the RFP. This section describes in complete detail the performance expected from the devices to be purchased under the RFP for the electronic physical security system. Performance specifications describe the function of each operating component.

For example, a typical RFP for an access control system begins with a description of the identity card carried by system users. A description of the card reader follows, then a description of the access point manager or electronic control device to which the card reader is connected. Indicate any preferences required for the manner in which card readers are associated with access point managers.

An example of this might be to distinguish between systems that require an interface installed at control points for managing the devices at that location. Some equipment manufacturers will require that their card readers be connected directly to the access point manager, while other manufacturers will require an intermediate device that transmits card information and lock control decisions to the door with all of the endpoint devices being connected to the intermediate panel. There are limitations and benefits of each approach, so the system designer must consider if either of these approaches would result in benefits to the system user and include those requirements in the performance specification.

After describing the performance requirements of the access point manager it may also be necessary to describe the manner in which these devices are connected to the host computer. In some cases, manufacturers will permit communications over local area networks (LAN). Some of the benefits of this design approach include using existing facilities for multi-building communication.

Finally, the performance specification describes the software features needed in the new access control system. You may use software feature names designated by certain manufacturers but must make a full description of how this feature should work. In so doing, it will become clear to the bidders why this feature is being requested since each manufacturer uses their own nomenclature for software feature.

Software features provide the greatest area for definition. There are simply too many variations of features to examine them all in this book but certain feature areas are important to all systems. A list of these areas follows:

1. In access control systems:
   - How is data is entered into the system?
   - What fields are available?
   - How can the fields be sorted?
   - What data is recorded by the system?
   - How can data be reported?
   - How the product governs "who" "goes where" and "when"?
2. In closed-circuit television (CCTV) systems:
   - How can camera images be selected?
   - How does the system searches for specific images?
   - What automated features are available for monitoring scenes?
   - What are the playback characteristics?
3. In alarm monitoring systems:
   - How are alarms displayed and announced?
   - How does the user respond to alarms?
   - What alarm information does the system record?
   - How is recorded alarm information reported?

Remember that these are "performance specifications" and those elements contained in the description relate to the benefits desired by that characteristic.

A description of a product's physical characteristics is not necessary unless there is compelling reason to include physical properties in the device description. For instance, some access control systems require that card readers be small enough to mount on narrow aluminum mullions for glass store front doors.

Specify the electrical characteristics of access point managers to ensure that there is adequate protection against damage due to lightning or power surges. A good example of a characteristic that is NOT necessary for performance specification is the physical size of the housing in which the access point manager electronics are mounted. Conversely, it may be acceptable to say access point manager housings may not exceed a certain set of dimensions when space in the equipment mounting location is limited.

9.4 CERTIFICATIONS

You may want to add third-party certifications to your specifications. Doing so allows you to rely on an independent organization to review and certify the equipment you will use as being manufactured to their standards. However, this should not be done arbitrarily, not all manufactures seek third-party certifications. Sometimes you may require a certification on a product that has little need for such independent reviews, thereby excluding what might be the right product for your applications. Here are some of the certifications available.

9.4.1 Certifications: UL

Consider minimum quality certifications. One widely recognized certification is Underwriters Laboratory (UL) Approval. UL (www.ul.com/) describes their services on their website as follows:

> A global leader in applied safety science, UL Solutions transforms safety, security, and sustainability challenges into opportunities for customers in more than 100 countries. UL Solutions delivers testing, inspection and certification services, together with software products and advisory offerings, that support our customers' product innovation and business growth.

UL describes their mission as follows:

- To promote safe, secure and sustainable living and working environments for people by the application of science, hazard-based safety engineering and data acumen
- To support the production and use of products which are physically and environmentally safe and to apply our efforts to prevent or reduce loss of life and property

- To advance safety science through research and investigation
- To concentrate our efforts and resources on public safety in those areas where we can make valuable contributions
- To work with integrity and focus on quality to enhance the trust conveyed by our certification marks and services
- To charge fair prices that allow us to meet our obligations, sustain our growth and invest in safety science and education
- To invest in our people and to encourage our people to invest in themselves
- To be a good example of corporate citizenship and social responsibility.

By requiring UL approval for your new equipment you have the benefit of a third-party verification on the caliber of the products from which you will make your selections.

Not all systems from all manufacturers meet UL criteria. However, such approvals are not always mandatory. Add these approval certifications to the RFP requirement if it will enhance the quality of the products received.

9.4.2 Standards: ISO

Another useful certification is the International Organization for Standardization (ISO) (www.iso.org/home.html). ISO is an independent, nongovernmental international organization with a membership of 169 national standards bodies. Through its members, it brings together experts to share knowledge and develop voluntary, consensus-based, market-relevant international standards that support innovation and provide solutions to global challenges.

While ISO does not provide "certifications" when manufacturers develop products they have the option to follow ISO standards. This provides a standardization and quality level that ensures they meet the worldwide expectation for high-quality products.

Much like UL, not all systems from all manufacturers meet ISO standards. However, such approvals are not always mandatory. Add these approval certifications to the RFP requirement if it will enhance the quality of the products received.

9.4.3 ADA Requirements

A third aspect of certification is the Americans with Disabilities Act (ADA) (www.ada.gov/). ADA protects people with disabilities from discrimination. This is not just a "standard", it is the law. Your installation must be ADA compliant or your company will be exposed to government intervention and civil litigation. Their website says: "The Department of Justice enforces the ADA through lawsuits and settlement agreements to achieve greater access, inclusion, and equal opportunity for people with disabilities".

The ADA Standards for Accessible Design – along with the Title II and Title III regulations – say what is required for a building or facility to be physically accessible to people with disabilities. The ADA Standards for Accessible Design ("ADA Standards") cover:

- Newly constructed buildings and facilities;
- Alterations – such as renovations and other changes that affect usability – made to buildings and facilities;
- Making architectural changes in existing state and local government buildings to provide "program access"; and
- Removing architectural barriers that are easily accomplishable without much difficulty or expense in existing buildings of businesses.

Since you are controlling access (and sometimes egress) from your facility, ADA compliance applies to your project. However, unless you plan to change the building and door configuration in your plans, ADA will not have much of an impact. Where you will need strict compliance is in the placement of control devices for doors such as card readers, keypads and egress devices. The rule of thumb that I always follow and recommend you to follow is to place such devices at no higher than the door knob of the existing doors. You can assume that the original architect followed ADA guidelines and so you are just following his/her lead.

Another point of impact is alarms. If a local alarm system is used, the alarm shall be both audible and visual. The audible alarm shall be at least 15 decibels. The visual alarm shall be a strobe-type fixture with clear or nominal white light. The maximum pulse duration shall be two-tenths of a second. The intensity shall be 75 candela. Vertically, the visual alarm shall be mounted 80 inches above the floor or 6 inches below the ceiling. Horizontally, a person should not be more than 50 ft from the visual alarm. Now, of course, this applies to alarms intended to notify occupants of some emergency and would not necessarily apply to security force alarms.

For more information on ADA requirements, see Federal Regulations 28 CFR Part 36, ADA Standards for Accessible Design.

9.5 DOOR DETAIL SCHEDULE

The Door Detail Schedule is the primary resource for access control and alarm monitoring end point information. These documents may be included either in the body of the RFP or as an attachment. Since these documents tend to change based on shifting user priorities and the discovery of other information regarding product capabilities in the market, including it as an attachment is usually the preferred approach.

However, it is important to communicate in the body of the RFP the existence of these schedules and what information may be found on it. For example, under this section the RFP may say:

> Attached to this RFP is a Door Detail Schedule which provides a list of all openings included in this system, the proposed field devices and the common control and display equipment.

The Door Detail Schedule also contains references to the equipment location on company floor plans and references the appropriate illustrations for elevation drawings of each type of door. The vendor will also find remarks associated with certain doors that will be helpful in pricing and planning the installation of the proposed system. By including these descriptions there can be little misunderstanding that another document exists that provides the necessary details that are included in the Door Detail Schedule.

9.6 CAMERA DETAIL SCHEDULE

The Camera Detail Schedule (CDS) is the primary resource for video end point information. These documents may also be included in the body of the work or as an attachment. Since the CDS also tends to change based on shifting user priorities and the discovery of other information regarding product capabilities in the market, also including it as an attachment is usually the preferred approach.

However, like the Door Detail Schedule, it is important to communicate in the body of the RFP the existence of the CDS and what information may be found on it. For example, under the section of Camera Detail Schedule the RFP may say:

> Attached to this RFP is a Camera Detail Schedule which provides a listing of all the camera views that is to be included in this system, an example of the images expected and a list of display and signal processing devices.

The CDS also contains references to the location on company floor plans and references elevation drawings for each camera location. The vendor will also find remarks associated with certain cameras that will be helpful in pricing and planning the installation of the proposed system.

9.7 DRAWINGS

Text documents can tell the entire story but sometimes “a picture is worth a thousand words”. Drawings are most often used to illustrate a point or a desired method of installation. So let's look at some drawings you could/should add to your specifications to make your desired outcome clear.

9.7.1 Marked Plot Plans and Floor Plans with Equipment Location

Blueprints are usually too large to be included in the body of the RFP. Blueprints are usually attachments to the RFP; however, in the age of sophisticated computer-assisted drawing (CAD) programs, blueprints can often be reproduced on standard 8½ × 11 or legal size pages. Under such circumstances, floor plans may be included in the body of the RFP. If the floor plans are an attachment, remarks are required in the RFP that refers to these attachments:

> Accompanying this RFP are floor plans which describe the location of equipment for the proposed system. Please note the reference numbers used on the Door Detail Schedule as they relate to the symbolic references on the floor plans.

Be consistent when marking blueprints with the symbolic references to indicate security system devices. Figure 9.1(a–e) provides an example of a symbol set that is gaining increased acceptance among security professionals. It is also important to provide a key or symbol reference on the drawings to aid in understanding the symbols.

9.7.2 Door Elevation Drawings

The marked blueprints will provide the vendors with a reference to the physical location of the field equipment. However, not all vendors are fully aware of the life safety considerations and general conventions used in placing equipment. Oftentimes, manufacturers provide drawings showing how equipment should be mounted. This is not true in all cases and there are frequent variations on standard arrangements that are necessary for unique situations. Equipment placement needs to be consistent for all components of a physical security system. This will increase the professional appearance of the installation and ensure compliance with all requirements. Include door elevation drawings, to describe what is expected for the physical installation of each device.

Figure 9.2 provides an illustration of a standard single leaf door with a door status switch, a card reader, a request to exit button and a power magnet lock. You should maintain a library of such drawings and provide a sample of these drawings for each equipment location in the system. In special circumstances where companies have unique requirements for equipment placement, make variations on these standard drawings when creating new system installations and system additions.

SIA/IAPSC CAD Security Symbols — RELEASE: 1, PAGE 1 OF 5

SYMBOL #	ASTM 967 1994 SUBMITTAL	ASTM 967 1995 SUBMITTAL	BLOCK NAME 1995 SUBMITTAL	DESCRIPTION M = MOUNT T = TECHNOLOGY/TYPE (SPECIFIC TO DEVICE) M: P = PEDESTAL, T = TURNSTILE, S = SURFACE, F = FLUSH, R = RACK, M = MULLION, D = DESK, W = WALL, C = CEILING, H = HIDDEN	SUGGESTED LAYER / COLOR
1. ANNOTATION					
1.01	NUM	A B C	REF	DEVICE REFERENCE A: DRAWING SHEET B: DETAIL C: DEVICE/ZONE NUMBER	170 / BLOCK
2. ACCESS CONTROL					
2.01	P	M T	CR	CARD ACCESS READER T: B = BARCODE W = WEIGAND P = PROXIMITY M = MAG STRIPE F = ELEVATOR FLOOR CALL H = ELEVATOR HALL CALL T = TOKEN S = SMART CARD	173 / GREEN
2.02		M T	BIO	BIOMETRIC ACCESS CONTROL DEVICE T: H = HAND GEOMETRY F = FINGER PRINT V = VOICE R = EYE RETINA I = EYE IRIS	173 / GREEN
2.03		M	KPD	KEYPAD DEVICE	173 / GREEN
2.04		M	CR-KPD	CARD READER WITH KEYPAD	173 / GREEN
2.05		M	CR-TA	CARD READER WITH TIME AND ATTENDANCE	173 / GREEN
2.06		####	DET	DETAIL SYMBOL	/
2.07		P M T	JBOX	JUNCTION BOX	/
2.08		M	STROBE	STROBE LIGHT	/

FIGURE 9.1 (a–e) Security Symbols.

SIA/IAPSC CAD Security Symbols					RELEASE: 1 PAGE 2 OF 5
SYMBOL #	ASTM 967 1994 SUBMITTAL	ASTM 967 1995 SUBMITTAL	BLOCK NAME 1995 SUBMITTAL	DESCRIPTION: M = MOUNT; T = TECHNOLOGY/TYPE (SPECIFIC TO DEVICE). M: P = PEDESTAL, T = TURNSTILE, S = SURFACE, F = FLUSH, R = RACK, M = MULLION, D = DESK, W = WALL, C = CEILING, H = HIDDEN	SUGGESTED LAYER / COLOR
3. ANNUNCIATION: CONSOLE/PANEL					
3.01			MUX	MULTIPLEX PANEL T: V = VIDEO A = ALARM C = CARD READER	176 / BLUE
3.02			C-PANEL	CONTROL PANEL T: B = BURGLAR F = FIRE P = PERIMETER D = DOOR	176 / BLUE
3.03			CPU	CENTRAL PROCESSING UNIT	173 / GREEN
3.04			KBD	KEYBOARD	173 / GREEN
3.05			PRNT	PRINTER	173 / GREEN
4. ANNUNCIATION: DEVICES					
4.01	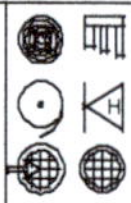		AUDIO	AUDIO DEVICE T: Z = BUZZER, B = BELL, C = CHIME, H = HORN, S = SPEAKER, L = LISTEN-IN, K = KLAXON, M = MICROPHONE, S = SOUNDER	177 / PURPLE
5. BARRIERS AND VEHICLE CONTROLS					
5.01			TRNSTL	TURNSTILE	170 / BLACK
5.02			REVDOOR	REVOLVING DOOR	170 / BLACK
5.03			TR-ARM	TRAFIC ARM	/
5.04			TR-LOOP	VEHICLE LOOP DETECTOR	175 / ORANGE
5.05			WIN-SCR	SECURITY WINDOW SCREEN T: S = SHADE B = BLIND (SEE 10.04 FOR ALARMED SCREEN)	/

FIGURE 9.1 (Continued)

SIA/IAPSC CAD Security Symbols					RELEASE: 1 PAGE 3 OF 5
SYMBOL #	ASTM 967 1994 SUBMITTAL	ASTM 967 1995 SUBMITTAL	BLOCK NAME 1995 SUBMITTAL	DESCRIPTION M = MOUNT T = TECHNOLOGY/TYPE (SPECIFIC TO DEVICE) — M: P = PEDESTAL, T = TURNSTILE, S = SURFACE, F = FLUSH, R = RACK, M = MULLION, D = DESK, W = WALL, C = CEILING, H = HIDDEN	SUGGESTED LAYER / COLOR
6. COMMUNICATIONS					
6.01		 M T	IC	INTERCOM T: M = MASTER S = SUB-STATION	178 / LT-GREEN
6.02		 M T	RADIO	TWO WAY RADIO	177 / PURPLE
7. ELECTRICAL					
8. LIGHTING					
9. MISCELLANEOUS					
9.01			SCHRED	DOCUMENT DESTROYER	170 / BLACK
10. SENSORS					
10.01		 M T	MD	MOTION DETECTOR T: M = MICROWAVE I =INFRARED U = ULTRASONIC X = EXIT	175 / ORANGE
10.02		 360%%D PIR	360.PIR	360 PIR MOTION DETECTOR T: X=PIR F= Y=360	175 / ORANGE
10.03		 M T	GBS	GLASS BREAK SENSOR T: S = SHOCK A = AUDIO	175 / ORANGE
10.04		 T	WIN-SCRA	SECURITY WINDOW SCREEN WITH ALARM T: S = SHADE B = BLIND (SEE 5.05 FOR NON-ALARMED SCREEN)	/
10.05		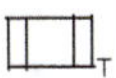 T	SD	SCREENING DEVICE T: M = METAL DETECTOR E = EXPLOSIVES DETECTOR X = X-RAY T = TAG DETECTOR (EAS) A = ACCESS	/

FIGURE 9.1 (Continued)

SIA/IAPSC CAD Security Symbols RELEASE: 1 PAGE 4 OF 5

SYMBOL #	ASTM 967 1994 SUBMITTAL	ASTM 967 1995 SUBMITTAL	BLOCK NAME 1995 SUBMITTAL	DESCRIPTION M = MOUNT T = TECHNOLOGY/TYPE (SPECIFIC TO DEVICE) M: P = PEDESTAL, T = TURNSTILE, S = SURFACE, F = FLUSH, R = RACK, M = MULLION, D = DESK, W = WALL, C = CEILING, H = HIDDEN	SUGGESTED LAYER / COLOR
	11. SURVEILLANCE				
11.01	CRT	M T	MON	MONITOR T: V = VIDEO D = DATA G = GRAPHIC M = MULTISCREEN	176 / BLUE
11.02		M T	CAM	CAMERA	176 / BLUE
11.03		M T	CAM-PTZ	CAMERA WITH PAN / TILT / ZOOM	176 / BLUE
11.04			VKBD	VIDEO CONTROL KEYBOARD	176 / BLUE
11.05			VMUX	VIDEO MULTIPLEXER	176 / BLUE
A.05			MPBL	MECHANICAL PUSH BUTTON LOCK	/
11.07		M T	REC	RECORDER T: V = VIDEO A = AUDIO	176 / BLUE
12.01		M T	SW-A	AUTOMATIC MONITORING SWITCH T: T = TEMP, G = GATE B = BAL. MAG H = HUMIDITY W = WATER L = LATCH	174 / RED
12.02		M T	SW-M	MANUALLY OPERATED SWITCH T: E = EMERGENCY L = LOCK F = FOOT M = MAT H = HOLDUP	174 / RED
12.03		M T	BUTTON	PUSH BUTTON T: P = PANIC D = DURESS R = DOOR RELEASE B = BELL PUSH	174 / RED

FIGURE 9.1 (Continued)

SIA/IAPSC CAD Security Symbols					RELEASE: 1 PAGE 5 OF 5
SYMBOL #	ASTM 967 1994 SUBMITTAL	ASTM 967 1995 SUBMITTAL	BLOCK NAME 1995 SUBMITTAL	DESCRIPTION M = MOUNT T = TECHNOLOGY/TYPE (SPECIFIC TO DEVICE) M : P = PEDESTAL, T = TURNSTILE, S = SURFACE, F = FLUSH, R = RACK, M = MULLION, D = DESK, W = WALL, C = CEILING, H = HIDDEN	SUGGESTED LAYER / COLOR
	13. DOOR AND LOCKING HARDWARE				
13.01	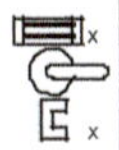		EL	ELECTRONIC LOCK T: M = MAGNETIC S = STRIKE L = LATCH SET H = HYBRID	173 / GREEN
13.02			EX-DEV	EXIT DEVICE T: E = ELECTRIFIED M = MECHANICAL D = DELAYED EGRESS X = HIGH SECURITY	/
	APPENDIX A: SAMPLE COMBINATION DEVICES				
A.01		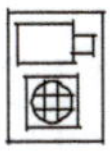	VID-IC	CAMERA WITH INTERCOM	/
A.02		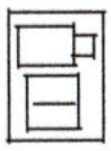	VID-CR	CAMERA WITH CARD READER	/
A.03		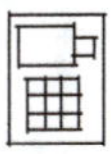	VID-KPD	CAMERA WITH KEYPAD	/
A.04	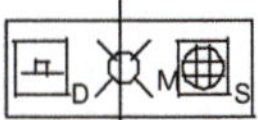		CB	CALL BOX W/ INTERCOM & STROBE	/

FIGURE 9.1 (Continued)

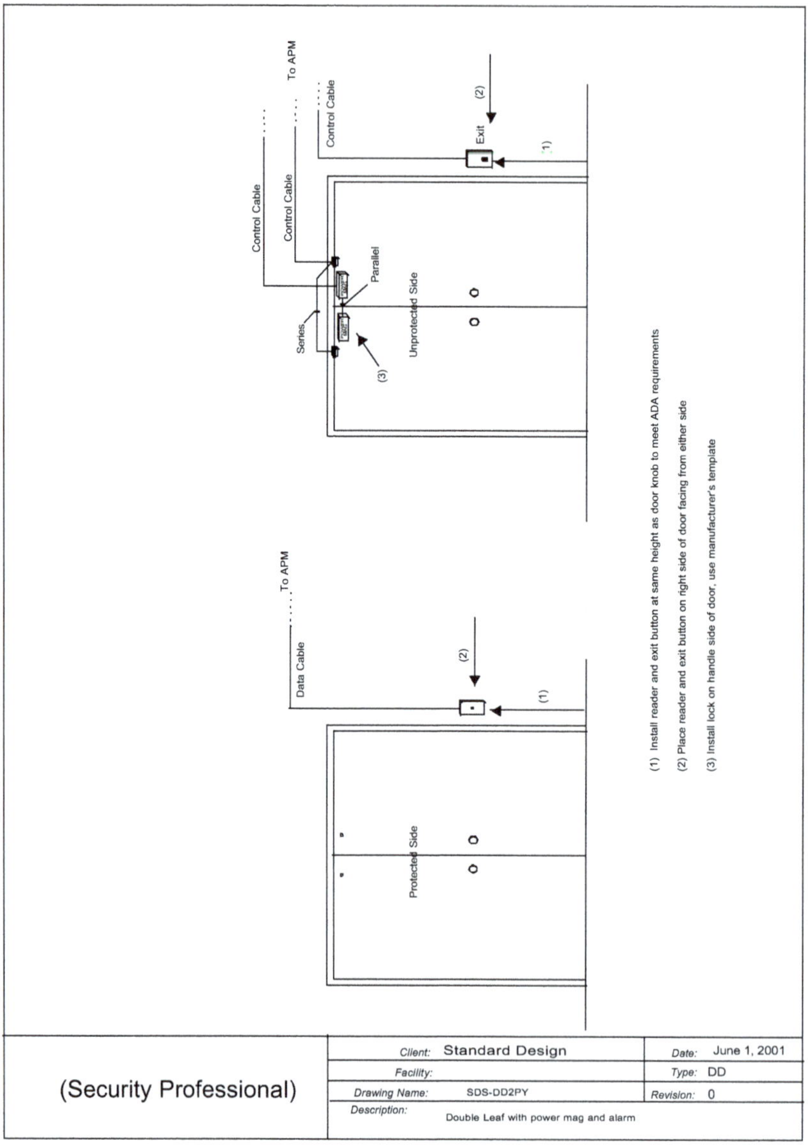

FIGURE 9.2 Door Elevation Drawing.

For instance, Figure 9.2 shows the card reader and exit button at door handle height. Placing these devices above the door handle height may be a violation of the ADA and expose the company to code violations or other statutory constraints. It is important for you to familiarize yourself with the applicable codes and standards regarding device placement. Further, while it may not violate an existing safety standard, incorrect placement of a lock or alarm contact may inadvertently defeat or diminish anticipated security benefits. Be aware of the manufacturer's recommended placement of products and indicate these placements on the drawing providing they do not conflict with applicable codes and the objectives of the security design.

9.7.3 Camera Elevation Drawings

As in the case of door detail drawings, Camera Detail Drawings are an essential element of the security survey documentation. Although life safety constraints are usually not an issue with regard to camera equipment placement, there are a number of other factors in camera placement that affect the overall effectiveness of the video system.

An example of placement criteria that may affect camera system performance is a camera viewing an object with backlighting. Without drawings to describe

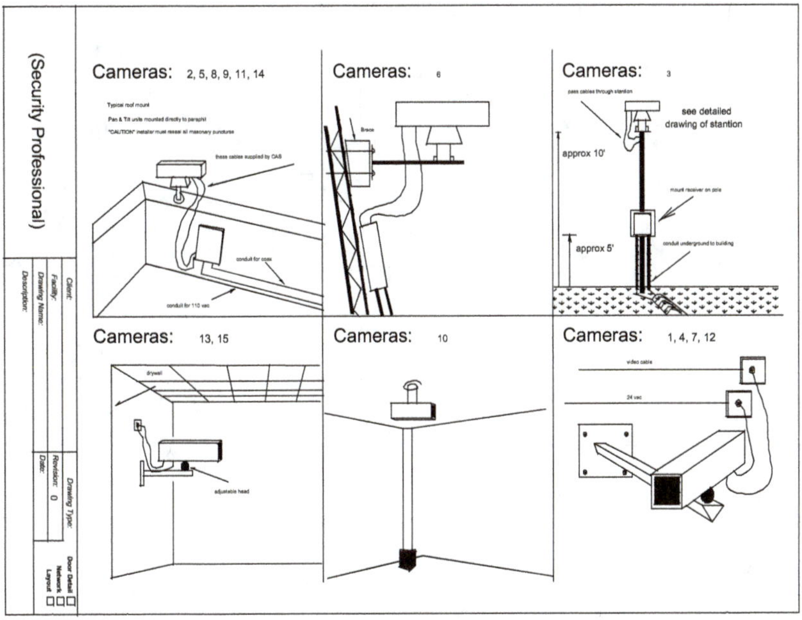

FIGURE 9.3 Camera Elevation Drawing.

specific placement, vendors may opt for a more convenient installation than what is optimally required for good camera views. In such cases, backlighting may hinder the view and the observer will frequently see silhouettes instead of a clear, identifiable image. Additionally, a fixed position camera installed within easy reach of a pedestrian can be either intentionally or inadvertently moved changing the camera angle to an unwanted view. Be aware of the correct placement of each camera and indicate that placement on the drawing. An illustration of a camera elevation drawing is shown in Figure 9.3.

9.7.4 Network Drawing

The network drawing serves to illustrate the connections between the communication devices of the electronic physical security system. The network drawing is most important when you are designing large complex systems with multiple floors or multiple buildings. Figure 9.4 provides a sample of a network drawing. Although not essential, the network drawing is especially helpful in illustrating the interrelationship between systems and when device communication is complex.

Network drawings provide a comprehensive illustration of the desired interconnection between devices in the electronic physical security system.

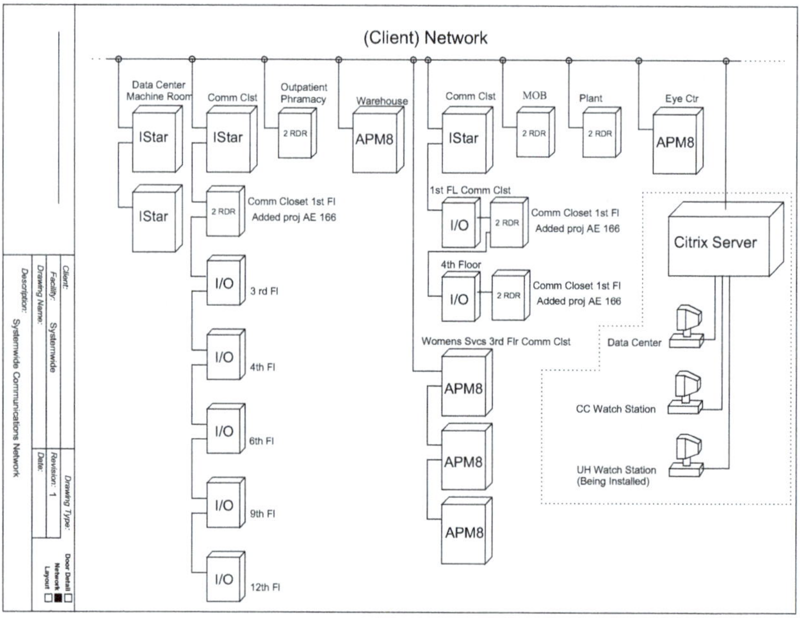

FIGURE 9.4 Network Drawing.

However, exercise caution in preparing a network drawing for open bids. These configurations are sometimes unique to manufacturers' systems. When special applications exist, such as multi-building environments, a network drawing clearly indicating the use of company-provided LAN would help the bidder understand that a LAN requirement is an integral part of the system specifications.

Network drawings include electronic communication devices but usually exclude low-voltage electrical connections such as cabling to door status switches, exit buttons and other similar devices. These illustrations are usually included in the Door Elevation Drawing. Add comments to network drawings that provide bidders with the opportunity to provide modified versions of these configurations. Doing so removes artificial limitations from the specification where no direct tangible benefit results from this unique wiring approach.

9.7.5 Command Center Drawing

The Command Center Drawing illustrates the physical layout of the equipment (including special security furniture) to achieve the identified objectives. This drawing should clearly indicate how to arrange the proposed equipment to provide optimum performance for the user. An example of a Command Center Drawing is shown in Figure 9.5

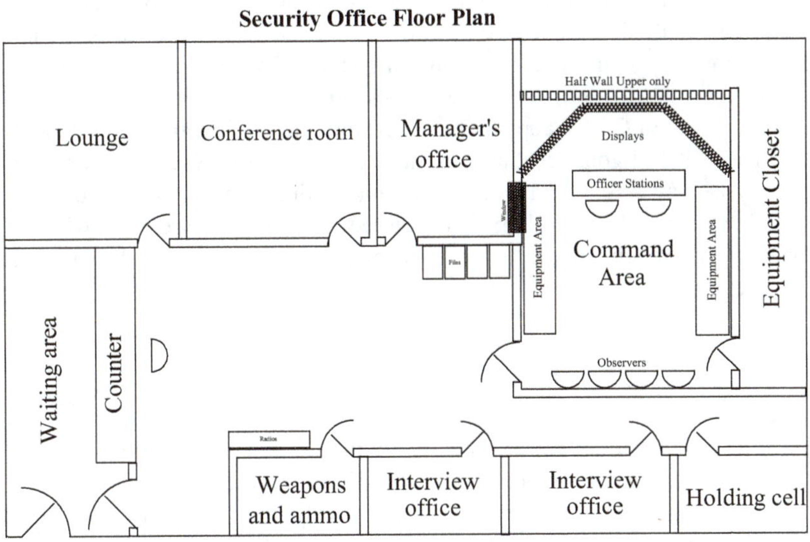

FIGURE 9.5 Command Center Drawing.

9.7.6 Common Equipment Elevation Drawings

Common Equipment Elevation Drawings are an illustration of how to arrange the equipment in the equipment locker rooms. In small systems, this illustration is usually not required but is helpful if special circumstances exist. It is an essential part of the equipment specification in larger systems. An example of a Common Equipment Elevation Drawing is shown in Figure 9.6. Some of the more useful considerations for the Common Equipment Elevation Drawings are as follows:

1. Mount equipment not more than 6 ft from the floor.
2. Conduit or similar cable raceways will be used to interconnect devices.
3. Allow space between the cabinets for access and system additions.
4. Label all cabinets.

9.7.7 Custom Circuit Drawings

In some instances, the system can only achieve the desired performance by a unique nonstandard wiring arrangement of certain components. An example of such a circumstance may be a “mantrap”. A mantrap is an arrangement of two locked doors connected by a vestibule. In this application, both doors may not be unlocked at the same time.

Most manufacturers can accommodate this by interconnecting the control and sensor ports in the access point manager (network panel). However, to illustrate this fully it will be necessary to provide a custom circuit drawing to show how the mantrap will work. Providing this level of detail helps to achieve the expected results when implementing the system.

In the case of CCTV applications, a custom circuit drawing may be needed when pan, tilt and zoom features are used in the CCTV system. In this application, you may wish to have a camera automatically pan, tilt and zoom to a particular image when an alarm is registered. The custom circuit drawing will illustrate which alarm contacts or access control system output signals will trigger the preset image.

9.8 CABLING

System cabling is a critical element in the installation of low-voltage security products. If the vendor uses poor-quality cable or the cable is installed improperly, the system will not communicate effectively and the installation will be plagued by numerous service calls.

Provide conditions in the RFP for cable routes. For most electronic systems, the current carried on these cables is miniscule and measured in milliamps. These

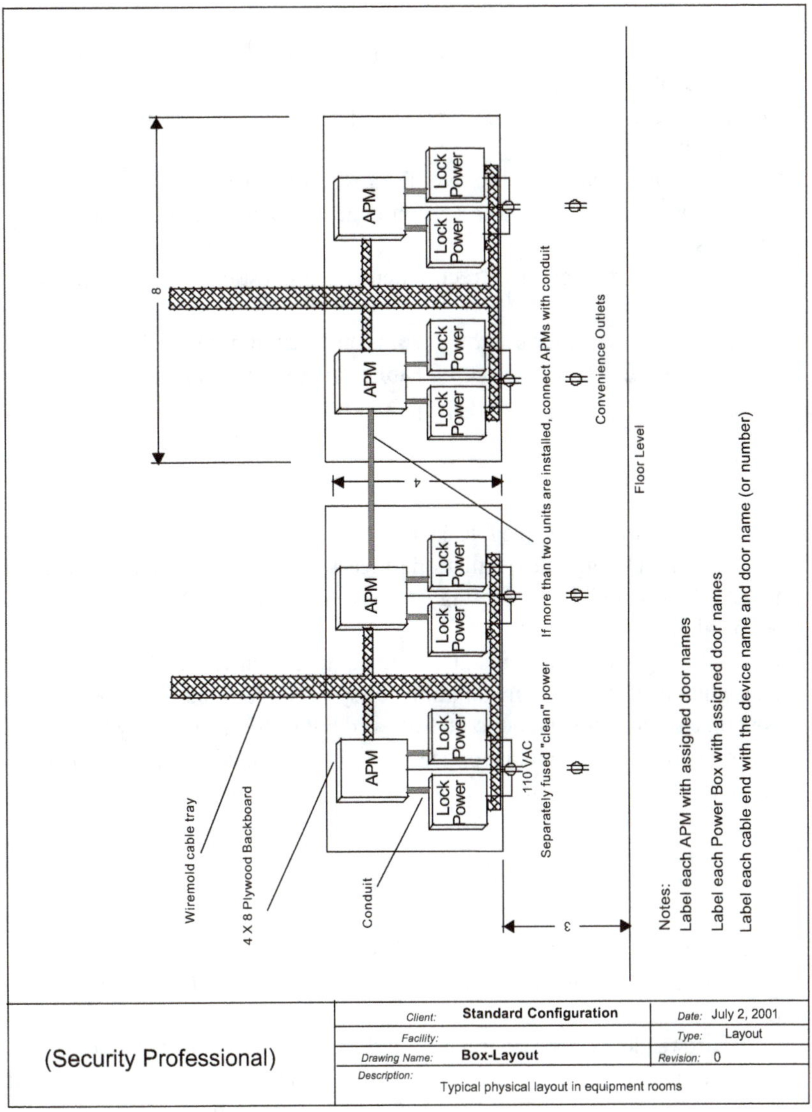

FIGURE 9.6 Common Equipment Elevation Drawing.

circuits carry digital information and a variety of external influences can degrade the data.

The National Electrical Code provides guidance on the installation of low voltage and cabling. Require the vendor to follow these guidelines in the RFP. Some additional guidelines are:

1. Low-voltage cable should not be strapped to or run parallel with high-voltage cable.
2. Do not place low-voltage cable in the same conduit with high-voltage cable.
3. Do not run low-voltage cable over fluorescent ballast.
4. Always use the manufacturer's recommended cable size and cable type for the system.
5. Follow the manufacturer's recommended suggestions for grounding cable shields.
6. Use spade tips when terminating cables on screw terminals.
7. Use cable studs when terminating cables on push-in connectors.

9.8.1 Cable Labeling

Require the vendor to provide a cable-labeling scheme for all cables to be marked using that scheme. During the installation process, the vendor's installers usually become very familiar with the cabling between devices. That familiarity leaves with the installers.

Cable labeling assists the installers in doing the installation but is more important when used after the installation for system additions and repairs. You may insist on a particular scheme to be followed but vendors generally have their own labeling methodology and as long as that methodology is clear, there is little reason to demand a specific method.

9.9 COMPONENT INSTALLATION CRITERIA

Each manufacturer will usually publish installation criteria for their system. However, here are some general rules you might want to include for installing devices.

Install card readers on the door handle side of the door at door handle height. There are cases where such reader placement is impractical or impossible. A good example is double leaf doors. To place the reader on the door handle side of the door would require a set of posts between the door leafs. Since none is available, the most acceptable alternative is to place the card reader on the right side of the double door adjacent to the doorframe.

However, there are still other circumstances where this is not possible because the door is at the end of a corridor with an adjacent wall on the right side. In these cases, require placement of the card reader as close to the door as possible but outside the "door swing" of the door leaf. This is a life safety consideration. Such placement will help to avoid injury to the users.

Install door status switch on the door handle side of the door as close to the end of the door as possible. The reason for selecting this location is that this edge of the door is farthest away from the hinge point and a small opening in the door will result in a perceptible opening between the magnet and reed switch. This is an important technique since it provides the earliest possible detection.

Although doors are the most common barricades, some do not lend themselves well to the installation of standard door status switches. An example is chain link gate monitors. These devices consist of armored cables mounted to chain link openings. Two "pigtails" are connected across the opening and must be disconnected to open the gate. Stipulate any mounting methods in the RFP that would affect the operation of these devices.

Many of the advanced security alarm monitoring systems prevent tampering with alarm monitoring circuits by using "supervised" alarm ports. Supervised circuits prevent a perpetrator from defeating an alarm system by placing bare end wires across the monitoring point as a shunt to prevent detection of an opening.

A supervised alarm port does not simply measure whether or not a circuit is present but the resistance value on that circuit. A resistor is installed at a predetermined location and has a specific value. This resistor is an electrical device that provides impedance to the current used to monitor the status of the reed switch. If a shunt is placed across the alarm contact or across the alarm cable at any point, it changes the resistance value of the circuit. This change is detected and an alarm is registered. In high-security applications using supervised alarm ports, require the vendor to install appropriate resistors at points recommended by the system manufacturer.

CCTV cameras should be placed out of reach of pedestrians to prevent tampering. Avoid installing cameras in areas where backlighting is present.

9.10 POWER QUALITY AND RELIABILITY

Explain any unusual power conditions that may exist and advise the vendor of their responsibility to notify the company about power quality requirements of the system. Do this to avoid situations where the company has large power-consuming devices connected to the same power feed as the vendor equipment. These devices cause variance in power quality that the system equipment finds intolerable. Require the vendor to specify the power tolerances and where power is required. Establish these requirements before the award of contract to avoid undisclosed additional costs to the company for providing power at these locations.

Specify backup power in the RFP for system critical components. State the time expected for backup power to engage when commercial power is lost and the amount of time the backup power will allow the system to continue to operate.

CAUTION ... backup power is not always required for locking systems. In cases where life safety issues apply, fire code may require locks to unlock in the event of a commercial power loss. The RFP must stipulate where to furnish backup power.

9.11 STARTUP RESPONSIBILITY

Specify startup responsibilities in the RFP and describe in clear specific terms what the vendor is required to do to make the system active. This may include programming card data and card readers, camera alignment and the adjustment of preset points on pan-tilt-zoom devices. Start-up responsibility should also include a definition of those preparations necessary for acceptance of the system installation. This could mean documenting and then programming the system for alarm messages and alarm map displays in access control systems. Indicate all the elements necessary for system turn on.

9.11.1 Card Testing

In some instances, the company has acquired other types of systems that use identity card credentials for a variety of purposes. In those cases, the RFPs stipulate that the new system must work with the existing cards. This is particularly important in systems where the population is very large (1,000 cards or more) and replacing all cards may be expensive and cumbersome.

If the system must work with existing cards, include a statement regarding testing the existing cards in the new system before installation.

9.11.2 "As Built" Project Drawings

You will document special circumstances as part of the RFP development but changes may take place in the system design during the installation. Require the vendor to update the system plans after the project is finished. These updates are referred to as "As-Built" drawings.

Require the bidder to provide as-built drawings when the work is finished. Also, include a requirement for a narrative that describes unique aspects of the wiring. These notes will be helpful when making additions or changes after the initial installation.

9.11.3 Test Criteria

Some manufacturers provide specific written tests for components after installation. Require the bidder to provide a copy of all manufacturers' test instructions with their bid. In the absence of manufacturers' recommended tests, require the bidder to supply the test criteria they will use to certify system acceptance. Compare this test criterion with the section in the last chapter called System Commissioning, amend these criteria if they do not appear to be adequate. Adequate acceptance testing is a condition of contract award.

9.12 SYSTEM ACCEPTANCE

Another area that frequently leads to contract disputes is what constitutes a "finished" job. To prevent misunderstandings, state in the RFP what constitutes system acceptance. This is the best indicator of a system installation being "finished". System acceptance should include at least the following elements:

1. Demonstration of the completed product installation
2. Successful completion of an acceptance test
3. Delivery of the required manuals
4. Delivery of specified training.

Describe the steps taken when evaluating the system at final delivery. This will be covered in more detail in the next chapter and you may want to include the "Commissioning" criteria in the RFP, but for now include at least the following steps in the RFP:

1. Deliver all the documentation specified in the RFP.
2. Conduct a pre-acceptance test. Conduct this test without company personnel. This will prevent embarrassing situations involving overlooked items in the installation. Correct these anomalies before company representatives witness the final acceptance test. For card readers (and other access control devices) the test includes presenting a valid and void card to all card readers to ensure that doors get unlocked when a valid card is presented and do not unlock when a void card is presented.
3. Test alarm monitoring points by deliberately violating protected openings throughout the system. Verify that the system senses the violation and displays it at the system consoles. In the case of multiple watch stations, several individuals may be required to observe system performance.
4. Have the vendor demonstrate CCTV systems to show the observation, recording and playback of recorded scenes.

5. If life safety systems are included in the system installation, test and certify these devices. Specifically, locking systems interfaced to the company's building fire alarm system should unlock when the fire alarm panel is in an alarm condition. Alarm conditions can be simulated without actually triggering the alarm. The fire alarm service company can create this simulation. Observe that all locks connected, automatically unlock.
6. Require the vendor to demonstrate software features of the new system. For access control systems, this includes the addition of new cards, assigning reader groups and time periods and how the user responds to alarms.
7. To test CCTV systems, observe all views, the recording and playback of all views and the movement of remotely controlled equipment. Also include a test of pre-sets for video alarm responses.
8. Conduct a "Final Acceptance Test" with the vendor and company representatives. Perform the same tests as described in the Pre-acceptance Test and demonstrate system operation for the company's approval.

9.13 GETTING APPROVAL FOR THE SPECIFICATIONS

When the RFP is finished, seek the approval of the management team before proceeding to the next step. This approval process is "crucial" in this stage of bid development. Call for a meeting of the management team to review the RFP. Provide all members of the committee with a copy of the finished bid before the meeting and then allow sufficient time for a review of the document before the meeting.

When presenting the RFP, promote an open debate on the validity of all assumptions and specifications listed. Your role is to explain what the recommended system will do and to guide the committee to an informed decision. It would help to remember that while selection committee input is valuable, it is also at this point uninformed. Explain the consequences of each choice and ensure that the company is well acquainted with the benefits and limitations of the proposed solutions.

9.13.1 Plan for Bid Evaluation

This is also the best time to establish the criteria for bid evaluation. We discussed this earlier in the design step and established the capabilities needed to achieve the design objectives. Meaningful objective measurements are needed to evaluate the proposed systems.

For example, the Physical Threat Assessment may have discovered that a disgruntled ex-employee attempted to sabotage the company's billing records by accessing the facility's main computer library and tampering with devices or records. Further, during the vulnerability assessment it was determined that a single card reader now controls the entry door to the computer library but there is free egress and the door status is not monitored.

Additional door security equipment is included in the recommendation for this situation, and an egress card reader. One of the recommended software features in this circumstance might also be anti-passback. This feature gives the System Administrator the ability to help enforce a rule that cardholders "must" badge in and out in alternating sequence for proper passage through the controlled door. You included the anti-passback system feature and must now describe how and where it will be used.

After presenting this recommendation, solicit feedback from the management team. Have the management team "weigh" the feature to establish relative importance in system operation. Do this for all features and use this weighted measure to evaluate the bids.

"Weighing" a feature means assigning a numeric value to the feature to describe its importance relative to other features. This weight will help you judge the significance of a particular feature in the vendor responses and lead to a more objective evaluation of all offers. Doing this for all proposed system features, you will learn which features are most important to the company.

If a system lacks certain features in the bid description and, based on this lack of capabilities it is necessary to reject the system, the weighted value for those features must be high. A threshold can be set that equals the sum of all mandatory features and vendor response scores with less than the threshold are disqualified. This level comparison provides an objective and fair evaluation process for all bids. Objectivity helps to make vendor selection "bulletproof" and provides substantial justification for recommending a vendor or system. While this is modestly important in commercial operations, it is vital when public funds are used. That would be applications in government offices (local, state and federal) and certain other hybrid operations that have high public visibility and partially use public funds.

Issue minutes of the meeting. Note any major changes made by the committee that differ from the original design in the RFP. Provide the evaluation weights for the selected features in the minutes. When the management team approves the RFP, release it to the company's purchasing department to begin the bid process.

After the meeting, adjust the RFP as required. Release the RFP to the marketplace. Confirm approval of the RFP in the minutes of the committee meeting. The minutes should reflect major changes by the committee that differ from your recommendation.

Now it is time to go to the market and get bids for your new system.

CHAPTER 10

Going Out for Bid

CONTENTS

10.1 INTRODUCTION TO THE BIDDING PROCESS

Bidding a new security system is not as easy as it might seem … the market does not have perfect knowledge of all the opportunities out there so you must make your bid known to the market. There are certain rules for bids that your purchasing department must follow, especially if you are using public funds such as a government contract or if you are a major corporation that receives large government purchases. Competitive bidding is often "required". It is true that competitive bidding is a good idea for the company but those organizations that are funded in part or in whole by public funds have a legal requirement imposed by the government for free and open bidding to give all companies a chance to compete. Your purchasing department will know the rules to follow.

If you do not have the benefit of a purchasing manager to tell you what to do, some good avenues to explore are the company's purchasing guidelines and your management team's advice. Legal issues aside, your goal is to get the best value for your company's investment dollar – this means the best equipment and service at the lowest price.

DOI: 10.4324/9781003490432-11

10.2 MAKING YOUR BIDDER'S LIST

In most cases, you will be representing major corporations or government entities. Of high importance to such organizations is the potential liability for improperly managed bids for major purchases. Given the complex nature and probable size of the security systems specified, it is likely that the systems under bid will be a major purchase. As a result, the rules of "Fair Play" are an essential part of the bid process. "Fair Play" is generally interpreted to mean that all bidders have an equal opportunity to vie for the company's business.

In some cases, there are circumstances that compel the company to have a particular preference for or against a vendor. The basis for these preferences may be previous experience with the vendor or other conditions not immediately apparent. Solicit comments on any biases during the bid review process. Document these biases in the meeting minutes and provide the rational. Suggest methods for excluding undesirable vendors.

An example of this may be a company that has a prior experience with a vendor where the vendor has failed to perform as expected. An examination of this circumstance may reveal that this performance failure is a result of inadequate labor. In such cases, add a vendor qualification or performance criteria to the Request for Proposal (RFP) that provides a rigorous requirement for personnel to handle the installation and/or servicing. The criteria for vendor qualification would include a requirement that no less than three technicians are available for service on the proposed system. Such a criterion will exclude all vendors with insufficient labor to serve the company's needs.

With full approval of the management team selection committee on the proposed bid, you will work with the purchasing department to release the RFP to the market. In some companies, there are strict guidelines for vendor selection and bid notification. In all cases, follow the company's purchasing policies. Before compiling a bidder's list or releasing notification of the bid opportunity, discuss the plans for the bid with the company's purchasing agent. The purchasing agent will have the final word on how to conduct the bid.

A good place to start in identifying your potential bidders are the vendors that currently provide services to the company. Before bid development, it is likely that local vendors have solicited, and in some cases been awarded, contracts for providing or maintaining existing security systems. Identify these companies through conversations with company employees.

Next, if you are a security professional, you should be keeping up with the market. You are most likely a member of ASIS International (www.asisonline.org/). The ASIS website describes membership as:

> Your trusted community for global security professionals. ASIS is where security professionals including CEOs, directors and managers collaborate on ideas, share lessons learned and build new partnerships. With many opportunities for cross-market networking across a global community of 34,000 members—spanning all industries including retail,

> healthcare, banking, cybersecurity and more—ASIS brings together those committed to advancing security worldwide.

This professional organization conducts an annual conference (currently known as GSX … for Global Security Exchange). In that conference all of the major manufacturers (and many of the smaller ones) display their products and services to promote their business. If you are not a member, you can still attend the tradeshow portion of the event and membership is not expensive and very useful.

Another trade show but usually intended for security dealers is Security Industry Association (SIA). Their website describes them as:

> The Security Industry Association (SIA) is the leading trade association for global security solution providers, with over 1,400 innovative member companies representing thousands of security leaders and experts who shape the future of the security industry.
>
> (www.securityindustry.org/)

This organization provides two conferences per year: ISC East and ISC West. Their website describes them as:

> The International Security Conference & Exposition (ISC) security events are the leading exhibitions for the security tradeshow industry, ISC Security Events are held in collaboration with premier sponsor SIA and are the only holistic security events strategically designed to provide products, technology, education and networking covering physical, IT and IoT security. ISC runs various regional events across North and South America, which range in a variety of different formats, each designed to connect you directly with suppliers and buyers in the security and public safety industry.

You may also recall from an earlier chapter you were encouraged to build a list of companies that provide security products and services, so, with that list and your list of existing vendors plus the information gathered from both these organizations, you can compile a "market list" of potential bidders for your new security system.

The approach I found most useful in soliciting bids is to contact what appears to be suitable manufacturers and ask them if they feel as though the system defined is a valid fit for their products and services. If they believe that there is a fit, then ask if they have a dealer in your area and provide them with contact information for seeking a bid opportunity. They will pass that information to the dealer and presumably they will seek a copy of your bid for their offer. When calling, ask for the head of the sales department and ask a key question during the conversation: "Do you have dealers in this area that will want to participate in our bid process?" Usually, the manufacturers will have a ready answer and can identify the dealers that will want to participate in this bid.

Having a local dealer is important ... these systems require periodic servicing, expansions, upgrades and other service-related tasks. You also need periodic support while using your system. All of these factors make having someone close by a necessity. Now there are situations where that is simply not possible, for example, if your site is located in a remote part of the country, but the point is still the same, you must pick a supplier that can and is willing to service your system as needed.

Greater participation by the market results in more options for the company. The vendor qualification list and performance criteria in the RFP will serve to cull this list to a manageable size. It is not necessary to artificially limit the number of bidders on a project except as the company directs.

The company's purchasing agent will do the bid release and will be responsible for documenting bid mailings and receipt of responses. This again serves to reinforce the unbiased nature of the bid and avoids putting you in a compromising position. But that should not stop you for soliciting bidders from as many sources as you can.

10.3 THE BIDDING PROCESS

After identifying potential bidders, advise the purchasing agent to release the bid advertisement. Coincident with that release, contact each bidder and inform them of the bid opportunity. Exercise caution when making these contacts and treat all vendors equally. Avoid any hint of bias.

Remember that you are "soliciting" offers; you opened the door when you contacted the manufacturers and now all the dealers are calling you to discuss your bid. An effective bid release will have as many participants as possible.

Before releasing a bid to market or even announcing your bid, have a plan in place. Select the dates for your bid milestones and remember holidays and weekends. You will want to give your bidders at least a 2-week notice on meetings and another 2 weeks to compose their bids. If the system is very large and complex, you might even add more time to that deadline. The milestone dates are:

- Bid Announcement
- MANDATORY Pre-bid Conference
- Bid Question Deadline and Response Deadline
- Bid Opening

10.3.1 Bid Announcement

Establish a formal fixed date for releasing the bid to market. You can solicit bids up to and beyond that date, but if a bidder calls for a bid document past bid opening, you cannot extend the deadlines just to favor that bidder. Have the bid package ready to go before the bid date, it should be complete in all respects and represent the entire proposal request.

It is usually best to insist on a formal written request. That request does not have to be complicated, you just need evidence that the request was made. A simple e-mail with a sentence asking for the bid is sufficient.

From time to time, other facts emerge that may alter some bid condition after the bid announcement and distribution of bids. You can change that by an amendment. Amendments are modifications to a bid but that also mean that if a bidder responds to the bid and meets the base criteria, the bidder must also acknowledge the amendment. So if you issue an amendment, add a section at the end for bidder acknowledgement signatures. Additionally, depending on the nature of the amendment, you may want to extend the other milestone dates to allow sufficient time for bidders to respond properly.

When a bid request is received (usually by the purchasing office), the request is recorded with the company name, contact person, address, telephone and e-mail information. Also noted is the date and time of the request. The bidder is then sent a copy of the RFP.

10.3.2 The Mandatory Pre-Bid Conference

Conduct a "mandatory" pre-bid meeting prior to the bid submittal date. The purpose of this meeting is to present the system bid opportunity to the bidders and to answer questions about the RFP or the bid process from the interested vendors. Invite the following company personnel to the pre-bid meeting:

- A member of the management team
- The company's purchasing agent
- At least one representative of the company's maintenance department
- At least one representative of the company's security department
- At least one member of the Information Technology (IT) department

You and the purchasing manager will moderate the pre-bid meeting jointly. Usually the purchasing agent takes the lead role in this moderation and you answer technical questions about the system. The other staff members are there to answer questions about their area of the company and the management team member is there only as an observer.

Require the vendors to sign a role sheet confirming their attendance. Review the entire RFP in an orderly fashion and answer questions from the vendors fully during the meeting. It is not necessary to "read" the document to the audience, instead bring up each section in turn and solicit questions. Questions given verbally in an open forum may be answered verbally; providing a full and complete answer is rendered. Since all bidders are present, there is little need to document every question and every response but you may find it useful to make notes of each question (the person asking is not relevant) and prepare a set of minutes for the management team.

However, in some cases the answers are not readily available and unanswerable questions are to be recorded and responded to in a written addendum that will be attached to the RFP. You may find that bidders do not understand some items. Document the question and answer in the RFP addendums in cases where these issues are complex or the question and response may have a significant bearing on the outcome of the award of the contract. Again, the bidder asking the question is not important.

At the conclusion of the pre-bid meeting, remind bidders that additional questions must be in writing. The deadline for questions must allow sufficient time to respond before bid opening.

10.3.3 Bid Question Deadline and Response Deadline

Formal questions will be sent to the Purchasing office for recording and management and they should forward those questions to you. It is a good idea for you to respond to all questions; if you don't know the answer, find it through one of the other team members and you compose the reply. Send your replies through the Purchasing office and they should forward them to all bidders. Respond to these questions as quickly as possible by RFP addendum and have Purchasing provide a copy of all questions and all responses to all bidders participating in the process. Since the pre-bid meeting is mandatory, send the responses only to those bidders attending the pre-bid meeting. As you can see, even at these early steps you are starting to "cull the herd".

10.3.4 Bid Acceptance and Bid Opening

The company purchasing office will receive the RFP responses from the vendors. The RFP has a specific bid date and time and some companies have stringent policies that prohibit the acceptance of bids beyond the allotted time. You must be aware of and honor these constraints. There have been many situations where such rigorous constraints were imposed and bidders presented their bid response only a few minutes late. Those responses were rejected and the bidder's offer was not considered. If your company has such rigorous constraints, emphasize these constraints at the pre-bid meeting.

Most companies have policies with regard to bid openings. Some bid openings are "public", while others are "private". In a public opening, bids are submitted by bidders and must be examined in part at the instant of opening. An example of this might be a government institution with strict public bid rules that require full disclosure in a public forum. Bidders may witness that their bid remained sealed until the bid date. Public bid openings serve to assure the bidders that their bid is given a fair and equal opportunity for consideration and that competing bidders are likewise excluded if they do not meet the minimum criteria. Learn the company's bid policies and follow them closely.

However, if there are no compelling reasons for a public bid opening, a private bid opening is usually preferred. It is less involved, simpler and allows you more time to examine bids before commenting. When conducting a private bid opening, sealed bids are not accessible until the close of bidding at the appropriate date and time. Sealed bids are to be opened in the presence of witnesses usually consisting of selection committee members and a representative of the company's purchasing department. This means, that company's purchasing agent will accept and hold all bids as received from the bidders. At bid opening, the seal is broken in the presence of these witnesses demonstrating that the bid information remained confidential until bid opening.

10.4 THE SINGLE-ITEM BID

Throughout this chapter we have discussed bidding a major system with multiple components and all the milestones needed to ensure the best deal for the company. But what about a single item bid with a very limited scope? An example of this might be a new or modified fence line. Do you need all this documentation and preparation for such a simple task? The short answer is "no".

In a limited scope of work with a single item, a simple RFQ is sufficient. Take the case of a fence line, seems simple right? Unfortunately it is not. How tall should the fence be, do we top the fence with razor ribbon or some other deterrent? What about the depth of the posts and how should they be set? The list is fairly long. Now to specify this product properly you must become a fencing expert, sounds like a lot of work doesn't it? So now we look at "Bid to Spec" that's a short hand version of an RFP.

Writing bid specs can be stressful – often, facility managers get stuck in the process while searching for the best products and equipment for their departments. Bids often secure suppliers for 1–3 years, meaning once you've made a decision you may be locked in. So where to start?

First, it's important to understand why items get put out to bid. It's simple; the process is designed to provide you with pricing and information on products that you have tested and evaluated. Bids encourage suppliers and vendors to put their best pricing forward for products and services that meet all the purchaser's requirements. The bid will typically go to the lowest bidder that meets all the bid specs.

We have all heard stories about facility managers struggling to maintain buildings with low quality or inadequate products simply because they were the cheapest on the bid. This is why it's absolutely critical to be familiar with the bid process and know how to write bid specs to get the products you need.

But in this case we don't want to become an expert on fences, so we modify our approach just a bit. We specify what we know we want then require the bidders to provide a detailed description of their offer and to include some of the construction choices they would make to accomplish our goals. This gives us detailed choices. We can see what material they recommend, the details of how the posts will be set and so forth. You will supply some of those details as requirements but you can evaluate the other choices recommended by the bidders.

With "specified" submittals in hand making the choice of the one best solution becomes easy. Now you can evaluate the bids the same way you would for a major project.

10.5 BID EVALUATIONS

Business decisions of this type are based on three variables: product, price and quality of service. Your evaluation will follow these principles. The measurement in a bid evaluation is "value", not just price. Certainly, price is a big component of value but the distinction is that value gives a much broader perspective in making a buying decision. Value requires examination of the quality of the offer and the reliability of the vendor. A "cheap bargain" is rarely a bargain at all. When price receives too much attention, and quality and reliability are in the background, the investment is often wasted.

When this happens, the company is actually worse off than when the project started. The installed system may not meet expectations, the budget is spent and the opportunity to do the job properly has passed. Company management rarely looks favorably on doing the same job over, at twice the price. A favorite phrase is, "if you're going to spend money, SPEND MONEY, don't fool around". This means that if you try to do a job cheaply, you spend more money in the end than if you simply took the time to properly determine needs then buy based on performance to needs. This is the definition of value.

10.6 TECHNICAL BID EVALUATION

Now come to hard part … well, maybe not that hard but certainly tedious. There is a temptation to dive right in and begin reading every bid cover to cover. You will usually find mountains of data, some of which you asked for, some of which you didn't! That is what makes the process hard, separating the wheat from the chaff. If this is your first bid evaluation, you will quickly understand why all the formality and structure was suggested in the previous chapters. Even with that structure the bidders will not always follow the guidelines. But remember this, you gave them guidelines not rules, so do not reject an offer based on "form" you must find the data you need in what might be 100 or more pages of submittals from each bidder. Some will do a good job,

Technical Bid Evaluation
(Simple CCTV Network Upgrade)

Questions Form	Manufacturer / Dealer	Desired Response	Panasonic / General Informatics	Exacq Tech / Allied Systems	Eagle Eye Networks / LAtech	Salient Systems / ADS	IPConfigure, Inc. / Insight Technologies	Pelco / AJ Labordette	Milestone / AJ Labordette	Bosch / MS Benbow & Assoc	Genetec / RAE Security	Salient / RAE Security	Weight, 1-10
1	LOCAL service on your product	Y	Y	Y	Y	Y	Y	Y	Y	Y	Y	Y	10
2	Will you service existing cameras	Y	Y	Y	Y	Y	Y	Y	Y	Y	Y	Y	7
3	Will you product integrate with S2	Y	Y	Y	N	Y	N	N	Y	N	N	Y	3
4	Operating system used (MS Windows = Y)	Y	Y	Y	Linux	Y	Y	Y	Y	Y	Y	Y	3
5	System Architecture 1 Component attached to network 2 Software based on Client's network 3 Cloud only	2	1	1 & 2	1	1	1 & 2 & 3	1	1 & 2	1 & 2	1	1	5
6	User access video browser based (Y)es	Y	Y	Y	Y	Y	Y	N	Y	N	Y	Y	10
7	No Limit on User IDs	Y	Y	Y	Y	Y	Y	Y	Y	Max 8	Y	Y	10
8	How are images stored 1 Separate on-site device 2 On Client's network 3 Cloud	2	1	1	1 & 3	1 & 2	1 & 2	1	1 & 2 & 3	1	1	1	5
9	Image extraction formats (common) acceptable	Y	Y	Y	Y	Y	No Stills	Y	Y	Y	Y	Y	5
												Feature Points Rank	58
EXTRA POINTS	Desired but NOT Required Features: (I)included, (A)availab I = full Value, A = 1/4 Value												
	Integration with the existing S2 system		I	A	N	N	N	N		N	N	A	5
	Can provide Pan, Tilt and Zoom control		I	I	I	I	I	I		I	I	I	10
	AI search of recorded video for specific criteria		I	A	N	A	N	A		I	N	A	7
	A mobility app		I	I	I	I	N	I		I	A	I	7
	License plate recognition		A	A	N	A	N	A		N	A	A	3
	Image manipulation on playback		I	N	N	A	Limited	A		I limits	N	N	5
	Extra Points Rank											Extra Points Rank	37

FIGURE 10.1 Technical Evaluation Spreadsheet.

others will not. Do the best you can do to find all of your evaluation criteria and make a reasoned and informed decision.

How do you do that? Begin by creating a spreadsheet (I am fond of Excel for this) putting the bidders names in the column heads and the criteria in the left column. In the second column add the "desired" answer next to the criteria. Then in the next column show the responses the vendors provided for the bid items. The last column is the "weighted value" your selection team gave to each feature or item. Your goal now is to reduce the number of offers to the top few (Figure 10.1).

Now let's examine the bids.

10.6.1 The First Cull: Basic System Components

The simplest place to start is the equipment count. You know how many cameras, card readers and other devices you specified, list those equipment counts on your spreadsheet. Look at how many were proposed by each bidder. Set aside those bids where the equipment count was not correct. Now this doesn't mean if you required 123 readers and the bidder quoted 117, there may have simply been a misunderstanding. If all bidders bid the same number, the mistake may have been in the RFP. So don't reject them but hold the bid aside until you are done.

It is possible to go back to a bidder and ask for a re-quote, especially if all other conditions are met. But this is not something you should do frivolously, seek the counsel of your purchasing manager for guidance. However, if you can confirm that the bidder omitted major elements of the system such as a telephone access system or recorders for the CCTV system, you can tentatively reject them.

Also, if you required any of the certification criteria in your technical specifications such as UL or ISO and the bidder submittals do not contain references to those certifications, you can (not must) disqualify the bid based on those criteria.

10.6.2 The Second Cull: Deal Breakers

Look for deal breakers. Next, during your bid review with the management team you identified certain "must have" items for your new system. List those items on your spreadsheet and review each bid to ensure that they comply with each item. Those that do not can be temporarily rejected at this step.

> A note on rejection …
> At this step, no one but you knows how each bid fares in your evaluation, keep it that way for now. You may find that a rejected bid is not as bad as it first seems after you have reviewed the other bids. So until you reach the "bottom line", keep your results to yourself. If you have set a bid aside based on these early culls, attach a note to the top of the bid that says why you have set it aside.

10.6.3 The Third Cull: Desired System Features Missing or Inadequate

The Work Breakdown Structure (WBS) was referred to as a tool for organizing information throughout the system development and bid management processes. The evaluation process makes use of the WBS. List the desired features by WBS section number and then inspect each bid for these items. Once again, if a feature is missing (i.e., anti-passback), note that on your spreadsheet under the heading for the respective bidder. The desired system features are listed by WBS number in the left-hand column followed by a description of the desired product or feature. Also in Figure 10.1, a "weighted value" was established by the selection team and a numeric value to the importance of each feature described. This is where you turn a subjective review into an objective assessment. Each bidder will receive points for how well they meet each feature requirement.

Review each vendor's bid in light of the required feature and determine if the vendor submittal falls below, meets or exceeds the criteria established for the desired feature. Assign the weighted value to determine how well the bid met the requirement. In some cases the feature is there but the way it is implemented is not entirely acceptable. You can "reduce" the point value for marginal features.

Responses that simply say "Our system can do this" are unacceptable and require further clarification. Again, seek the advice of your purchasing manager and obtain clarification from the bidder.

When your examination is done, you add up the points and have a ranking for how well the bidder met the selection criteria and that ranking is "weighted" by the importance of each feature. Remember, you already eliminated the deal breakers in the previous step so this ranking becomes the final technical measurement.

Provide a fair and equal opportunity to all bidders. Remove as much subjectivity in the evaluation process as possible. Obtain clarification for responses that appear to be inadequate or result in a negative conclusion based on the information provided. Give the bidder an opportunity to correct misunderstandings about the submittal so that a more objective evaluation could be possible.

When requesting additional information or updates to a bidder's submittal, channel your request through purchasing. The purchasing agent is a good filter to keep you within the bounds of your purchasing rules.

Upon receipt of the vendor's reply to these queries, either amend or confirm the initial conclusions reached about the vendor's willingness and ability to respond adequately to the RFP requirements. When the tabulation is complete, calculate a score for each vendor by adding the weighted value of the desired feature for the vendor's response.

At the conclusion of this technical evaluation, prepare a report to the management team that clearly illustrates the results of the bid process, the method used to evaluate data and the conclusions arrived at to make the appropriate system or vendor recommendation. End the report with a description of the follow-up action required and how the next step in the process will be handled. At this point the one best offer might not be evident. The recommendation may consist of three or more vendors, who all meet the minimum criteria for the desired system. This step is a "pass/fail" criterion and does not seek to select the one best solution yet.

In summary, you began with the broadest possible bidder's list. The bidder's criteria and submittal criteria were used to cull the first layer off that list. Then, the technical evaluation culled a second layer of potential bidders. This resulted in a "short list" of potential bidders for detailed examination. This technique will save time for you and expense for the company. It permits the broadest possible participation and then filters the results to closely scrutinize only the most likely candidates.

> CAUTION ...do not disclose the results of the evaluation to the vendors at this time. There may still be unrevealed differences in the vendor's offers and the selection list may change as further examinations take place. Bidders that did not make the initial cut may be added to the list if there are adjustments in the evaluation process.

Now that we have the technical evaluation, let's look at how much money we have to spend for each bidder and the terms of business.

10.7 BUSINESS PLAN EVALUATION

A Business Plan evaluation is usually more straightforward than a technical review. The bid elements are more objective and quantifiable. Make a side-by-side comparison of each offer and, where appropriate, comment on the bidder's submittal.

Once again, start with a spreadsheet formatted as before with the criteria in the left margin and the bidders across the top. Subjectivity is usually not an issue in this part of the evaluation but variations in bidder responses may introduce differences that cannot be easily reconciled. To ensure that all bidders are provided with a fair and equal opportunity to bid on the RFP, bidder responses that appear to be inadequate or appear to result in a negative conclusion based on the information provided in the bid response should be communicated back to the bidder before making a final decision on the viability of the bid (Figure 10.2).

10.7.1 Price

Price comparisons are not as easy as they may first seem. Yes, this is a firm-fixed-price bid but that is just the start. In the trade there is a phrase "low ball a bid". That means you quote an initial price that is very attractive but you make up for it with maintenance and future additions. Hence, the bid provided a projection of additional card readers, cameras and so forth to seek the future costs of system additions.

So on your spreadsheet, start with the Initial Purchase Price as the first line. Some systems have mandatory online services that must be purchased with the system, so your second line should be monthly (or annual) fees.

> Note:
>
> To have an even comparison, convert all costs to "annual costs" so that you have a "First Year Cost", "Second Year Cost" and so forth. As discussed in earlier chapters you can expect a location life of about 7 years for most systems before they need a major upgrade or replacement. So your goal here is to understand what the lifecycle cost of the system will be from each bidder.

Total Cash Outlay for the following criteria:
7 year location life
Add 14 cameras

	Panasonic	Eagle Eye Networks	Salient Systems	Bosch	Salient
Acquire System	General Informatics	LAtech	ADS	MS Benbow & Assoc	RAE Security
Initial purchase price	42,500	18,199	49,659	34,019	46,350
License Fees					
Year 1	-	6,760	-	-	-
Year 2	-	6,760	-	-	-
Year 3	-	6,760	-	-	-
Add 14 Cameras, 2 per year — Initial purchase price					
Year 1	613	480	292	300	300
Year 2	613	480	292	300	300
Year 3	613	480	292	300	300
Camera License Fees — **Fee Amount**	-	**65**	-	**95**	**50**
Additional Cameras					
2 — Year 1	-	130	-	190	100
4 — Year 2	-	260	-	380	200
6 — Year 3	-	390	-	570	300
Total Cost to Own for 7 Years	44,339	40,699	50,535	36,059	47,850
Maintenance					
Year 1	Warranty	Warranty	Warranty	Warranty	Warranty
Year 2	3393.10	3469.00	1,489.78	3133.00	2500.00
Year 3	3721.41	3469.00	1,534.48	3313.00	2500.00
Year 4	4093.55	3469.00	1,580.51	3493.00	2500.00
Total Cost to Maintain for 7 Years	11,208	10,407	4,605	9,939	7,500

	Panasonic	Eagle Eye Networks	Salient Systems	Bosch	Salient
Final Analysis	General Informatics	LAtech	ADS	MS Benbow & Assoc	RAE Security
Total Cost to Own for 7 Years	44,339	40,699	50,535	36,059	47,850
Total Cost to Maintain for 7 Years	11,208	10,407	4,605	9,939	7,500
All costs for 7 Years	55,547	51,106	55,140	45,998	55,350
Rank	5	2	3	1	4

FIGURE 10.2 Business Plan Evaluation Spreadsheet.

10.7.2 Maintenance

Next add the annual maintenance costs. Most bidders will not quote prices for service beyond 3 years because their costs will change. If your system is large enough, you can negotiate long-term maintenance fees but that might be asking too much. If you get a 3-year forecast, that will give you a starting point and you can extrapolate the future years from the first 3 years. In some cases bidders are reluctant to quote a forecast for "full service" contracts. That means the cost of the equipment is included in the maintenance contract costs. A work around for this is to separate the labor from the material and ask for a labor-only forecast. At the same time require the bidder to provide a projection of the failure rate of end point components (card readers, cameras, etc.). You can use that data to do your own forecast.

10.7.3 Future Costs

Then add in the projections you provided the bidders for costs of future additions to your spreadsheet and show their price quote for each year's addition. Again be careful to look for annual fees as well as initial purchase price.

It is simply not possible to provide you with a fixed format because of the pricing variations of bidders. Know that your goal is to define the TOTAL COSTS for year 1 though year 7 in a side-by-side comparison for all bidders who have passed the initial criteria. I suspect you can now see why you culled bidders when you started to get to a short list.

10.7.4 Terms

Now review items like payment terms, equipment storage, delivery interval … all the elements raised by the management team and selection committee. These items rarely make a difference between bidders but from time to time one of the bidders may have an unusual perspective on the project and it must be pointed out during the bid comparisons.

10.7.5 Conditions and References

This is where you define the "Quality of Service". Begin with the criteria in your bid document. Did you require a local office? Did you list a minimum number of technicians? Are you asking for 24/7 service? List your criteria on your work-sheet and inspect the bids for evidence of that criteria. Again, omitted data can be requested subsequent to the initial submittal of the bidder failed to provide enough information.

After evaluating the bids, check the bidder's references. Contact the previous buyers listed by the bidder and discuss their performance during the installation and, if applicable, the performance of the installed system. Create a form for this investigation similar to the example in Figure 10.3.

Interview Guide Physical Security System Selection Process
Vendor Questions

(Consultant)
(Date)

Questions are to be addressed to the service manager who will handle the system:

Administrative:

1. What is the address and telephone number of the primary service contact office?
2. Who is the top management person at this office and how long have they held that position?
3. What is the address and telephone number of other offices in the state of Louisiana that could service our facilities?
4. Who are the top management persons at each subordinate office and how long have they held that position?
5. What are the hours of operation of each service office?
6. Do service calls come directly to the field offices or are they channeled through a dispatch center?
7. What is your average response time for a routine service call (document studies would be helpful) for a **M**aintenance **C**ontract customer?
8. What is your "guaranteed" response time for a service call for an MC customer?
9. What is your response time for a major system outage for an MC customer?
10. What is your average recorded time from initial call to "problem cleared"?
11. Is there a charge for after-hours service calls for an MC customer?
12. Will it make a difference in service response if (the Company) provides the installation?
13. If you perform the system installation, what documentation do you produce prior to the installation?
14. If you perform the system installation and follow-up maintenance, do you maintain and update your system documentation (show examples)?
15. Your bid included a price for system maintenance, is that price negotiable if (the Company) assumes some of the maintenance responsibilities?

FIGURE 10.3 Sample Contact Form.

Labor:

1. How many technicians are at the primary service office?
2. What is the training history of each technician with regard to the system you are proposing?
3. How many technicians are at the subordinate offices?
4. What is the training history of each technician at the subordinate office with regard to the system you are proposing?
5. What continuing education program do you have for technicians?
6. Do you assign technicians on a first come basis or are technicians assigned specific accounts?
7. What duties other than "maintaining access control systems" are your technicians required to do?
8. Approximately how many accounts does each technician handle?
9. What is your performance measurement index for a technician?
10. What is the average employment length "on the job" for your technicians?
11. If your service office is not open 24/7, how do you handle after hours service calls?
12. Who are your top 3 MC service customers in each office that will serve an (The Company) facility and what is there approximate MC value?

Material:

1. Where do you stock spare equipment for the system you are proposing (address or address(es))?
2. How many spare readers (of the type you are proposing) do you stock?
3. How many network panels (of the type you are proposing) do you stock?
4. If you perform a service call for an MC customer, and use a spare from your stock is there a charge for material?
5. If an MC customer receives a spare from your stock, is it a new product or refurbished?
6. If an MC customer receives a new or refurbished spare from your stock, is the original product repaired and returned or is there simply a "swap" of possession?
7. What is the warranty on a replaced product?

END OF INTERVIEW

FIGURE 10.3 (Continued)

Interview Guide Access Control System Selection Process
Referred Customer Questions
(The Company) Vendor Selection Committee

(Consultant)
(Date)

Questions are to be addressed to the System Administrator (users):

1. When was your system installed?
2. How did you select this vendor for your system?
3. Why did you select this vendor?
4. What features were you most interested in when selecting your system?
5. Did the vendor do your installation or did you contract with others?
6. Do you use your access cards as ID cards?
7. Do your ID cards have photos and does the vendor supply this photo system?
8. Approximately how many card readers are in your system?
9. Which card reader technology are you using?
10. Are all the card readers located in the same building?
11. How did you handle inter-building communications (if applicable)?
12. How many workstations do you have?
13. Are there any off-site workstations?
14. Do you use your system for alarm monitoring?
15. Do you use your system for CCTV control?
16. Do you use your system for elevator control?
17. What is the model name of yousystem software?
18. What version of the vendor's software are you using?
19. How long does it take for the vendor to deliver additions to your system?
20. Generally, has the system met your expectations?
21. How often does the vendor communications system fail?
22. What system limitations have you found that you cannot overcome?
23. How difficult is the system to learn to use?

FIGURE 10.3 (Continued)

24. How would you rate the vendor's user training program (1–10, 10 being the best)?
25. How would you rate the vendor's telephone support for user problem (1–10, 10 being the best)?
26. Do you have a maintenance contract with the vendor?
27. Where is the vendor service office that maintains your system?
28. What are their hours of operation?
29. Who do you call to place a service request?
30. What is your average response time for a routine service call?
31. What is your response time for a major system outage?
32. How many visits does it take the vendor to clear a problem?
33. About how many service calls do you have in an average month?
34. Do the technicians seem knowledgeable about the system?
35. Has the vendor ever charged you for items you felt should have been covered by your MC?
36. Does the vendor have adequate records on your system installation (cable runs, interconnections, etc.)?
37. Do you generally get the same technician for each service call or are they randomly assigned?
38. Have you ever had to place an after-hours service call, and what was the response time?
39. Have parts been readily available for your system?
40. Would you make the same decision again to use this vendor?

END OF INTERVIEW

FIGURE 10.3 (Continued)

10.8 CONFIRM YOUR CONCLUSIONS

You will find that most people are willing to talk to you about their experience. Some will praise their vendors, others may complain. Take all comments with a grain of salt. There are always undisclosed biases (pro and con) in these conversations. Remember this is not an interrogation, you are looking for impressions from others who have experienced working with the bidders.

Prepare written comments for the bidder on each point in the Business Plan where it appears that the bidder has not met the requirements. Send that letter to the respective bidder through the purchasing agent. This gives the bidder an opportunity to correct misunderstandings about the submittal and reinforce the desirability of their offer.

Upon receipt of the bidder's reply, amend or confirm the conclusions reached about the bidder's willingness and ability to respond adequately to the RFP requirements. The principal objective in doing this detail level comparison is to ensure that the process is as objective, fair and even as possible for all prospective bidders.

10.9 VENDOR PRESENTATIONS

After evaluating the written proposals, request a product demonstration from the bidders identified as the most likely candidates to meet the requirements of the RFP. Develop a presentation agenda that focuses on the features that are most valuable to the company. Based on that agenda, create an evaluation form that the selection committee will use to review the vendor's presentation. This helps to guide the selection committee in the presentation process (Figure 10.4).

The agenda will allow for breaks at 60-minute intervals and permit the bidder approximately 15 minutes at the end of the presentation to discuss features not shown on the agenda. They may also use this time to sum up their presentation.

When scheduling meetings with the vendors, set no more than two presentations each day: one in the morning and one in the afternoon. Limit the vendors to a maximum of 2.5 hours for the entire presentation. This will reduce "buffer overload" and permit the management team to attend to other duties between presentations.

Begin the presentation with an introduction of the selection committee by name and title and remind the bidder that you are the prime contact for all follow-up calls pertaining to this bid. Allow the bidder to "take charge" of the presentation process but moderate the proceedings to ensure that the agenda is followed.

At the end of the presentation, collect the evaluation forms and tabulate the results. Prepare a final report on the comparison of the systems presented, incorporating the evaluation of the written proposals and the product demonstration. The report will amplify, confirm or amend the initial evaluations (from the written responses) and conclude with a final recommendation for the most responsive bidders.

10.10 WRAP UP

At the conclusion of the evaluation, combine the comparison summary of the technical evaluation with the conclusions reached in the business plan evaluations. Prepare a written report for the management team identifying the most responsive bidder, how they rank against each other and the benefits of selecting one over another.

Illustrate the method used to evaluate the bids. Conclude with the follow-up action and how to handle the next step in the process. Remember that the recommendation may have more than one bidder if all comparison elements are equal. The recommendation may also conclude that the benefits do not justify the cost of the project and the recommendation may suggest another approach. Your job is to help the management team make the best decision based on the information available.

Call for a meeting of the system selection committee, present the evaluation and the final recommendation. At the conclusion of the meeting, ask the

Selection Committee Presentation Evaluation

	Feature Point Value Assignment Points	Assigned
1 General Description and Capabilities		
1.2 Guard Tour Capabilities	50	
1.2 Image Management Capabilities	100	
1.2 CCTV controls	50	
1.2 Specialized parking software	30	
1.2 Datagathering and data management	20	
2 Cards		
2.1 Can proposed system read owner's cards	500	
3 Card Reader		
3.1 Touch pad	2	
3.1 Indala prox	2	
3.1 Static safguard	2	
3.1 Tamper resistant, 2 stage	8	
3.1 Indoor/outdoor compatibility	2	
3.1 Red and green status lights	8	
3.1 Offline operation	10	
3.2 Network compatible with prox readers	5	
3.3 Integrated PIN	3	
3.3 Duress code on PIN	2	
3.3 PIN only locations	2	
4 Access Point Controller		
4.1 Offline enable	5	
4.1 Local buffer(min 1,500 transactions)	10	
4.1 On-board clander clock	5	
4.1 Leapyear calendar adjustments	1	
4.1 Daylight savings time calendar adjustments	2	
4 1 Battery backup for memory, 30 da	10	
4.1 Battery backup for operation, 6 hr	9	
4.1 LED display for communications	10	
4.1 LED display for lock status	8	
4.1 LED display for power	10	
4.1 LED display for alarms	5	
4.1 LED display for output relays	5	
4.1 Removable backup memory batteries	7	
4.2 Modular plugs	5	
4.2 Multiplexing or SDLC network design	1	
Alarms field expandable for alarms	6	
Alarms alarm input interlock	4	
Alarms alarm only model	4	
Alarms supervised alarm inputs	5	
Capacity initial card capacity of 5,000	5	
Capacity expandable card capacity of 12,500	5	
Hardware cabinet lock	8	
Hardware tamper switch	4	
Hardware local port for lap top interface	5	

FIGURE 10.4 Presentation Evaluation Form.

Hardware	Local port for printer interface	3	
Hardware	On board lock power, AC/DC, fused	1	
Hardware	Exit button input on separate port	8	
Hardware	Upgradable RAM chip	10	
Hardware	UL Approved	8	
Outputs	Field expandable for relays	1	
Readers	Number of readers supported, 4 is desired	7	
5	**Data Communications Network**		
5.1	Network architecture with hub & subsystems	1000	
5.1	Centralized database with source access	1000	
5.1	ODBC-Compliant Database	1000	
5.1	Direct Link to Peoplesoft		
5.2	Password at subsystem level	20	
5.2	Multiple terminals on subsystem processors	20	
	AC Network Architecture from Literature		
Alarm	Hub initiated dial up	10	
Capacity	Card reader capacity, minimum 500	10	
Comm	Propriatary line protocol (not desired)	4	
Hardware	Modular expasion of reader capacity	8	
Software	PC level network display	10	
Software	Can down load individual new card data to sub	100	
Software	Can bulk down load database updates to sub	100	
Software	Can modify tables with other db programs	100	
Software	Password-protected software access	10	
Software	Authorized levels for password acces	10	
Software	Auto log off	9	
Software	Operator Messages	5	
Software	Operator Audit Trail	6	
Software	Help Function	10	
Software	Database archiving	4	
6	**Access Control Functions**		
6.2	Who goes where, when	100	
6.2	Time schedule	10	
6.2	Holiday schedules	10	
6.2	Cardgroups	20	
6.2	Access by void valid	20	
6.2	Access by time of day	20	
6.2	Access by day of week	20	
6.2	Access by door	20	
6.2	Access by PIN and card	5	
6.2	Access by biometrics	5	
6.2	Photo with card file, ODBC exchange	50	
6.2	Auto door control by time	9	
6.2	List biometrics available	1	
6.3	Anti-passback	10	
6.3	Local anti-passback	4	
6.3	Global anti-passback	10	

FIGURE 10.4 (Continued)

6.3	Timed anti-passback	4	
6.3	Anti-passback with forgivness	4	
6.3	Anti-passback with exceptions	5	
6.3	Zoned anti-passback	10	
6.3	Auto expiration	8	
6.3	Calculated occupancy, Parking	4	
6.3	Monitor only reader, Guard Tour	1	
6.3	Elevator controls	7	
	<u>Subsystem Software</u>		
Alarm	Auto dial hub on alarm	10	
Alarm	Exit device release with alarm shunt	10	
Alarm	Door ajar detection	10	
Card file	User definable card fields	10	
Card file	Exporting card data	4	
Card file	Temporary cards	1	
Card file	Limited use cards	1	
Card file	Escort / visitor cards	2	
Controls	Output controls by keyboard	7	
Controls	Output controls by timer	10	
Controls	Output controls alram event	8	
Controls	Output controls by card swipe	4	
Controls	Output point identification by name	1	
Controls	Operator door control	9	
Controls	Reader lockout	1	
7	**<u>Alarm Monitoring Functions</u>**		
7.1	Monitor external devices	5	
7.2	Supervised and unsupervised monitoring point	10	
7.3	Alarm display	5	
7.4	Alarm announcement, audible	5	
7.4	Alarm announcement, visual	10	
7.4	Alarm announcement, verbal description	10	
7.4	Alarm announcement, acknowledgement	8	
7.5	Alarm maps, drawn	1	
7.5	Alarm maps, import	1	
7.6	Alarm shunting by time of day	10	
7.7	Alarm display at hub and substation	1	
8	**<u>Reports</u>**		
8.1	System status report	5	
8.1	History reports	20	
8.1	User defined reports	10	
8.2	Hub report on subsystem settings	5	
8.2	Hub report on traffic	5	
8.2	Hub report of history data from subsystems	20	
8.3	Subsystem report history filter: date, time, card	20	
8.4	Specialized reports, guard, elevator	15	
8.5	ASCII stream output for report	10	
		5030	0

FIGURE 10.4 (Continued)

committee if they are ready to decide to proceed. As with the decision to conduct the bid process, expect delays in the final choice. Usually by this time, there are no big surprises and the choice is "who to buy from" not "should we buy".

Prepare minutes of the meeting and follow up the selection committee at reasonable intervals to determine acceptance of the final recommendation if they do not make a decision at the meeting. After receiving final approval, release a recommendation to purchase the system to the company's purchasing office with full instructions on how to establish the contract with the selected bidder.

Once a decision has been made, a formal rejection letter to the unsuccessful bidders is a simple business courtesy. Although the bidder will not win the contract, the formal rejection helps them know where to end their efforts and expectations. A formal notice of rejection, if properly written, will also encourage the rejected bidder to participate in future bid opportunities. In the next chapter we will discuss "when" to send this rejection and why you should wait. But be prepared with a letter in hand so that when the time is right you can discharge this courtesy. The next step is system implementation.

CHAPTER 11

System Implementation

CONTENTS

11.1 INTRODUCTION

Well, we are finally here! You identified the assets, examined the vulnerabilities and designed the proper system to mitigate those vulnerabilities. You then worked through the acquisition process, identified the correct vendors and received the management team's approval and budget to implement your new security system, But ... even when a physical security system is properly designed and successfully acquired, it can fail to achieve the desired results because the implementation was poorly carried out. The preceding chapters were dedicated to the identification of the right system components and the professional delivery of those devices. Now you must focus attention on project management and implementation to ensure proper delivery and professional installation of these new security tools.

11.2 AWARDING THE CONTRACT

Review the Request for Proposal (RFP); this forms the basis of the agreement between the company and the vendor. Prepare the procurement recommendation

DOI: 10.4324/9781003490432-12

for the company's purchasing manager and request that the purchasing manager issue a "Letter of Intent" to purchase the system from selected vendors. This will provide the vendor with notification to proceed with pre-award submittals. *Refrain from notifying the unsuccessful bidders of the results of the contract award until the successful bidder accepts the order.*

Sometimes bidders make mistakes that are not apparent and they do not realize the mistake until after their bid has gone to review. However, when they are awarded a contract they look more closely at what they proposed and in so doing discover their error. Under these circumstances they will sometimes simply not accept the contract. Maybe their price was too low or they missed something in their labor estimate. Regardless of the reason, it's not an order until it is signed sealed and delivered!

By the way, that is the reason for a Bid Bond. If this situation occurs, you can use that bond to award the contract to the second most responsive bidder and if there is a price difference the bonding company must pay you that difference. Thus, requiring a Bid Bond assures you that a third party has monitored the bidder in the past and what they offered is what they will deliver at the price it was offered.

It is important to note here that actually enforcing the bid bond is the company's option, not a requirement. People make mistakes, the bond is here to confirm that the company does not have to pay for those mistakes. But if you have not incurred any costs and you find that the selected bidder cannot fulfill the contract, you may want to "let them off the hook" without calling in their bond. There may be a time in the future when you need them and holding them to the strict bond conditions will not reflect well on them. If the company suffers no penalty and you get what you want with the next lowest bidder, allowing them out of the offer is a gesture of good will and may serve you in future dealings with this company.

If the RFP requires preinstallation submittals, follow up receipt of those submittals before awarding the contract. Inspect the submittals for conformity to the requirements of the RFP and require the vendor to correct any errors or deficiencies. The mandatory submittals described in earlier chapters are:

1. Completions Schedule (firm installation schedule)
2. Schedule of Earned Values (when will payments be requested for each billable item)

Notify the company's purchasing department when the submittals are in order and request preparation of the purchase order with instructions to the vendor "not to proceed until after attending an initial walkdown meeting and receiving a Notice to Proceed". Now recommend that the purchasing manager notify the unsuccessful bidders of the contract award in the letter we discussed in the last chapter. It is helpful, though not imperative, for you to also telephone the prime contact of each bidder and thank them for their efforts.

11.3 GETTING STARTED

The most important aspect of system implementation is communication between the company, you and the vendor. Good communication ensures that changes in the design and unforeseen problems can be quickly and easily resolved. The relationship is not adversarial but cooperative. All parties want a smooth successful installation and one of your primary duties is to facilitate that process. The company wants a useful, effective system and the vendor needs to make a reasonable profit.

To begin the communication process, convene an Initial Walkdown meeting with the vendor and select members of the company's system selection committee. Begin with a review of the terms and conditions of the RFP. Confirm that everyone understands what is expected of them to successfully implement the security solutions. At the conclusion of the meeting, visit all equipment locations and discuss how to carry out the installation and the concerns for operational aspects of the installation. This process is called the Initial Walkdown.

Prepare a report on Initial Walkdown for the management team and enumerate all the concerns expressed by the meeting attendees. If additional information or decisions are required before proceeding, document the responses in follow-up letters to the vendor and the management team, including Purchasing.

Prepare a request to the purchasing manager to release a "Notice to Proceed" to the vendor. This signals the vendor that their submittals are acceptable and they may begin the investments needed to deliver the proposed systems.

11.4 MILESTONE REVIEWS

There are no rigid rules that apply for every installation; each installation requires individual review planning. The vendor's work schedule is a good resource for this coordination planning; this was part of the submittal After Award of Contract. The RFP also required periodic meetings with the vendor's on-site project manager; they probably have a plan in mind already for project coordination. Discuss the best times for coordination meetings with the vendor. Establish a firm meeting schedule coordinated with anticipated work completion milestones.

In addition to the milestone inspections, plan to perform periodic spot inspections to confirm progress. These are informal walkdowns to review the work. Exercise caution during these inspections. Remember that the workmen report to the vendor and should always be given instructions from the vendor's project manager. If an installation error is discovered, that error should be reported immediately to the vendor's project manager and not directly to the workmen. An exception to this might be if a workman is about to cut a doorframe to install a lock on the wrong door. Direct communication with the workman would save everyone concerned time and money but report the error to the vendor's project manager for verification.

The inspection process described below is the customary and usual method for installation of most types of physical security systems. After inspecting the installation for each milestone, create a "punch list" of unfinished items or items that require correction. The term "punch list" is used to identify uncompleted or defective items discovered during an inspection of an installation. By addressing these items early in the installation process, confusion is reduced and errors are eliminated more easily.

After each milestone inspection, conduct a meeting with the vendor's project manager and representatives from the company's selection committee. This will aid in the communications process and keep the company informed about the progress of the installation.

11.4.1 Milestone Meeting 1: Cabling Complete

The project usually begins with cabling. When the vendor announces that cabling is complete, inspect the cable installation, paying particular attention to the following items:

1. Is the cable type that was proposed by the vendor (or recommended by the manufacturer) the cable that was used?
2. Is each cable labeled so that it can be easily identified at both ends?
3. Has the installer allowed enough slack in selected cables for future additions?
4. Is there excess cable (coils of communications cable in ceilings can act like antennas for radio frequency (RF) and electromechanical interference (EMI), thereby interfering with the proper communications between the devices)?
5. Is the cable properly suspended in ceiling areas?
6. Has cabling been provided to all equipment locations?

After completing the inspection and coordination meeting, report the progress of Milestone 1 to the management team and plans to follow up any action required.

11.4.2 Milestone Meeting 2: Equipment Staging Complete

If the RFP required bench testing and staging of the system before installation, follow up the vendor to determine when the equipment is in hand. Require the vendor to provide an inventory by serial number of each major piece of equipment.

When the vendor is ready for a staging inspection, visit the vendor's place of business and observe that all devices are working properly. Allow for the absence of software setup but all major components should be tested and confirmed operational. At the conclusion of the test, record the names of the individuals performing the test and the results of the test. Note any system defects and the vendor's commitment to replace defective equipment. Prepare a report on the progress of Milestone 2 for the management team. Provide the results of the test and plans to follow up any action required.

11.4.3 Milestone Meeting 3: Equipment Mounting Complete

When the vendor announces that the equipment is mounted, conduct Milestone 3 inspection and coordination meeting. Some areas of concern are as follows:

1. Is the mounting cosmetically acceptable?
2. Are all components securely mounted?
3. Does equipment mounting interfere with the operation or access to other devices?
4. Is the installed equipment the same products demonstrated during staging process?

After completing the equipment mounting inspection and coordination meeting, report the progress of Milestone 3 to the management team and plans to follow up any action required.

11.4.4 Milestone Meeting 4: Final Termination Complete

When the vendor announces that the final termination (connecting the low-voltage cabling to the equipment) is complete, conduct Milestone 4 inspection and coordination meeting. Some areas of concern are as follows:

1. Are all cables terminated at each device?
2. Is each cable labeled so that future system expansion is easy to do?
3. Do the termination areas appear neat and orderly?
4. Are the control boxes clearly labeled identifying the purpose of each box?
5. Is there a chart in each control box indicating the end devices connected to it?
6. If tamper alarms were specified on the control boxes, are they installed?
7. Are there locks on the control boxes?

Please note:

At this point, power should not be applied to the devices. The vendor will be permitted to connect to commercial power when all devices are wired and ready for use.

When Milestone Inspection 4 is finished and the coordination team has agreed in the follow-up meeting that the system is ready to be "turned on", the vendor should be given permission to power up the system and begin the testing and troubleshooting phase. Report the results of Milestone 4 to the management team and plans to follow up any action required.

11.4.5 Unscheduled Visits

Periodically visit the jobsite to determine progress and inspect the work. A good rule of thumb is to do an unescorted inspection on a weekly basis. Much can be learned by a simple visit and it will be relatively easy to gage the progress of the work by seeing what has been accomplished since the last visit. Report problems found to the vendor to aid in the installation process but remember that these are unscheduled visits outside regular milestones. In managing labor resources, a vendor may allow intermediate progress to lapse on one project while emphasizing another more urgent project. There is no reason for recrimination if milestone deadlines are met. Your project may be the next one to get special attention to meet the milestone dates.

11.4.6 Final Inspection

When the vendor has announced that the system is ready for final inspection, call for a "pretest" of system operation. The pretest saves time and trouble for all concerned by ensuring that the final acceptance test will be conducted without incident. Conduct all of the steps of final testing. Develop a final punch list that describes items requiring attention before final delivering.

11.5 SYSTEM COMMISSIONING

11.5.1 Goals and Purpose

A security system consists of a variety of barriers, access control points, surveillance tools and protocols to protect and defend assets from identified threats. Some of these components are mechanical in nature, while others are electro-mechanical and still others are electronic in nature. It is imperative that each component performs as expected if the security system is going to do the job it was designed to do. System commissioning covers all these elements and is based on the Procurement Specification that was prepared as a result of the threat assessment, system design and security system recommendation for the project.

The main objective of system commissioning is to provide an orderly handover of a planned security system from the system vendor or contractor to the owner, guaranteeing its operation in performance, reliability and information management. Additionally, commissioning represents the fulfillment of quality and operational requirements of the project by the vendor or contractor and provides a basis for recommending final payment to the vendor.

Project commissioning assures that all systems and components of a planned security system are installed, tested and operational according to system specifications as provided by the design consultant, owner or final client. A commissioning process may be applied not only to new projects but also to additions, renovations or revamping of existing systems.

In practice, the commissioning process is a set of observations and tests to confirm the function of every operational component of the project. This includes individual functions on devices like card readers and cameras up to complex system operations such as access control software and artificial intelligence (AI) interpretations of video images.

Generally, walls, doors, barriers and other purely mechanical components of the system that were referred to in the specifications are confirmed as an adjunct to other more sophisticated components such as access control and alarm monitoring. For example, if a card reader was required on a door, it is expected that the door is fully operational and commented on only if there is an obvious flaw in the door installation discovered during the access control inspection.

However, in some cases, certain mechanical components are included in the commissioning observations if there is a particular need defined in the specification such as a continuous hinge or extended screws that attached the door frame to the wall construction. Without such criteria, the mechanical components are simply assumed to be satisfactory and it is left up to the building contractor to ensure that these components are up to the current building codes.

11.5.2 Methodology and Standards

Each system is unique; a checklist of verification points is prepared before each commissioning walkdown. While the checkpoints will vary with each system, certain standards apply for all system components; below are the general guidelines for those standards.

The commissioning process begins at the outer point of each system such as a card reader in an access control system, then the function is traced through the system components until arriving at the user interface. Then automatic functions, reports and other user operations are tested and confirmed. At the end of the process a document is issued to client or end user that the system is fully operational and ready for use. The following requirements are applicable for each system component test (Figure 11.1).

Access Control Test

1 Verify access and egress, test valid and VOID cards
2 Confirm door closer
3 Verify door latches when it falls
4 Verify every transaction at every door
5 Verify fire alarm Interface

Door Description	Location Ref on Drwg	Commissioning Test	Comments
Exterior Perimeter			
Ped Gate fm Villere St.	1	PASSED	
Vehicle Gate fm Villere St.	2	FAILED	Reset the access time. See report.
Vehicle Gate fm Columbus St.	3	FAILED	Reset the access time. Connect the phone line and program the dialer. See report.
Building Security Perimeter Floor 1			
Main Entrance East Door	5	PASSED	
Main Entrance West Door	6	FAILED	Correct install of remote lock switch. See report.
Office Access to Student Area	9	FAILED	Reader on wrong side of door, see report.
Admin Office	12	PASSED	
Rear Door to Student Area	14	FAILED	Reader on wrong side of door, see report.
100 Stair 1 Egress	15	PASSED	
Employee entrance	16	FAILED	Repair door lock and then confirm reader and lock function together. See report.
W Door Collab. Courtyard	20	PASSED	
E Door Collab. Courtyard	23	FAILED	Lock failing.
Service Entrance? Stair 5 Exit	24	PASSED	
Stair 2 to Student Area	28	FAILED	Card reader on wrong side of door, reconfiguration needed. See report.
Receiving Door to Student Area	31	FAILED	Latch handle jamming. See report.
Service Entrance	32	FAILED	Electric lock on wrong leaf, no pull handles to open. See report.
Side Entrance	35	FAILED	Door lock jamming, top dog. See report.
Freight Gate	36	FAILED	Connect the phone line and program the dialer.
Not on the controlled door schedule, Media/ Coffee Room.		FAILED	Door in the wrong place. See report.

FIGURE 11.1 Test List for Commissioning.

11.5.3 Access Control

Door locks are verified locked for access and then card readers are tested to confirm they recognize authorized cards and unlock the door; then unauthorized cards are confirmed as rejected specifically, these are cards that are designed for that system but are not authorized for that area.

If the company has access control equipment installed, obtain a void card (one that is not supposed to work) and a valid card (one that is supposed to work) and test each controlled door. The void card should be rejected and the valid card should be accepted. Also verify the locking device used to secure the door. When the door is in a normal and locked condition, is it possible to defeat the lock by ordinary means and gain access?

Egress is tested to confirm that either free egress is allowed or, for controlled egress, that the door cannot be opened unless the appropriate egress method is used (e.g., door hardware, card reader, exit button, etc.). This is confirmed against the Door Detail Schedule. Confirm reader placement complies with ADA requirements.

The user interface is then verified to confirm that all transactions (access granted or denied) are presented in real time to the user (note that display may be turned on or turned off at the discretion of the user). Reports as specified in the design are confirmed so that subsequent investigations into door usage may be made at a later date.

Control tables in the system software are also verified. At least one table of authorized times must be present and properly labeled for 24 hours 7 days a week access. If other time requirements were provided to the vendor at the time of design submittal, they too should be verified.

At least one table for access areas must be present and properly labeled for all doors. If other access group requirements were provided to the vendor at the time of design submittal, they too should be verified. Other software features such as user database that are included with the design orders should likewise be verified against the installed system.

11.5.4 Life Safety

In access control systems there are electromechanical locks that are used to hold doors closed and locked to secure an area. Sometimes those locks "compete" with life safety goals and for that reason, those locks are connected to the building fire alarm system. Each door so connected must also be tested to confirm that when the fire alarm is triggered the door will automatically unlock. Do this test for each fire alarm interfaced door in the system.

This is usually done by triggering the fire alarm or fire suppression systems to confirm that these systems have the ability to unlock the controlled

Alarm Monitoring Test

1 Verify all door alarms are shown at control

2 Verify all door alarms are shown at central station panel

Door Description	Location Ref on Drwg	Commissioning Test	Comments
Main Entrance East Door	5	PASSED	
Main Entrance West Door	6	FAILED	No alarm signal registering
Office Access to Student Area	9	PASSED	
100 Stair 1 Egress	15	PASSED	OWNER WANTS ADDITONAL SECURITY FEATURES AT THIS DOOR. See report.
Employee entrance	16	FAILED	Alarm locked in open position
Electrical Room 155	17	PASSED	
AHU 1A	18	FAILED	No alarm signal registering
Storage	19	PASSED	
W Door Collab. Courtyard	20	FAILED	Security components exposed, see report.
W Rollup Door Collab. Courtyd	21	PASSED	
E Door Collab. Courtyard	23	FAILED	Security components exposed, see report.
Service Entrance? Stair 5 Exit	24	PASSED	
Electrical Room	25	FAILED	No alarm signal registering
Mechanical Room	26	FAILED	No alarm signal registering
Maintenance / Repairs	27	FAILED	No alarm signal registering
Stair 2 to Student Area	28	PASSED	
Exterior Service Yard	29	Door Missing	plans changed, door not there
Roll up Door to Service Yard	30	FAILED	No alarm signal registering. NOTE: originally there was only one roll up door at this location, now there are two Alarm missing from second door.
Receiving Door to Student Area	31	PASSED	
Service Entrance	32	FAILED	No alarm signal registering
Stair 3 Egress N	33	FAILED	No alarm signal registering
Side Entrance	35	PASSED	
Stairwell 6	37	PASSED	
Room 102	PIR	Could not test	For after-hours alarms only
Room 103	PIR	Could not test	For after-hours alarms only
School Office Lobby	PIR	Could not test	For after-hours alarms only
The doors below were added to the system after this schedule was prepared.			
Courtyard to Machine Lab	N / A	PASSED	
Courtyard to Welding Lab	N / A	PASSED	
Courtyard to Lumber Storage	N / A	PASSED	
Courtyard to Carpentry Lab	N / A	PASSED	
Courtyard to Electrical Lab	N / A	PASSED	
Courtyard to Stairwell	N / A	PASSED	

FIGURE 11.2 Test List for Commissioning, Alarm Monitoring.

doors. Do these tests with the knowledge and consent of the facility managers, the response team and any outside service that monitors these alarms. The maintenance personnel that service the detection systems can usually trigger these systems without sounding a general alarm and disrupting the company's staff.

11.5.5 Alarm Monitoring

The door monitoring device is visually verified to confirm that what was specified was actually installed. For example, some doors require "concealed" door status switches (DSS), while others require special DSS devices such as armored contacts for roll up doors; if the appropriate DSS is not in place, you should note an exception to your commissioning form (see Figure 11.2).

Verify the door is closed and door status is verified on the security display as being closed. Then use the access device on the door to request access, open the door and confirm the display shows the door is open. Finally, hold the door open past the door shunt time and confirm that the display shows an alarm of "door opened". Allow the door to close and reset the alarm then egress the door and confirm that the display shows the door opening without an alarm (this, of course, assumes that this door is not using egeess control).

Panic alarms are verified to show as a "Panic or Distress" alarm at the appropriate location.

The user interface is then verified to confirm that all alarms (door status, panic and other alarms as defined by the system specifications) are presented in real time to the user (note that display may be turned on or turned off at the discretion of the user). Reports as specified in the design are confirmed so that subsequent investigations into alarm violations may be made at a later date.

11.5.6 Video Surveillance

Each fixed focal image required by the Camera Detail Schedule is verified by first confirming that an image with the appropriate labeling is presented at the user interface. That image is then inspected for clarity and field of view.

When inspecting for field of view attention should be given to overly broad images; that is, if an 8 mm lens is specified and a 6 mm lens is used, the area to be viewed may be too broad, and hence the target in the image is too small. The target area follows the rule of thumb that a subject in the designated field may occupy no less than 10% of the total image. This is to ensure that subjects can be recognized from the images provided and can trigger automatic closed-circuit television (CCTV) analytical functions such as real-time recordings.

If night viewing is an issue, defined by the system specification, another walkdown after-hours in the dark may be required.

Where pan, tilt and zoom features are included in the design, the same verifications are made as described for fixed images and the ability to move the camera and zoom the lens is confirmed with attention to the range of fields of view.

Recorded images are then verified for clarity, ease of search and the ability to stop playback and print or capture recorded images on another media (such as a compact disk (CD) or thumb drive). The maximum recorded time is confirmed where prescribed in the system design (see Figure 11.3)

CCTV Test

1 Confirm image is present
2 Verify clarity
3 Verify field of view
4 Verify recording and play back

Camera View	Location Ref on Drwg	Commissioning Test	Comments
Exterior			
Bus Entrance to Employee Parking	7	PASSED	Move signs
Employee Parking E	16	PASSED	Move signs
Interior Floor 1			
Floor 2			
Interir Courtyard Entrances (N / S)	60	FAILED	Camera missing
Stair 3 226	61	FAILED	Camera is present but does not show up on system
Lounge	68	FAILED	Camera missing
Simulation Room	69	FAILED	Camera is present but does not show up on system
Floor 3			
Guest Parking, Student Walkway E	1	PASSED	
Exterior Perimeter, (Plan) SE Corner	6	PASSED	
Primary Entrance East Side	110	PASSED	
Bus Drop and Emergency Exit	117	PASSED	
Student Area W	76	N/A	Plans changed, no camera but there is no floor to view. Camera removed from system
Main Entrace	20	PASSED	
Entry Vestibule	21	PASSED	
Visitor Lobby	22	PASSED	
Rear Access to Admin	23	PASSED	
Corr. 101 East E	43	PASSED	
Corr. 101 East W	44	PASSED	
Media Lounge	45	PASSED	
CAD 3 Storage	46	PASSED	
Primary Student Egress	48	PASSED	
Stair 2 144	49	PASSED	
Lounge	50	PASSED	
Carpentry Lab	100	PASSED	
Welding Lab	101	PASSED	
Elevator 2	102	PASSED	
Receiving Cabinets	103	PASSED	
HVAC Lab	104	PASSED	
Electrical Lab	105	PASSED	
Kitchen Storage Area	82	FAILED	Camera missing. NOTE: location is now Roof. Need new location for camera for this view
Lounge	109	FAILED	Camera missing
Elevator	70	PASSED	
Graphic Design Lab Storage	90	PASSED	
Programming and Development	108	PASSED	

CCTV Test

1 Confirm image is present
2 Verify clarity
3 Verify field of view
4 Verify recording and playback

Camera View	Location Ref on Drwg	Commissioning Test	Comments
Corridor 301 Center W	115	PASSED	
Corridor 301 Center E	116	PASSED	

FIGURE 11.3 Test List for Commissioning, CCTV.

11.5.7 Audio Surveillance

Each area under audio surveillance is verified to confirm minimum recognition of sound and clarity. Using a decibel meter, normal conversation is about 60 db, sounds at that level should be reproduced and confirmed recognized by the system. The sound should again be reproduced at progressively lower levels until the threshold is found. Minimal acceptable level is above 30 db. Words and numbers are then presented to the surveillance station for verification of clarity.

If audio recording is included in the system design, recorded sounds are then verified for clarity, ease of search and the ability to stop playback and export to another media (such as a CD or thumb drive). The minimum recorded time is confirmed where prescribed in the system design.

11.5.8 Intercom Systems

Each intercom station is verified to confirm the ability to signal the control station or, if applicable, another intercom station. The station should be checked to verify ease of use and instructions for reaching the control station. Likewise, the ability to "call" the station from the control location should be confirmed. Clarity of speech should be confirmed by normal conversation between the intercom station and the control station. If a remote door release is included with the intercom station, this too should be confirmed at the time of testing. Confirm placement complies with ADA requirements.

11.5.9 Employee Identification

The implementation of this security system component includes the creation of identity cards and the quality of the card and clarity of printed information on the card. A new card should be created as part of the test. If a photograph is included in the design criteria, a photo of the individual card holder should be taken. The card should then be examined for photo clarity, text clarity and the inclusion of all card holder information in the design criteria.

Where applicable, lanyards, clothing clips or other wearable devices should be confirmed available. If the card is an access card, it should be authorized in the system and the use should be confirmed at a convenient card reader. The final product should be examined for unique characteristics as well as the resistance value of the design to prevent unauthorized duplication by ordinary means (such as a photocopy).

11.5.10 Visitor Controls

Visitor control systems allow the user to properly identify and vet visitors to the facility; it generally consists of a means to record visitor ID information and verify that the visitor is authorized to enter. While this is most often a matter of protocols there is usually equipment involved such as cameras, databases and related devices.

The system should be tested by registering as a visitor and, if applicable, determining if that visitor has permission to enter. Then the recordkeeping of the device should be examined to confirm the ability to recall a visit and run reports described in the specification, such as how often this visitor came to the facility.

11.5.11 Communications

This verification is intended to confirm that the response team (security force) is accessible by telephone or other forms of communication to be alerted to the presence of a threat or impending potential threat. Means and methods expected are published telephone numbers, signage with contact information and security phones. The bulk of the commissioning attention should be paid to security phones.

Specifically, call boxes and stand-alone stations that either are directly connected to the security station or have automatic dialers to reach the response team. The units should be tested by operating them and ensuring that the response team receives the call. Where applicable, the operation of alert lights and horns in conjunction with phone usage should be confirmed.

11.5.12 Lighting

If the security system design included adding or upgrading lighting, the security system commissioning should include confirmation that the lights were installed and are operating on a timer or sensor to turn on during darkness. Additionally, a light meter should be used to confirm the intensity of the new or upgraded lights and that they meet the light-level requirement of the system design after sunset.

11.5.13 Signage

If signage is part of the design criteria, all signs described in the specification should be verified. In addition to confirming placement the commissioning should assess the surrounding foliage and other structures to ensure visibility and the sign itself should be examined for clarity in print and character size. The material used in making the sign should be assessed (if material specs are not part of the design orders) and confirmed weather resistant.

11.5.14 Special Circuits

In some instances, the standard operation of commercially available devices will not meet the security objectives; in those cases special connections are required to achieve the sought-after goals.

The performance of each special circuit should be examined to confirm it produces the results defined in the specifications. The actual wiring is less important to the commissioning than the resulting equipment performance. Where performance is not acceptable, the circuit should be rejected with a request for redesign.

11.5.15 Software Test

The software test covers some of the items you already tested, but this time you are looking at the system from the operator's point of view. Your goal is not necessarily to test every software feature of the system but rather those features included in your RFQ as being necessary for the security system you specified. Figure 11.4 is an example.

Software Test

		Passed
Access Control		
	All card transactions displayed, granted and denied	
	All alarm transactions are displayed	
	Access table, 1 group, all doors	
	Time period table, 1 24-hour zone	
	User database	
	Change door state	
	Report card useage	
	Report card holders	
Alarm Monitoring		
	All alarm points displayed when in alarm	
	Demonstrate clear an alarm	
	Demonstrate auto shunt alarm	
	Report alarms by door	
	Report alarms multiple doors	
CCTV		
	Verify recorded images	
	Playback by camera	
	Playback by multiple cameras	
	Search by time	
	Export to separate media	
	Verify maximum recorded time	

FIGURE 11.4 Test List for Commissioning, Software Test.

11.6 FINAL REPORT AND DELIVERY

A report to the management team should then be prepared that details the findings of the commissioning. System components found that are not operating as specified should be identified with explanations and descriptions of the rejection. In those cases a subsequent commissioning walkdown should be held until all errors are corrected.

If all the system components are acceptable, the report should so state and final payment release to the vendor recommended. This will conclude the system commissioning.

11.6.1 Delivery, Who Should Attend

Invite the vendor's sales representative, project manager and support personnel to the final test. Invite members from the selection committee who are assigned the duties of monitoring the system installation.

Arrange to have a two-way communication between the groups doing the tests. Most large companies and many vendors have radio/telephone systems that can be used for this purpose.

11.6.2 When Should the Test Be Conducted

It is best to conduct the test during a week that does not have company holidays. This will allow the vendor a day for last minute preparation and time to correct any anomalies discovered during the final acceptance test before a weekend. Start the test early, it may take full day in large systems. You can also do the delivery inspection on multiple days if necessary.

11.6.3 What Should Be Covered

Demonstrate all operational aspects of the system. Tests were conducted and errors were identified and corrected during the commissioning, so this is simply a formality so that the company knows the new system is in and working. It is also the "period at the end of the sentence" for the vendor.

11.7 POST-INSTALLATION SUBMITTALS

Based on the requirements of the RFP, vendors will provide additional documentation at the end of the installation. In this example, the vendor was required to provide an “as built” drawing. This is a modification of the original wiring arrangement and reflects the changes from the original design resulting from unforeseen installation conditions. The as-built drawings will be invaluable when modifying or adding to the system later.

Confirm the vendor training arrangements and discuss training commitment dates with the company’s security managers. Verify that the vendor and security staff set class dates.

The system is now operational but should remain “turned off” following the acceptance test and delivery. But let’s define “off”. In most cases the best alternative is to leave all the electronics powered on but the locking devices powered down so that the doors operate as they did before the installation. Shunt the alarm systems so they are not recorded. Turn the system on when the training is complete and the security staff is ready to place the system into service.

11.8 SECURITY SYSTEM PERSONNEL

In previous chapters, the term “the system” referred to the devices the company needed to purchase in order to provide the recommended security solutions. To implement the proposed solutions, the system also needs people. People manage the systems. People determine the most appropriate constraints to program into the system to meet security objectives. People respond to alarm conditions perceived by the system.

“The system” is the combination of the devices and the people that work with them. Your role does not end with the successful implementation of devices – it is just one step in the process. You must also address the human side of the equation.

11.8.1 Identify the System Administrator

The system administrator (SA) serves as the central point for all decisions concerning system operation. The SA may seek advice and counsel from various department managers where system components are; however, the SA is responsible for implementing the decisions. The SA reports to the Chief of Security or Risk Management Manager and sometimes is the manager of the department.

You should work with the management team to identify the SA. Advise the company that the responsibilities of the SA are not casual and will demand considerable effort from the designated person. In other words, the SA, especially for larger systems, should not be a human resources clerk assigned this role as a sideline project to their other duties. The SA is a dedicated individual, usually in the company’s security department, who is prepared to devote at least 50% of their work time to managing the physical security system.

11.8.2 Identify the Help Desk

In complex systems with multiple work stations and especially in systems that provide work stations to departments (in some cases department heads control their own card authorization), identify a Help Desk. The Help Desk works with the SA and provides software support and guidance to other participating departments. In some cases, the Help Desk is actually the SA since they are most familiar with system operation in the company.

11.8.3 System User Training

The company relies on you to guide the implementation of the new physical security system. You must rely on the system vendor to teach the software programming steps and mechanical details of the selected system to the users.

There is simply too much information available for all such systems for you to be a knowledgeable expert in the intricate details of the ever-changing software world of physical security. Make sure that the company receives full user training from the vendor or the manufacturer of the system and provide oversight to that training.

There are two levels of user training: System Administrator and Operator. The names of these levels may differ from one company to another but the concept is essentially the same. An SA manages all the functions of the physical security system and has the top-level password that will permit them to change all system user functions.

An Operator is usually an officer standing a post watch who must respond to alarms in the system and requests from authorized employees to alter the system's performance. For instance, a controlled door that normally requires an access credential must remain open for an extended period to permit moving large or heavy objects in and out of the facility. To prevent company security from responding to repeated alarms from this door, the employee would request that security disable the alarms and hold the doors unlocked while the opening is used. The post officer usually has the authority to decide to unlock the door and operator training should include instructions to do this.

Discuss these procedures with the SA. Alter the vendor's training agenda before delivery of the training class if it does not appear to address all users' needs. This modified agenda will help the training technician focus attention on the most needed procedures.

Attend a portion of each level of training class provided. Conduct exit interviews with the attendees to determine their satisfaction with the training. When the system is in service, some spot testing should help determine if the product training was effective. If the users cannot use the system tools effectively, request additional product training from the vendor.

11.9 CREATING USER DOCUMENTATION FOR SYSTEM MANAGEMENT

Personnel in all companies, but especially in larger companies, tend to move between jobs. As a result, knowledge gained in the procedures and use of company tools can be lost when employees transfer or leave the company. This is especially important when the lost employee is the SA or Help Desk technician.

System documentation is an important part of your job. An adequate "structure" is essential in the proper management of any complex physical security system, and having a carefully documented structure will help orient new employees.

11.9.1 Identifying the Authorized Population

To identify the authorized population, start with organizing cardholder access control data.

> Note:
>
> This technique applies regardless of the technology used (keypad, biometrics, card reader). For this example, we will assume that the system selected is a card reader-based product.

Many of the sophisticated physical security systems available today provide a substantial database for collecting and displaying a variety of information about cardholders. Designate the information needed for the security system database carefully. Just because you "can have" 50 items of information on every employee in the new security tool, it does not follow that you "must have" that much information on everyone.

Certain pieces of information are essential in the proper handling of any security system database. This would include:

1. The names of cardholder
2. Their company department affiliation
3. An internal identifier used to designate the employee (usually an employee number)
4. The authorized access constraints for each employee

Some companies use social security numbers as employee numbers. In those cases, seek the advice of the company's human resources department to minimize liability and exposure for using employee social security numbers in the security database. Some other recommended fields for the security system database are:

1. Items used to identify an unconscious employee discovered on company grounds
   - Sex: male or female
   - Height
   - Complexion: light, medium, or dark

2. For situations involving vehicles, include:
   - Vehicle make, model and color
   - Vehicle license plate number
   - Parking sticker ID number

Maintaining vehicle data can be troublesome. Use vehicle data only if employees park their vehicle on company premises and the company is responsible for the security of the parking area. Coincident with this requirement, recommend that the company employ a vehicle parking sticker system to recognize authorized vehicles in the employee parking area.

Omit nonessential information that has limited value to the security function. Be especially careful about personal information to which the company has access and is available to security. Examples include the following:

- Data of birth
- Wage data
- Home address
- Home telephone number

Good arguments can be made for using information like this for identification during a crisis but it is a slippery slope. If someone with access to this database discloses personal information to unauthorized personnel, the company has significant liability exposure. Help the SA develop a list of information types, otherwise known as "fields", that the SA considers valuable in assessing identification in a crisis. Discuss this list with Human Resources before committing to a plan of action.

Identify cardholders and then segment them into like groups. The groupings usually reflect department or job functions. Cluster the groups based on the anticipated access permissions, that is, deciding where they can go. It is not necessary to make the door access decision at this step, only to group like cardholders together. By assigning individuals to groups, it will be easier to manage and make decisions on large populations of cardholders (Figure 11.5).

11.9.2 Organize Card Reader Data

The primary purpose of an access control system is to help the company control who, goes where, when, within their facility. Card data provides the answer to

Women's services Department

NAME_LAST	NAME_FIRST	Title	Department	Nursery Staff 1	Pedeartics 2	GYN 3	OB 4	Neo Nat 5	Labor and Delivery 6	Emergency 7	Clinic 8
	Alma	Nursing Asst 2	Nursery	1							
	Krisden	Rn 2	Nursery	1							
	Lynn	Rn/Mclno Section Mgr	Nursery	1							
	Madelena	Clerk Chief 1	Nursery	1							
	Elimaris	Rn 3	Transitional Nursery	1							
	Shannon	Rn 2	Transitional Nursery	1							
	Portia	Rn 1	Transitional Nursery	1							
	Christine	Nursing Unit Aide	Transitional Nursery	1							
	Cecila	Clerk Chief 1	Pediatrics		1						
	Bridgette	Nurse Registered	Pediatrics		1						
	Marleen	Rn/Mclno Asst Sect Mgr	Pediatrics		1						
	Sandra	Rn 2	Pediatrics		1						
	Meagan	Rn 2	Pediatrics		1						
	Brenda	Practical Nurse--Licensed, 3	Pediatrics		1						
	Beverly	Rn 2	Pediatrics		1						
	Mary	Nursing Asst 2	Pediatrics		1						
	Angela	Rn/Mclno Asst Sect Mgr	Gyn-Inpatient			1					
	Natasha	Psychiatric Aide 3	Gyn-Inpatient			1					
	Leslie	Practical Nurse--Licensed, 1	Gyn-Inpatient			1					
	Geraldine	Nursing Asst 2	Gyn-Inpatient			1					
	Sharon	Clerk Chief 1	3 West Ob				1				
	Wanda	Rn 3	3 West Ob				1				
	Dianne	Practical Nurse--Licensed, 2	3 West Ob				1				
	Theresa	Rn/Mclno Asst Sect Mgr	3 West Ob				1				
	Michelle	Rn 2	Neo-Natal Icu					1			
	Cecille	Clerk Chief 1	Neo-Natal Icu					1			
	Mitzi	Rn 2	Labor And Delivery						1		
	Letha	Clerk Chief 1	Labor And Delivery						1		
	Denise	Rn-Clinical Nurse Spec	Labor And Delivery						1		
	Glenda	Rn-Supervisor 2	Emergency Medicine-Peds							1	
	Kim	Nurse Registered	Emergency Medicine-Peds							1	
	Sheena	Clerk Chief 1	Emergency Medicine-Peds							1	
	Brenda	Nursing Asst 2	Ob-Gyn Clinic								1
	Gustavia	Clerk 4	Ob-Gyn Clinic								1
	Gralina	Clerk 4	Ob-Gyn Clinic								1
	Julie	Rn-Supervisor 2	Pediatric Clinics								1
	Brenda	Rn-Clinical Coordinator	Pediatric Clinics								1
	Colette	Rn 2	Pediatric Clinics								1

FIGURE 11.5 Cardholder Matrix.

"who" was assigned the card. (Remember, in a card-based access control system the card represents the employee.) The system can certify the card but not the individual carrying it. Higher forms of access permissions can help achieve user recognition.

Organize reader data to establish "where" a card may go within the facility. All sophisticated access control systems in the market today provide opening control by requiring that authorized individuals present a valid credential (including biometric measurements) to the device controlling the opening. Construct a matrix for access decisions by using a copy of the Door Detail Schedule developed during the system design phase of this installation. Figure 11.6 presents an example of this Door Group Schedule.

In Figure 11.6 the doors are listed in the left-hand margin as they are in the Door Detail Schedule. However, the columns across the top now bear a different nomenclature. The decision matrix columns include the group names of authorized groups within the system. Request the SA make decisions on which groups access each control area.

Work with department heads and other company employees to verify the access decisions. In Figure 11.6, a "1" is used to denote permission is granted and a blank field is used to denote permission is not granted. The choice of symbols is arbitrary but creating these tables in a Microsoft Excel worksheet allows easy manipulation and data sorting with numerals versus alpha characters. Any set of symbolic references can represent a "yes" or a "no".

Door Group Schedule

By: (Consultant Name)
Client: (Company Name)
Revision: 0
Work Location: (Area)
Date: (Date)

Project: (Project Designation)

Door Description	Group 1	Group 2	Group 3	Group 4	Group 5	Group 6	Group 7	Group 8	Notes
First Floor:									
old pediatrics	1	1							
old pediatrics	1	1							
morgue ramp exit	1		1						
east entrance	1	1	1	1	1	1	1	1	
front entrance	1	1	1	1	1	1	1	1	
west entrance	1	1	1	1	1	1	1	1	
admitting	1								
medical records admin	1		1						
walk in clinic	1			1					
family doctor	1			1					
walk-in clinic 2	1			1					
east entrance to oncology	1				1				
west entrance to oncology	1				1				
Radiology Oncology	1				1				
fire stair -	1	1	1	1	1	1	1	1	
walkway	1	1	1	1	1	1	1	1	
psyc triage	1								
west rear stair	1					1			
loading dock	1					1			
ER Admit	1					1			
Triage Station	1			1	1		1		
Admitting	1						1		

FIGURE 11.6 Door Group Schedule.

11.9.3 Time Zones

Time zones define "when" an authorized credential has permission to access (or egress) an opening. Exercise caution when establishing time zones; do not be overly restrictive. The following example may be helpful in understanding what "overly restrictive" means.

Assume that the company is a manufacturing facility with 24 hour operations, manned by three 8-hour shifts. Also assume that the first shift begins at 8:00 a.m. and concludes at 4:00 p.m. Monday through Friday. In an overly restrictive environment, the individuals authorized to work during shift 1 will be given a time zone assignment of 8:00 a.m. to 4:00 p.m. Monday through Friday. Such restriction does not allow for employees who work odd shifts when it is convenient for the company or the employee. This also does not allow for employees arriving and departing at mid shift.

As a result, departments must report all changes in shift assignment to company security to change access permissions. The resulting flood of shift change information can easily overwhelm an SA. Further, department managers who authorize shift changes may neglect to inform security that a change has taken place. This will delay workers from reporting to their assigned location at the proper time.

A more acceptable approach to assigning time zones is to determine if significant breaches in security will occur if an employee accesses the facility at times other than their normal working hours. If there are no compelling reasons to restrict the hours an employee may enter a facility, then assign the employee or group 24-hour access permission.

Conversely, many companies operate on a standard business hour schedule, 7:00 a.m. to 6:00 p.m. It would be unusual for employees to access the facility after-hours and on weekends. In such cases, assigning most employees to a normal working hour time period is the most acceptable means of restriction.

Some exceptions may be made for managerial personnel and others who have frequent need to access the facility after normal working hours and, since most sophisticated systems today permit multiple time periods, one time period may be assigned for after-hours while another is assigned to regular hours employees.

There are no hard and fast rules; it is a question of practical judgment. What the reader should take away from the foregoing is that you may restrict access based on time when it is apparent and necessary but you should not arbitrarily restrict access based on time when there are no good reasons to do so.

You can assist company personnel in making Time Zone decisions by providing a data entry tool or form for compiling the data (see Figure 11.7 for an example of a Time Zone form).

Security System Procedures
Department Submittal, Security Control Time Zones

Revised:	
Version:	2-4
Submitted:	10/30/23

Department: (Department Name)

Time Zone	Description	Start Time	End Time	M	T	W	T	F	S	S
1	Normal Working Hours (NWH)									
2	Alarm Only Door Monitoring 2									
3	Auto Door Unlock Times 1									
4	Auto Door Unlock Times 2									
5	Auto Door Unlock Times 3									
6	Cardholder 24 / 7 hour Access	0:01	24:00:00	X	X	X	X	X	X	X
7	Cardholder Limited Access NWH									
8	Cardholder Limited Access 1									
9	Cardholder Limited Access 2									
10	Cardholder Limited Access 3									

FIGURE 11.7 Time Zone Form.

11.9.4 Assigning Access Permissions

Use a top-down approach when designating authorized access permissions. Work with members of the system selection committee to determine how to handle access permissions. In some cases, conflicts arise between department managers regarding access to their assigned areas. The system selection committee sets the policy for these decisions.

Following the guidelines established by the committee, determine the controlled areas each cardholder group may access. Assist the department managers in establishing these permissions. Resolve conflicts between departments and document the decisions. To help with the documentation, refer to Figure 11.8 for an example of a permissions form.

Typical Access Permission Form for Department Heads

(Client Name) **Department Submittal, Access Privilege Request**		
	Revised:	11/03/23
	Version:	1
	Submitted:	11/03/23

Please list the security privileges for all of the cardholders:

(1) If a card was previously issued

Card holder Name	ID Number (1)	Time Zone	Reader Group

"Add lines as required"

FIGURE 11.8 Access Permission Table.

Avoid unduly restrictive access permission tables and counsel the department managers against overcomplicating the permission tables. Frequently, company managers will request highly specific access constraints that unnecessarily limit the times and locations that an authorized employee may be granted access. Their lack of experience in establishing these controls coupled with the zeal to support the company's new approach to security is often the contributing cause. The rule of thumb in making these decisions is to restrict an employee from accessing the facility only during those times when their presence might provide an unwarranted security risk.

11.9.5 Video Observation and Recording

If a CCTV system was included in the system recommendation, watch officers would require instructions on what to observe and how to manage the recording devices. Help the SA prepare a set of instructions on how to observe and categorize incidents.

For example, the SA may want to pay special attention to a vulnerable area along a fence line. The post orders should include a requirement to view an area several times a day and note suspicious activity. This observation is required in the absence of alarms and is intended to categorize conduct or activity in these areas for later investigations.

Provide a plot plan showing the location of each camera within or around clearly identified structures. Make the "perspective" of each camera clear to the watch officer.

Image recording accompanies most CCTV applications. Some system maintenance is required at the user level, such as archiving image files on a routine basis. Help the SA develop a process for managing the recorded images. This process depends on the type of system implemented. Images are transferred to CDs or copied to other media as required by the system. The user training classes teach the techniques available on the installed system but the SA and you must decide on how best to use those capabilities.

11.9.6 Alarm Response

In the planning and implementation process, the system design recommended devices to monitor and control openings. Openings were monitored to ensure that they were not opened during periods when the facility should be secured. However, simply monitoring the doors and recording when unauthorized openings were made will not fully address most security situations.

Alarm recognition is an integral part of the overall physical security system. The physical security system will provide information regarding unauthorized use of controlled openings. It is essential to recognize these breaches in security and clearly identify the area to take appropriate action.

During the design phase, the Door Detail Schedule established the identity for each opening. The identity given to each opening included the common name used by employees for that opening. Some new members of the security force monitoring the system may not be familiar with all the names used to describe openings. A clear description of each secure point helps the watch officer dispatch a roving patrol to the area in question.

Security systems provide alarm messages in response to the violation of a secured opening. These alarm messages begin with a text description of the alarm point. If the company is located on a campus with multiple buildings, a building name or number is usually associated with each building.

The first element of the description is the building name or number (in multiple building sites). Next, indicate the floor number and whether the door is internal or external. If the door is external, indicate the side of the building (by compass point) where the door is located. Even without specific recognition of the violated door, knowing the building and facing side where the opening is located will be most helpful in initially dispatching the patrol officer to investigate. Designations can continue with floor number and subject area. For example:

> "Admin Building, first floor, external door, southeast corner"

Again, the level of description is a matter of judgment. The SA will know the level of familiarity of the facility by the company security staff. Anticipate some employee turnover in the security staff. At any time, a new employee who is unfamiliar with the internal names may be the watch officer on duty during an alarm event. The description should be clear enough so that a person who is not familiar with all aspects of the facility could find the violated door with relative ease.

In addition to a text description of the violated door, integrate floor plans or facility maps that provide a graphic representation of the alarm location. Most of the sophisticated security systems available today provide a means to link an alarm event to an embedded floor plan or facility map. Work with company departments to create the necessary images for linkage to the new physical security system. In these cases, the vendor can usually assist the company in establishing this graphic link.

11.9.7 Responding to Alarm Events

After identifying the alarms, the security staff must respond to the incident. Work with the SA to describe in detail what response should occur when alarm event takes place. Usually, these instructions are limited to a few short sentences, for example: "Unauthorized Access Building 127, first floor north, Main Entrance. Officer to Investigate Immediately and Report Findings to the Command Post".

Help the SA write procedures such as these for each alarm event that could occur in the system. Once written, seek concurrence of the department manager in charge of the area where the security opening is located. See Figure 11.9 for an example of an Alarm Message Submittal form.

The message may include contact information for department employees. In the case of highly toxic or dangerous biological agents inside a protected area, the procedures may also include contacting the department manager, the police or the fire department. When layering these additional contact requirements on an alarm

Security System Procedures
Department Submittal, Security Control Alarm Messages

Revised:	11/03/23
Version:	2-4
Submitted:	11/03/23

Department: (Department Name)

Message Number	Alarm Message
1	
2	
3	
4	
5	
6	
7	
8	
9	
10	
11	
12	

FIGURE 11.9 Alarm Message Form.

response, remember that contact individuals might not be available during an alarm event. Use a descending list of contact personnel and have several contacts for the watch officer.

In addition to the personnel response during alarm events, many of the physical security systems can automatically trigger devices that will help to detect, deter and delay a perpetrator. For instance, systems can automatically turn on lights, sound sirens or trigger CCTV systems to focus in on the area of incident as soon as the incident occurs.

The mandate for private security is substantially different from the mandate for publicly funded police officers. Private security endeavors to protect the people and property of the companies for whom we work. Apprehending criminals is not the primary concern. The goal of private security is to prevent criminals from perpetrating their crimes on the employer and, by extension, the employees. It follows then that an immediate response by some device that should cause the perpetrator to flee a scene before a crime is committed may be preferable to having a patrol officer "catch them in the act". Work with the SA to determine the means needed to detect, deter, delay and respond to criminal activity.

11.9.8 System Reporting

After the security system devices are in service, software management is essential for a successful operation. Most of the sophisticated physical security systems provide a set of system reports that identify system programming decisions.

The first set of system reports describes how the readers are grouped together and how time zones are arranged. The second set identifies the credentials used in the system and the authorized access permissions. Other system reports include alarm descriptions and the timing of automatic events based on alarm information or time of the day. These are the standard system reports. Help the SA select a list of standard reports and develop a schedule for periodically reprinting these reports. Base the frequency of reprints on the expected number of changes in system programming over a given time.

Obtain a ringed binder and create an index to store the reports. Help the SA prepare a copy of each report for the binder. This will be a useful tool when discussing system arrangements during company meetings.

In addition to programming reports, activity reports are also a part of system management. In most systems, when an alarm event occurs, the system records the date, time and location of the alarm. When the company security acknowledges that alarm, they are required to make an entry in the system and describe the action taken before clearing the alarm. Use alarm event reports when evaluating facility-wide security violations and security force responses.

Additionally, all systems on the market provide some form of transaction history. This transaction history is a database of events that occurred during system operation. The most useful reports from transaction history are "exception reports".

An exception report focuses on those transactions that occurred outside of the normal range of business activity. For instance, if an employee attempts to use their credential to enter an opening without permission, the system will record that attempt. In most cases, security officers do not investigate such incidents since it is often a user error. However, the exception report will reveal trends in employee activity. The report filter will isolate unauthorized attempts to gain access to restricted areas and identify employees repeatedly attempting to violate access restrictions. This could indicate that security must conduct an investigation.

In some situations, the physical security systems monitor other systems, thereby centralizing information for all safety and security matters on the company's premises. For instance, the physical security system can monitor the status of alarm and trouble indicators of building fire alarm systems. The security system can produce a report showing the behavior of these systems over time. Fire alarm systems that are not physically inspected on a frequent basis may show repeated troubles before actually going into alarm or failing. By running periodic reports on these other systems, company security can focus the attention of the facilities department on systems that may be on the brink of failure. By addressing such concerns early, the company can avoid false alarms and reduce potential disruption of work.

11.9.9 Programming

Work with the SA to supervise the programming of all the decisions into the system. Remember that training alone will not guarantee good results and the SA needs support and guidance from an experienced professional.

11.10 SYSTEM MANAGEMENT PROCEDURES

The preceding sections have addressed how the physical security system is to be implemented from a logistical point of view. However, even projects that are implemented exceedingly well can fail if the appropriate management procedures are not in place to work with the new system. It is essential to have management controls for all elements of the new physical security system to prevent unauthorized persons from having access to critical control processes.

11.10.1 Establish Procedures to Issue Credentials

The security credential that is most widely used today for system identification is the access card. There are a variety of other access devices as described earlier in this book that do not require the physical presence of a card but instead are authorization numbers or biometric measuring. The same rules apply for each of these other access credentials that apply to access cards. For this discussion, we shall confine our remarks solely to card-based systems.

In most sophisticated physical security systems, a user must enter information about the credential into the system for the credential to work properly. Although it seems that an un-programmed card is useless, it is not. Advise the SA to handle new access cards carefully.

Some physical security systems have a default mode when communication is lost. In default mode, the higher-level qualifications for access permissions are ignored. Under these circumstances, any access card sold to the facility will automatically have access permission in all doors. Some companies use security credentials without photos as a form of physical identification. If a perpetrator wishing access to a facility steals a security card, the perpetrator may approach an unwary employee and suggest that their card is not functioning today and would like the employee to help them gain access to the facility. This is an employee training issue but is also a credential safeguard issue.

The physical security system may have substantial safeguards, but a perpetrator with deliberation and intent can circumvent those safeguards more easily with a stolen card. Keeping an accurate inventory of available identity credentials is an important part of safeguarding system operation.

As part of the SA's recordkeeping process, instruct them to keep a complete and accurate list of all orders placed and received for security credentials. The SA should note the order information that requested the security cards and indicate the starting and ending number of the card sequence. Match that inventory to the system card report described earlier and maintain a list of lost or destroyed cards. The SA will then be able to identify every card that was acquired for the system, its current condition and final disposition.

Assist the SA in preparing a set of procedures that describes how and when to issue a new security credential. Require departments that hire new employees to complete a Card Request Form. Include in this form the signature of the department manager authorized to grant access to their area, and what access permissions are available for the employee (see Figure 11.10). Require the new employee to present this document to company security for a security credential.

The procedure should include how to maintain the authorization form after issuing the security credential. A card form file or binder is the simplest choice. File the form alphabetically for quick and easy recalls during updates and replacements.

(Client Name) Department Submittal, Security Card Request	Revised:	11/02/23
	Version:	1

1. Department Requesting Card:

Date Card Requested
Department
Employee Name
Employee Title
Employee ID Number

Type of Card Request:

New ☐
Replacement ☐
Old Card Number:

Security Assignment:
(See departmental records for codes)

Reader Group
Time Period

Authorization:

Supervisor Name (print)

Supervisor's Signature ____________________

2. Human Resources Card Assignment:

Date Assigned
Card Number Assigned

Picture Used:
From File ☐
New ☐

HR Representative Assigning Card:
Print Name

Initial ____________

3. Security Department:

Date Security Privilege Assigned
Security Representative:
Print Name

Initial ____________

Security Department Emergency Call Log:

Telephone requests from other departments to change the security status of this card:

Date	Caller	Department	Request	Responding Officer

FIGURE 11.10 Card Request Form.

11.10.2 Procedures for Lost or Replaced Security Credentials

Anticipate that cards will be lost or destroyed. Include in the procedures the steps needed to replace a lost or damaged card. Use the card request form for card replacement. In most cases, the employee's department manager should be required to sign this document authorizing card issuance or replacement for their subordinate. Such procedures provide department managers with additional information regarding the security awareness of their employees. An employee who constantly loses or destroys identity cards may be subject to disciplinary action.

A technique used successfully is to require an employee wishing a replacement card to pay a fee for the new card. Although these fees help recover some of the cost incurred in this card replacement, the primary purpose is to deter negligent employees. Seek broad acceptance to this policy before recommending that the SA implement it.

Include disabling the lost or damaged card in the replacement card procedure. Even in cases where card damage is minimal (my dog chewed it, I left it in my pants and the dryer warped it, I used it as an ice scraper last week and it split), disable that card number in the physical security system. It is to the company's advantage to have only one legitimate credential recognized for each employee of the company.

11.10.3 Procedures for Dismissed Employees

Employee turnover is an unpleasant fact in companies today. Sometimes an employee leaves a company voluntarily and is ready, willing and able to return all company property, including security credentials. At other times, a dismissal occurs that is contrary to the employee's wishes and that employee is less agreeable to these requirements. Under such circumstances, employees often fail to return their security credentials. Moreover, in situations where the termination results in hostility from the terminated employee, a level of threat exists. In these cases, securing the facility specifically against that employee is prudent.

In most cases, access to a facility may be denied by a simple set of commands entered at a workstation of the physical security system. However, those commands are always based on instruction from company managers and in a situation like the one previously described, those managers may not be aware of the urgency needed for such a request.

Assist the SA in establishing firm access denial procedures with the human resources department of the company. Encourage the SA to repeatedly inform company managers of the importance of notifying company security quickly when such a termination takes place.

Changes in card authorizations (including removing access privileges) should be communicated to company security in written form. This is a form identifying the credential to remove from the system. However, in situations like the one described above, time is of the essence. Part of the procedures should require the terminated employee's department to contact security by telephone and immediately initiate a removal of access permissions for the terminated employee. Require a confirming form from the department but deny access based on verbal instructions.

In addition to procedures for denying access, a portion of that procedure should deal with retrieval of the physical credential from a dismissed employee who has failed to surrender it upon dismissal. Much like a perpetrator whose falsified credential may be used for dishonest purposes, a dismissed employee with intent to do harm is familiar with the policies and procedures of the company and can be a far more damaging opponent than an outsider with criminal intent.

Assist the SA and human resources department and, if necessary, the company's legal department in effectively handling security during terminations. Assist the SA in preparing written procedures based on these discussions.

11.10.4 Procedures for Changes in Access Permissions

We have thus far dealt with the possession of the credential but it is also important to deal with the authority level assigned to that credential to fully implement company policy. In addition to employee turnover, employees move around a company (especially in large organizations) through promotions and transfers and these changes may have a significant impact on their access permissions. Written permission for changes in an employee's access privilege is as important as providing an employee with an appropriate credential.

Require department signatures when defining changes in access permissions. Permission changes and new card authorizations can easily be included on the same form to minimize paperwork.

11.10.5 General Protocols

In Chapter 5 we discussed preparing protocols based on company policy, now it is time to implement those protocols. You will want to schedule training not only for the security staff but also for all employees.

A method I have used successfully is to create a video for the management team to pass to each employee. It can explain what this new security system does, the importance of using it properly and the value to each employee in ensuring that the company's assets and employees are safe and secure.

If there are special guidelines for visitors (they should be short and to the point) about what to do or what not to do in a given situation, have those guidelines printed out and make it a Standard Operating Procedure (SOP) to distribute copies of the guidelines to each visitor. This will not only protect their safety and the company's assets but will also serve to protect the company if they are sued for not taking reasonable care to protect a visitor to their premises.

11.11 SYSTEM TURN ON

After all processes are in place, training is complete for the staff and the written procedures are finished, schedule a visit with the vendor to turn the system on. In companies with less than 100 employees, it may be helpful to call a brief company-wide meeting to allow you to introduce the new system to all employees. This introduction should include some discussion of security procedures and the means and methods for using the various credential identification devices located throughout the facility. This meeting should emphasize the company's desire to provide a safe and secure work environment for the employees and the security of company property.

In larger companies, such meetings may not be possible but a written presentation of these same concepts is appropriate. The formal introduction of this system should come from the highest level possible within the company to reinforce the company's commitment to the new security commitments.

11.12 EVALUATING THE IMPLEMENTATION

Perform weekly reviews of system operation for approximately one month after system implementation. These reviews should include sampling and reading system reports to identify potential problems with system performance and discussions with employees to identify system anomalies. Recall the system vendor to perform changes or corrections to system programming and equipment installation where needed to more closely meet company objectives.

Review the performance of individuals managing and operating the system. Meetings with the SA can oftentimes reveal concerns or confusions about the installation.

Construct a practical application test for the system operator. Each operator should be tested in the early weeks to ensure that they understand the training they received. Specifically, certain aspects of system use such as opening doors from a keyboard or the meaning of certain alarm messages should be included in a quiz for each officer on an individual basis. The purpose of these exercises is not to evaluate the employee but rather to evaluate the employee's need for additional training. At the conclusion of each examination, prepare a report to the SA for handling knowledge deficiencies found in their subordinates.

Confirm the system's acceptance by department managers and other employees. Conduct at least one interview with all of the company managers involved in the selection and acquisition process for this physical security system. Also, meet with the managers in key departments to determine the level of satisfaction and acceptance with the delivered system.

Prepare a final report for the management team regarding the success of the implemented solutions. If appropriate, identify new ways to use the system to satisfy additional company needs revealed in the implementation process.

11.13 FOLLOW-UP EVALUATION AND TRAINING

When the new physical security system is fully implemented and all the procedures and personnel training are in place for the system to operate as expected, the job is essentially finished. However, the astute security professional knows that circumstances change over time and certain adjustments in system performance may be required.

Revisit the company on a periodic basis to test the satisfaction with the installed system. Determine if the system requires changes or improvements to meet the ever-changing demands of security requirements.

Review the selected vendor's performance with regard to corrective and preventive maintenance. Frequently, promises made during bid submittals are not always remembered in exactly the same way they were presented by the vendor. For the first year of the system installation, plan on quarterly reviews to determine service satisfaction. Determine the company's level of satisfaction with the vendor's current level of service and if competing offers may be required for future system additions and maintenance.

11.14 THE LAST WORD

The security professional provides a way to bring together needs and solutions. To the company, the security professional represents the marketplace. They want the right products that will provide a safe and secure environment for their employees and their possessions without excess costs. To the marketplace, the security professional represents the business opportunity to sell their products. They want a fair opportunity to show what they can do to meet the needs of the company. The security professional has a fiduciary responsibility to select the most appropriate products and services in an unbiased manner that offer the best value for the company.

The techniques presented in this book help you reach those goals. A good business deal is one where all parties leave the table feeling that they have gained something. As a security professional, you should always strive for a win-win situation. Above all, a security professional must have integrity, honesty and a sense of fair play.

Technical skills and the knowledge and experience gained in physical security are an essential part of the job. However, ethics are paramount in any business arrangement. Even the best designed system will fail if the business arrangements are not equitable. Be forthright in dealing with the company and the vendors and remember that you are a business consultant as well as a security expert.

Index

Note: Page numbers in *italics* indicate figures on the corresponding pages.

www.ingramcontent.com/pod-product-compliance
Lightning Source LLC
LaVergne TN
LVHW021726021026
849161LV00004BA/731

* 9 7 8 1 0 3 2 7 9 0 7 7 0 *